THE COURTS
AND
THE CANADIAN
CONSTITUTION

D1560299

THE CARLETON LIBRARY

A series of Canadian reprints and new
collections of source material relating
to Canada, issued under the editorial
supervision of the Institute of Canadian
Studies of Carleton University, Ottawa.

THE COURTS
AND
THE CANADIAN
CONSTITUTION

A SELECTION OF ESSAYS

EDITED AND WITH AN INTRODUCTION BY

W. R. LEDERMAN

The Carleton Library No. 16 / McClelland and Stewart Limited

The Canadian Publishers
McClelland and Stewart Limited
25 Hollinger Road, Toronto 16

PRINTED AND BOUND IN CANADA
BY
T. H. BEST PRINTING COMPANY LIMITED

CONTENTS

NOTE ON THE EDITOR

William R. Lederman was born in Regina in 1916, and obtained his LL.B. from the University of Saskatchewan in 1940. A Rhodes scholar, after service overseas with the Royal Canadian Artillery during the Second World War, he received his B.C.L. from Oxford University in 1948.

W. R. Lederman is now Professor and Dean of the Faculty of Law at Queen's University, Kingston, a post he has held since 1958. He is a member of the Saskatchewan, Nova Scotia, and Ontario Bars, Queen's Counsel in Ontario, and Chairman of the Legal Education and Training Section of the Canadian Bar Association for the year 1963-64. He has contributed articles to a number of learned journals, including the *Canadian Bar Review* and the *McGill Law Journal*. He was also one of the contributors to *Legal Essays in Honour of Arthur Moxon* (1953) and *The Political Process in Canada; Essays in Honour of R. MacGregor Dawson* (1963).

INTRODUCTION

In this collection of essays and addresses, I have tried to be faithful to a restricted but important theme. The selections all bear directly on the general nature of Canada's federal constitution or on the general process of the interpretation of it in the Judicial Committee of the Privy Council and the Supreme Court of Canada. Limitations of space were necessarily severe, and I make no claim of special virtue for these particular essays over others of equal merit that were not chosen. Moreover the list had to be short for another reason. I decided early to reproduce in full, or at least in very substantial measure, whatever essays I did select, and thus to avoid making the collection a thing of bits and pieces.

What is offered then is a good sample, but only a sample, of the writing on the federal constitution of our country that is to be found for the most part in learned journals and similar publications not readily accessible to the public or even to the growing numbers of university undergraduates. This book is published in the belief that such contributions by scholars learned in the law, in history, or in political science should be made more accessible.

I sincerely thank the authors and publishers whose consents for reprinting the items in this volume were so readily given. Specific acknowledgements are made as appropriate at the start of each item.

To provide a background for the essays to follow, I attempt in the balance of this introduction to explain briefly the Canadian judicial system and the general nature of the process of judicial review of legislative powers in a federal country.

THE CANADIAN SYSTEM OF COURTS

The British North America Act, 1867, states in its preamble that the original federating provinces "have expressed their Desire to be federally united into One Dominion under the

Crown . . . with a Constitution similar in Principle to that of the United Kingdom." This passage looks not only to the future but also to the past. It reminds us that, before Confederation, the British North American colonies had already enjoyed a considerable history of self government under English constitutional principles. English governmental institutions – Governors, Councils, Assemblies, and Courts – had been authorized for the colonies either by decrees of the King and his Imperial Privy Council or by express statutes of the Imperial Parliament. Our particular concern here is with the courts. By the middle of the nineteenth century at the latest, and in some cases earlier, the British North American colonies had established superior courts on the model of the historic English Central Courts of Justice, usually by appropriate colonial judicature statutes approved in London. This means that the English superior court as it was after the Act of Settlement (1701) became in due course a most important feature of our great English constitutional inheritance.

The English judicial system is characterized by a separation of powers in favour of the independence of the judiciary – à separation of the courts from control or influence by either legislative or executive bodies. Sections 96 to 101 of the B.N.A. Act establish our Canadian superior courts, and a reading of these sections (quoted hereafter) reveals the hallmarks of several hundred years of English judicial development. The judges are to be appointed from the autonomous legal profession, they are not civil servants. They enjoy guaranteed salaries and permanent tenure until death or an advanced age (seventy-five years), whichever comes first. They can be removed earlier only by joint address of Senate and House of Commons for grave misbehaviour. The result is that our judges need only have regard to reason, conscience, and the evidence in their duty-bound endeavours to interpret laws according to the meaning and purpose expressed or implied in those laws. This is the essence of judicial independence.

The interesting thing is that this separation of powers permitted the establishment of an essentially unified judicial system for Canada in 1867 without offence to the federal idea.[1] The

[1] See also W. R. Lederman, "The Independence of The Judiciary" (1956), 34 Can. Bar. Rev. 769 and 1139, at 1158-1160.

existing courts in each province were continued by section 129 of the B.N.A. Act, subject to certain other provisions of the act that divided power and responsibility for the judicature between provincial and federal authorities. Section 92(14) gave the provinces "exclusive" legislative power over "the Administration of Justice in the Province, including the Constitution, Maintenance, and Organization of Provincial Courts, both of Civil and of Criminal Jurisdiction, and including Procedure in Civil Matters in those Courts."

This is a very wide power, but it is subject to certain important subtractions in favour of the federal authorities. Criminal procedure is an "exclusive" federal legislative category by section 91(27); and sections 96 to 100, inclusive, make collaboration of the federal executive and Parliament necessary to complete the establishment of provincial superior, district, or county courts. Section 101 gives the federal parliament an overriding power to establish certain federal courts. These sections require quotation in full:

96.   *The Governor General shall appoint the Judges of the Superior, District, and County Courts in each Province, except those of the Courts of Probate in Nova Scotia and New Brunswick.*

97.   *Until the Laws relative to Property and Civil Rights in Ontario, Nova Scotia, and New Brunswick, and the Procedure of the Courts in those Provinces, are made uniform, the Judges of the Courts of those Provinces appointed by the Governor General shall be selected from the respective Bars of those Provinces.*

98.   *The Judges of the Courts of Quebec shall be selected from the Bar of that Province.*

99(1). *Subject to subsection two of this section, the Judges of the Superior Courts shall hold office during good behaviour, but shall be removable by the Governor General on Address of the Senate and House of Commons.*

   (2). *A Judge of a Superior Court, whether appointed before or after the coming into force of this section, shall cease to hold office upon attaining the age of seventy-five years, or upon the coming into force of this section if at that time he has already attained that age.*

4 - THE COURTS AND CONSTITUTIONS

100.   The Salaries, Allowances, and Pensions of the Judges
       of the Superior, District, and County Courts (except
       the Courts of Probate in Nova Scotia and New Bruns-
       wick), and of the Admiralty Courts in Cases where the
       Judges thereof are for the Time being paid by Salary,
       shall be fixed and provided by the Parliament of
       Canada.

101.   The Parliament of Canada may, notwithstanding any-
       thing in this Act, from Time to Time provide for the
       Constitution, Maintenance, and Organization of a
       General Court of Appeal for Canada, and for the
       Establishment of any additional Courts for the better
       Administration of the Laws of Canada.

To summarize, the result is that minor courts in the provinces, such as those of magistrates or justices of the peace, are
entirely within provincial control. District, county, or superior
courts of the provinces, including provincial appellate courts,
require the collaboration of provincial and federal authorities
for their establishment and maintenance. Then at the apex of
the structure is the "General Court of Appeal for Canada," the
Supreme Court of Canada, entirely constituted by the federal
parliament and executive.

There is not, generally speaking, any division of jurisdiction
in these courts corresponding to the division of legislative powers between the provincial legislatures and the federal parliament. In general they "administer justice" concerning all types
of laws, whether such laws fall legislatively within the purview
of provincial legislatures or the federal parliament. Indeed, the
final appellate jurisdiction of the Supreme Court of Canada in
this plenary sense cannot be impaired or excluded by provincial
legislation. It is true that the federal parliament could go a long
way, perhaps all the way, in placing exclusive original jurisdiction to administer laws legislatively within its range in the hands
of purely federal courts, under the closing words of section 101.
To a quite limited degree this has happened in the case of the
Exchequer Court of Canada, but, with this exception, there is
no significant vertical division in the Canadian judicial system
corresponding to the division between the separate systems of
state and federal courts in the United States. This brings us
then to consideration of the role of our superior courts as
interpreters of the federal constitution.

JUDICIAL REVIEW OF LEGISLATIVE POWERS IN CANADA

The English Superior Courts after 1688 did not review the validity of legislative acts of the Imperial Parliament. Nevertheless, in the exercise of long-standing jurisdiction, they did continue to review and strike down the acts of lesser governmental officials and bodies when such acts exceeded the powers granted. In the colonies, the citizen complaining of such excess of powers would go first to the superior colonial courts of original jurisdiction, from which an appeal could eventually be taken to the Judicial Committee of the Privy Council in London as the final appellate tribunal of the overseas empire. As one learned writer expressed it in the late nineteenth century:[2]

It is the primary condition of all legislation by subordinate and provincial assemblies, throughout the British empire, that the same shall not be repugnant to the law of England. This condition is enforced . . . by the decision of the local judiciary of the colony, in the first instance, and ultimately of Her Majesty's Imperial privy council, upon an action or suit at law, duly brought before such a tribunal, to declare and adjudge a colonial, dominion, or provincial statute, either in whole or in part, to be ultra vires and void, as being in excess of the jurisdiction conferred on the legislature by which the same was enacted. . . .

Hence final authority for our courts to rule upon the extent of legislative powers has valid historical roots. But also such power of judicial review has roots in the necessities of a federal system. Neither the federal parliament nor the provincial legislatures could be permitted to act as judges of the extent of their own respective grants of power under the B.N.A. Act. If they were, soon we would have either ten separate countries or a unitary state. The authority to speak the last word on the extent of legislative powers in a federation cannot be left with the very legislative bodies whose powers are in question. Hence, resort for this purpose to an independent judicial tribunal is indicated. For us this means resort to our traditional superior courts on the English model, the nature of which was explained earlier. Final review of the distribution of legislative powers by such courts is a specially entrenched principle present by necessary implica-

[2] Alpheus Todd, *Parliamentary Government in the British Colonies* (2nd ed.; London: Longmans, Green & Co., 1894), p. 302.

tion in the Canadian constitution. As Mr. Justice McGillivray has expressed it, speaking in the Alberta Court of Appeal,[3]

. . . consideration of the legislative capacity of Parliament or of the Legislatures cannot be withdrawn from the Courts either by Parliament or Legislature. In my view this statement may rest upon the safe ground that by necessary implication from what has been said in the B.N.A. Act, the Superior Courts whose independence is thereby assured, are just as surely made the arbiters of the constitutional validity of statutory enactments as Parliament and the Legislatures are made law enacting bodies. If, as I think, it is not open to question that neither Parliament nor Legislature may provide as the concluding words of an enactment that it shall be deemed to be intra vires *by all Courts in the country then neither the one nor the other of these legislative bodies can reach the same end by denying access to the Courts for the determination of constitutional questions.*

When we think of constitutional interpretation today, we think also of the Supreme Court of Canada as our final court of appeal. But it is well to recall that the Supreme Court was not established until 1875. What happened immediately at Confederation was that the pre-Confederation provincial superior courts were continued after 1867, subject to the new arrangements provided by sections 96 to 100 of the B.N.A. Act. Moreover, the direct pre-Confederation channels of appeal from the provincial appeal courts to the Imperial Judicial Committee in London were not disturbed and remained open. This continued to be the position until 1935 in criminal cases and until 1949 in all other cases. The result has been that many appeals in constitutional cases by-passed the Supreme Court of Canada altogether, and those that did not were usually taken on appeal from the Supreme Court to the Privy Council anyway. So, until Privy Council appeals were finally abolished in all cases at the end of 1949, the Supreme Court of Canada lived always in the shadow of the Judicial Committee. Accordingly it was the latter body that, for the most part, developed the Canadian federal constitution to its present state by authoritative interpretation. Let us now look briefly at the complex nature of the task that confronted the Judicial Committee in this respect. There are

[3] *I.O.F.* v. *Lethbridge*, [1938] 3 D.L.R. at pp. 102-3; affirmed in the Privy Council, [1940] A.C. 513.

inherent difficulties involved for any judicial body charged with the duty of final interpretation in a federal country.

Some authorities complain that the Judicial Committee, during some eighty years of interpretation, contradicted both the intentions of the Fathers of Confederation and the text of the B.N.A. Act by showing a heavy bias in favour of provincial powers at the expense of federal powers. I doubt that this allegation can ever be proved or disproved. Certainly there was widespread consensus in 1867 – a compact if you will – that a new Canada on federal principles was to have both effective central power and significant provincial autonomy, the latter with particular reference to the French Canadians. But the precise terms of the consensus or compact – as expressed in the Quebec Resolutions of 1864 and the corresponding sections of the B.N.A. Act of 1867 – were not all that clear. Neither before nor after the event in 1867 did these provisions prove to be free of uncertainty or ambiguity.

Recently, Professor P. B. Waite has published a book surveying public opinion about the proposed federal scheme in all parts of British North America in the period 1864-67, as revealed in dozens of newspapers and other relevant publications of the time.[4] This distinguished study shows (to me at least) that important differences about the nature of the proposed federal scheme were apparent in the immediate pre-Confederation period under review. There were centralizers and provincial autonomists even then, taking different meanings from the Quebec Resolutions of 1864. These differences persisted and reappeared after Confederation in conflicting opinions about what the terms of the B.N.A. Act called for.

Of course some things were clear enough in 1867, but nevertheless important uncertainties, overlaps, and ambiguities simply remained unresolved at that time. In due course they came to light. The much-abused Viscount Haldane expressed an important truth when he said in 1915:[5]

The draftsman had to work on the terms of a political agreement, terms which were mainly to be sought for in the resolutions passed at Quebec in October, 1864. To these resolutions and the sections founded on them the remark applies . . . that

[4] P. B. Waite, *The Life and Times of Confederation, 1864-67* (Toronto: University of Toronto Press, 1962).
[5] *John Deere Plow Company Ltd.* v. *Wharton* [1915] A.C. 330 at p. 338.

if there is at points obscurity in language, this may be taken to be due, not to uncertainty about general principle, but to that difficulty in obtaining ready agreement about phrases which attends the drafting of legislative measures by large assemblages. It may be added that the form in which provisions overlapping each other have been placed side by side shows that those who passed the Confederation Act intended to leave the working out and interpretation of these provisions to practice and to judicial decision.

Indeed, Viscount Haldane's point can be carried somewhat further. Laws have to be expressed in words of some degree of generality, particularly basic constitutional laws, so that frequently the interpretative tribunal has important discretions to exercise. This is especially so as time moves on and conditions in the country change from those obtaining when the constitutional document was drafted. As the great jurist Hans Kelsen has said (writing of the Charter of the United Nations) : [6]

Since the law is formulated in words and words have frequently more than one meaning, interpretation of the law, that is determination of its meaning, becomes necessary. Traditional jurisprudence distinguishes various methods of interpretation: the historical, in contrast to the grammatical, an interpretation according to the "spirit," in opposition to a literal interpretation keeping to the words. None of these methods can claim preference unless the law itself prescribes the one or the other. The different methods of interpretation may establish different meanings of one and the same provision. Sometimes, even one and the same method, especially the so-called grammatical interpretation, leads to contradictory results. It is incumbent upon the law-maker to avoid as far as possible ambiguities in the text of the law; but the nature of language makes the fulfilment of this task possible only to a certain degree.

. . . .

The true meaning of a legal norm is usually supposed to be the one which corresponds to the will of the legislator. But it is more than doubtful whether there exists at all such a thing as the "will of the legislator," especially where the law is the result of a complex procedure in which many individuals participate,

[6] Hans Kelsen, *The Law of The United Nations* (London: Stevens & Sons, Ltd., 1951), pp. xiii-xv.

such as the procedure through which a statute is adopted by a parliament or the procedure through which a multilateral treaty is negotiated and signed by many plenipotentiaries and ratified by many governments. The intention of the one or more who draft the text of a legal instrument is not at all identical with the will of the legislator, that is the will of those competent to make the draft a binding law, and who often fulfil this function without adequate knowledge of the text. In any event interpretation can take into consideration the intention of those who drafted the law or the will of the competent legislator only if intention or will is expressed in the terms of the law. However, the fact that the wording of a legal norm allows several interpretations proves that its actual framer or the competent legislator has not been able or willing to express his intention in a way excluding any interpretation not in conformity with his intention. In such a case, none of the several interpretations can be assumed to be the only one that corresponds to the intention of the framer or the will of the legislator. The ambiguity of a legal text moreover, is sometimes not the unvoluntary effect of its unsatisfactory wording but a technique intentionally employed by the legislator, who, for some reason or other, could not decide between two or more solutions of a legal problem, and hence left the decision to the law-applying organs. If there are two or more possible interpretations, the law-applying organ has always the choice among them.

The fact that the legal norms are formulated in words having frequently more than one meaning is the reason why every legal instrument has its own life, more or less independent of the wishes and expectations of its begetters. That the law is open to more than one interpretation is certainly detrimental to legal security; but it has the advantage of making the law adaptable to changing circumstances, without the requirement of formal alteration.

Professor Kelsen's wise words point to the high importance of an independent and sophisticated process for construing a federal distribution of legislative powers. Only by such a process can results be reached that are sensitive to the needs and conditions of the country from time to time. The Judicial Committee had successes as well as failures in this regard, and in any event that tribunal should not now be disparaged for having failed to find answers in the text of the B.N.A. Act that just were not there to be found.

Nevertheless, it must be said that the Supreme Court of Canada as our final tribunal of interpretation has a vital quality for this purpose that the Judicial Committee did not have. The judges of the Supreme Court are Canadians who live all their lives with the problems and conditions of the country that is governed by the B.N.A. Act as its federal constitution. Because of the inevitable discretions inherent in the processes of constitutional interpretation, this should bring more wisdom and realism to the task than would otherwise be possible.

At present the Supreme Court of Canada is constituted by ordinary federal statute,[7] and the judges of the court are appointed by the Governor General in Council, that is by the federal cabinet. As a result, there are some misgivings to the effect that the Supreme Court of Canada is not as truly independent of the Parliament and Government of Canada as it should be in a federal country. In this respect the Supreme Court of Canada may seem to compare unfavourably with the Judicial Committee of The Privy Council in London.

My own view is that these misgivings are unfounded. The Supreme Court of Canada is pre-eminently a superior court in every sense. Our whole constitutional tradition means that the Canadian Parliament would never dare to tamper with the Supreme Court Act in any way prejudicial to the true independence of the Court or its judges. Nevertheless, the statute of the Court could be specially and formally entrenched in appropriate clauses of the Canadian constitution, if it were thought useful to do so. As for the appointment of Supreme Court judges, I consider this power should remain with the Prime Minister of Canada and his Cabinet, responsible as they are to the Parliament of Canada representing all parts of the country. It should be noted that the present statute of the Court requires one-third of the judges to be appointed from the Bar of the Province of Quebec, thus ensuring the presence of judges learned in the French civil law of Quebec. In any event, the main point here is that, once a highly qualified person has been appointed to the independence and security of the Supreme Court of Canada, he must simply be trusted to rise to the challenge of the office with integrity and intelligence. This applies

[7] *The Supreme Court Act*, Revised Statutes of Canada, 1952, chapter 259.

to constitutional interpretation as much as to the disposal of ordinary appeals.

Accordingly, whatever changes lie ahead in the general constitutional field, I believe that the Supreme Court of Canada should be continued in its present function and power of final constitutional interpretation. No institution is perfect, but an independent superior court of appellate jurisdiction on the English model, manned by Canadian judges, offers the best tribunal available for holding the balance between Canada and the provinces in our federal system. To a very important extent, such balance is a function of constitutional interpretation. Formal constitutional amendment is at best an occasional major operation. Constitutional interpretation on the other hand is a continuing and detailed process that must be available every day.

Nevertheless, I do not intend by the foregoing to imply that every important working decision about the meaning of our federal constitution is made, or should be made, by a court, in particular the Supreme Court of Canada. Great numbers of such decisions must be made at every level of government by a great variety of ministers and officials, with the aid of their legal advisers. The important point is that the relatively few issues taken to the Supreme Court of Canada are critical, because this is the final resort in a show-down. Moreover, Supreme Court decisions, being final, are controlling in the field of interpretation, laying down the principles and guide lines to be respected at other levels of government, and by private citizens as well.

W. R. LEDERMAN,
Queen's University,
September, 1964

PART ONE

GENERAL NATURE OF THE BRITISH NORTH AMERICA ACT AS A FEDERAL CONSTITUTION

The British North America Act, 1867,

(30 and 31 Victoria, c. 3, as amended)
Sections **91** *to* **95**.

Powers of the Parliament

91. It shall be lawful for the Queen, by and with the Advice and Consent of the Senate and House of Commons, to make Laws for the Peace, Order, and good Government of Canada, in relation to all Matters not coming within the Classes of Subjects by this Act assigned exclusively to the Legislatures of the Provinces; and for greater Certainty, but not so as to restrict the Generality of the foregoing Terms of this Section, it is hereby declared that (notwithstanding anything in this Act) the exclusive Legislative Authority of the Parliament of Canada extends to all Matters coming within the Classes of Subjects next herein-after enumerated; that is to say, –

1. The amendment from time to time of the Constitution of Canada, except as regards matters coming within the classes of subjects by this Act assigned exclusively to the Legislatures of the provinces, or as regards rights or privileges by this or any other Constitutional Act granted or secured to the Legislature or the Government of a province, or to any class of persons with respect to schools or as regards the use of the English or the French language or as regards the requirements that there shall be a session of the Parliament of

Canada at least once each year, and that no House of Commons shall continue for more than five years from the day of the return of the Writs for choosing the House: provided, however, that a House of Commons may in time of real or apprehended war, invasion or insurrection be continued by the Parliament of Canada if such continuation is not opposed by the votes of more than one-third of the members of such House.

1A. The Public Debt and Property.

2. The Regulation of Trade and Commerce.

2A. Unemployment insurance.

3. The raising of Money by any Mode or System of Taxation.

4. The borrowing of Money on the Public Credit.

5. Postal Service.

6. The Census and Statistics.

7. Militia, Military and Naval Service, and Defence.

8. The fixing of and providing for the Salaries and Allowances of Civil and other Officers of the Government of Canada.

9. Beacons, Buoys, Lighthouses, and Sable Island.

10. Navigation and Shipping.

11. Quarantine and the Establishment and Maintenance of Marine Hospitals.

12. Sea Coast and Inland Fisheries.

13. Ferries between a Province and any British or Foreign Country or between Two Provinces.

14. Currency and Coinage.

15. Banking, Incorporation of Banks, and the Issue of Paper Money.

16. Savings Banks.

17. Weights and Measures.

18. Bills of Exchange and Promissory Notes.

19. Interest.

20. Legal Tender.

21. Bankruptcy and Insolvency.

22. Patents of Invention and Discovery.

23. Copyrights.

24. Indians, and Lands reserved for the Indians.

25. Naturalization and Aliens.

26. Marriage and Divorce.

27. The Criminal Law, except the Constitution of Courts

of Criminal Jurisdiction, but including the Procedure in Criminal Matters.

28. The Establishment, Maintenance, and Management of Penitentiaries.

29. Such Classes of Subjects as are expressly excepted in the Enumeration of the Classes of Subjects by this Act assigned exclusively to the Legislatures of the Provinces.

And any Matter coming within any of the Classes of Subjects enumerated in this Section shall not be deemed to come within the Class of Matters of a local or private Nature comprised in the Enumeration of the Classes of Subjects by this Act assigned exclusively to the Legislatures of the Provinces.

Exclusive Powers of Provincial Legislatures

92. In each Province the Legislature may exclusively make Laws in relation to Matters coming within the Classes of Subjects next herein-after enumerated; that is to say, –

1. The Amendment from Time to Time, notwithstanding anything in this Act, of the Constitution of the Province, except as regards the Office of Lieutenant Governor.

2. Direct Taxation within the Province in order to the raising of a Revenue for Provincial Purposes.

3. The borrowing of Money on the sole Credit of the Province.

4. The Establishment and Tenure of Provincial Offices and the Appointment and Payment of Provincial Officers.

5. The Management and Sale of the Public Lands belonging to the Province and of the Timber and Wood thereon.

6. The Establishment, Maintenance, and Management of Public and Reformatory Prisons in and for the Province.

7. The Establishment, Maintenance, and Management of Hospitals, Asylums, Charities, and Eleemosynary Institutions in and for the Province, other than Marine Hospitals.

8. Municipal Institutions in the Province.

9. Shop, Saloon, Tavern, Auctioneer, and other Licences in order to the raising of a Revenue for Provincial, Local, or Municipal Purposes.

10. Local Works and Undertakings other than such as are of the following Classes: –

   (*a*) Lines of Steam or other Ships, Railways, Canals, Telegraphs, and other Works and Undertakings connecting the Province with any other or others of the Provinces, or extending beyond the Limits of the Province;

   (*b*) Lines of Steam Ships between the Province and any British or Foreign Country;

   (*c*) Such Works as, although wholly situate within the Province, are before or after their Execution declared by the Parliament of Canada to be for the general Advantage of Canada or for the Advantage of Two or more of the Provinces.

11. The Incorporation of Companies with Provincial Objects.

12. The Solemnization of Marriage in the Province.

13. Property and Civil Rights in the Province.

14. The Administration of Justice in the Province, including the Constitution, Maintenance, and Organization of Provincial Courts, both of Civil and of Criminal Jurisdiction, and including Procedure in Civil Matters in those Courts.

15. The Imposition of Punishment by Fine, Penalty, or Imprisonment for enforcing any Law of the Province made in relation to any Matter coming within any of the Classes of Subjects enumerated in this Section.

16. Generally all Matters of a merely local or private Nature in the Province.

Education

93. In and for each Province the Legislature may exclusively make Laws in relation to Education, subject and according to the following Provisions: –

1. Nothing in any such Law shall prejudicially affect any Right or Privilege with respect to Denominational Schools which any Class of Persons have by Law in the Province at the Union:

2. All the Powers, Privileges, and Duties at the Union by Law conferred and imposed in Upper Canada on the Separate Schools and School Trustees of the Queen's Roman Catholic Subjects shall be and the same are hereby extended to the Dissentient Schools of the Queen's Protestant and Roman Catholic Subjects in Quebec:

3. Where in any Province a System of Separate or Dissentient Schools exists by Law at the Union or is thereafter established by the Legislature of the Province, an Appeal shall lie to the Governor General in Council from any Act or Decision of any Provincial Authority affecting any Right or Privilege of the Protestant or Roman Catholic Minority of the Queen's Subjects in relation to Education:

4. In case any such Provincial Law as from Time to Time seems to the Governor General in Council requisite for the due Execution of the Provisions of this Section is not made, or in case any Decision of the Governor General in Council on any Appeal under this Section is not duly executed by the proper Provincial Authority in that Behalf, then and in every such Case, and as far only as the Circumstances of each Case require, the Parliament of Canada may make remedial Laws for the due Execution of the Provisions of this Section and of any Decision of the Governor General in Council under this Section.

Uniformity of Laws in Ontario, Nova Scotia and New Brunswick

94. Notwithstanding anything in this Act, the Parliament of Canada may make Provision for the Uniformity of all or any of the Laws relative to Property and Civil Rights in Ontario, Nova Scotia, and New Brunswick, and of the Procedure of all or any of the Courts in those Three Provinces, and from and after the passing of any Act in that Behalf the Power of the Parliament of Canada to make Laws in relation to any Matter comprised in any such Act shall, notwithstanding anything in this Act, be unrestricted; but any Act of the Parliament of Canada making Provision for such Uni-

formity shall not have effect in any Province unless and until it is adopted and enacted as Law by the Legislature thereof.

Old Age Pensions

94A. It is hereby declared that the Parliament of Canada may from time to time make laws in relation to old age pensions in Canada, but no law made by the Parliament of Canada in relation to old age pensions shall affect the operation of any law present or future of a Provincial Legislature in relation to old age pensions.

Agriculture and Immigration

95. In each Province the Legislature may make Laws in relation to Agriculture in the Province, and to Immigration into the Province; and it is hereby declared that the Parliament of Canada may from Time to Time make Laws in relation to Agriculture in all or any of the Provinces, and to Immigration into all or any of the Provinces; and any Law of the Legislature of a Province relative to Agriculture or to Immigration shall have effect in and for the Province as long and as far only as it is not repugnant to any Act of the Parliament of Canada.

Our Changing Constitution

F. R. SCOTT

In a presidential address before this Section of the Royal Society, whose members are drawn from so many different fields of knowledge, one is tempted to choose a subject that can be treated in a manner less technical than would be expected by a more specialized audience. This paper is about our changing constitution, but from a point of view broad enough, I hope, to cut across many of the boundaries that divide us. I have selected for discussion certain aspects of our constitutional development that are particularly relevant to problems we face today, the most important of which is the "repatriation" of the constitution itself. Part of my paper – indeed much of it – will be historical, a reminder of things past, even a *recherche de la constitution perdue*; part will be autobiographical; and part of it will be rash enough to include foretellings, and perhaps forebodings, of the future. As I shall frequently refer back to a date of which we shall shortly be celebrating the centenary, namely 1867, the first all-Canadian year, I feel that a short title to my talk might simply be "Life with Fathers."

I had the good fortune, as a young student in the McGill Law Faculty, to be introduced to constitutional law by the late H. A. Smith, until recently Professor of International Law at London University. He was not only a stimulating teacher but a jurist with a strong sense of history, who looked through the legal terminology of the constitution, and of its judicial interpretations, to the body politic it was designed to create. It was he who taught me to see the problems which the Act of 1867 was intended to remedy, to look at the conditions in the British North American colonies in the 1860's, and to seek the intentions of the Fathers of Confederation not only in the words of the statutes but also in all the material available to historians, includ-

Presidential address to The Royal Society of Canada, 1961.
From: *Proceedings of The Royal Society of Canada*, Third Series, Volume 55 (1961), pages 83-95. By permission of the author.

ing the Confederation debates and other *travaux préparatoires*. He was well aware that English and Canadian courts exclude references to most of this material, and he has strongly urged[1] that this rule of exclusion should be changed to the more sensible practice, well established in continental jurisdictions, of permitting the judges to admit all historical evidence and to use their own discretion in respect of it.

Professor Smith was among the first commentators in Canada to point out that the trend in Privy Council interpretations of the B.N.A. Act – he was writing just after the disastrous judgment of 1925 in the Snider case had reduced federal jurisdiction to its lowest point – had been towards a type of constitution quite different from that which the Fathers of Confederation had clearly intended. To use his own words: "Whether the principle of federal government devised by our forefathers or that more recently established by the Privy Council is the better for Canada is a question of policy beyond the scope of this article. I hope that I have written enough to show that they are not the same."[2]

The Fathers had stressed the importance of the federal government's being given ample authority for the great task of nation-building[3] that was entrusted to it. Unlike the American Congress, the Parliament of Canada possessed the residue of powers not otherwise distributed, as well as its specified powers. The Privy Council, in certain leading cases, had paid so much attention to the preservation of provincial autonomy, as though this was the chief or only aim of the Fathers, and had so expanded provincial jurisdiction over property and civil rights, as virtually to transfer the federal residuary power to provincial hands, at least in peacetime. Apart from the residuary clause, Privy Council judgments drastically curtailed federal jurisdiction over trade and commerce, fisheries and agriculture. Such a *volte face* could only have occurred in a court which substituted its own idea of the intentions of the Fathers from that which was on the record it barred itself from examining.

[1] "Interpretation in English and Continental Law," *J. Comp. Leg.*, Third Series, vol. IX (1927), p. 153. See also "The Residue of Power in Canada," 1926 Can. Bar Rev., 432 at p. 433.

[2] "The Residue of Power in Canada," 1926 *Can. Bar Rev.* 432 at p. 439.

[3] Cartier, Brown, Galt, and other Fathers of Confederation used the word "nation" to represent all Canada. See references in F. R. Scott, "Political Nationalism and Confederation," *C.J.E.P.S.*, VIII, 3 (1942), pp. 387-90.

Professor Smith's thesis took some time to win acceptance in legal and academic circles. The historical record, it is true, was not wholly clear, either before or after 1925. A change of heart seemed to occur when the Privy Council in the years 1930-32 attributed to federal competence two matters of national and indeed international importance, namely aeronautics and broadcasting,[4] but this was a short-lived respite. After the judicial massacre of Mr. Bennett's "New Deal" legislation in 1937,[5] weakening if not destroying federal competence over unemployment insurance, interprovincial marketing, and the implementing of Canadian treaties, there were few commentators left in Canada who had not put themselves on record as sharing Professor Smith's point of view.[6] Instead of being "a living tree capable of growth and expansion," as the constitution was described in 1930, it was now likened to a ship of state sailing on larger ventures but still retaining the "watertight compartments" which were an essential part of her original structure. So, as Professor McWhinney points out,[7] the "marine metaphor" of Lord Atkin offsets the "arboreal metaphor" of Lord Sankey. The Sirois Report in 1940, perhaps not wanting to wound provincial susceptibilities, came to the remarkable conclusion that the historical interpretation and references to the intentions of the Fathers of Confederation proved nothing, and that anyway the enquiry was not worth pursuing.[8] The enquiry, in my opinion, was very well worth pursuing and is still more worth pursuing as we come to face the problem of nationalizing the constitution. In turning our back on history we may forget values and experiences which are still valid.

I think perhaps in this debate, now almost forgotten but having a relevance I shall attempt to show in a moment, there were some important considerations overlooked. A constitution establishes a structure and framework for a country based on certain values. If, like ours, it is largely a written constitution for a federal state, it is a law for making laws, looking to the

---

[4] Both judgments are reported in 1932 A.C., pp. 54 and 304 ff.

[5] See the Appeal Cases for that year: also comments in 1937 *Can. Bar Rev.*, pp. 393-507.

[6] I have compiled a list of these authorities in "Centralisation and Decentralisation in Canadian Federalism," 1951 *Can. Bar Rev.*, p. 1095 at p. 1108 n. 44.

[7] *Judicial Review in the English-Speaking World* (2nd ed.: Toronto, 1960), p. 74.

[8] *Report of the Royal Commission on Dominion-Provincial Relations* (Ottawa, 1940), vol. I, pp. 32-6.

future exercise of the powers distributed for the attainment of the desired ends. The value of the historical approach is not that it necessarily settles the points of contention that the courts must wrestle with, or that it renders more precise the meaning of words and expressions whose ambiguities are only brought to light by experience, though it sometimes may help even here. The value is rather in the broad objectives it discloses, the political concepts shown to have gone into the making of the constitution, which point in the general direction that the courts would be expected to follow.

The great constitutional values that the Fathers of Confederation considered important cannot easily be disputed. Those men valued provincial autonomy, of course, or there would not have been a federal state. But they equally clearly valued a federalism that leaned towards strength at the centre when the choice had to be made, or they would not have placed the residue of powers in federal hands, unified the court structure, and provided for federal appointment of Lieutenant-Governors and disallowance of provincial laws. They held the duality of cultures to be a value; they wanted protection for certain school and language rights. The two cultures, moreover, were to enjoy equal status in the Province of Quebec, despite the numerical superiority of the French-speaking element there. They clearly intended Canada to possess a system of parliamentary democracy, for the whole Act, as well as the Preamble, contemplates the free working of parliamentary institutions with all that that implies in the way of fundamental liberties. And that the new federal government was to be the chief builder of the national economy, having the main responsibility for our future material well being, is abundantly evident from all that was said at the time as well as in the provisions of the Act relating to economic matters. In the words of Dr. Mackintosh, speaking of the Fathers of Confederation: "They had conceived a great and daring project: the development of inter-provincial trade, the acquisition of the West from the Hudson's Bay Company, the construction of a transcontinental railway and the administration of a scheme of immigration and land settlement."[9] It is in the light of these values and objectives that the main criticism of the constitutional commentators was directed at the results of so much of the judicial interpretation.

[9] In *Federalism: An Australian Jubilee Study*, ed. Geoffrey Sawer (Melbourne, 1952), pp. 87-8.

Among French-speaking lawyers and jurists the study of constitutional law has, quite naturally perhaps, been accorded less time and received less attention than the broad field of the civil law, Quebec's proud and exclusive possession. The aspects of the constitution which most occupied French Canada until comparatively recently were those dealing with language and school rights, and with Canada's status in the Empire and Commonwealth. Under the powerful and colourful leadership of Premier Duplessis, however, and emerging from the extreme centralization of World War II, ardent defenders of Quebec's autonomy discovered their provincial government as a potent symbol (with a flag) and protector of their rights and revendications. The full value of certain Privy Council trends in interpretation came to be appreciated, though the developing opinion did not stop there. When Quebec's Royal Commission of Inquiry on Constitutional Problems in 1956 did make the kind of political, social, and economic analysis of the constitution to which English-speaking Canadians had been more habituated, it produced, in both French and English, the five weighty volumes of its Report that we call the Tremblay Report.[10] Though little known, I suspect, outside Quebec, and perhaps confined to certain circles inside, this Report is in my opinion as important reading for serious students of our constitution as any other work we possess – at least if you believe, as I do, that thoughts in people's heads are potent forces making for constitutional change.

Like the Sirois Report, to which it is in effect a point by point reply, the Tremblay Report crystallizes a certain attitude of certain people at a certain time, and also like the Sirois Report, its recommendations are not all going to be accepted. It puts forward a view of Canadian federalism based (if I may be forgiven an over-simplification) upon the treaty-between-races concept, the notion that the constitution is primarily designed to preserve and promote the duality of cultures. Note that this concept is not the same as the concept of provincial autonomy, since the notion of cultural partnership does not favour any province except Quebec. From the treaty concept, however, conclusions are drawn which would require a relinquishment of federal control and jurisdiction far greater than any to be hinted at even in Privy Council judgments and such as would have

[10] *Report of the Royal Commission of Inquiry on Constitutional Problems* (Quebec, Queen's Printer, 1956), and Annexes.

astounded the Fathers of Confederation. The duality of cultures was, as I have said, one of the values, and a great value, accepted at Confederation, but then it was not believed to be incompatible with the other values also affirmed at the time, one of which was that our federalism should be strong at the centre rather than weak. The Tremblay Report is one possible view, if not of what Canadian federalism is (though in some degree this claim is made), but of what it ought to be; it touches on matters which are so much a part of our national life as never to be far from our political choices; and it adds a number of challenging ideas to that total stream of thought and discussion in Canada, whose variety of claims and whose contradictions make our constitutional history and law so interesting.

I know it sounds a little old-fashioned still to be talking about the Fathers of Confederation and the kind of country they foresaw. The choices they made are not necessarily the best for today. But it seems to me both interesting and relevant to know why they made them, so that if we decide to reject or alter their scale of values, we do so deliberately and consciously. We seem to be facing constitutional issues comparable, in some ways, to theirs. We are certainly having to think out our relationship with the United States afresh. Canada in the 1860's received the opposite treatment from that which is now accorded us: instead of seducing us by the embrace of great corporations, which has brought so many of us to bed with affluence, the Americans then cast our forefathers out into the economic wilderness by cancelling the Reciprocity Treaty, just as England had earlier rejected them by repealing the corn laws. So there we were in the 1860's, English- and French-speaking Canadians, Maritimers and distant western colonials, having to meet the challenge of continental isolation with boldness and imagination, or else to remain in a petty provincialism exposed to all the dangers of stagnation and ultimate absorption.

I am still impressed, every time I reflect upon it, with the largeness of outlook of the men who believed, though they had only the simplest and slowest means of communication with remote parts of a vast country, that they could make of the bigger northern half of the continent something like what the Americans had made of the southern half so far as economic development was concerned. At that time the prime mover in the whole business had to be the new government at Ottawa; provinces were necessary for the preservation of local customs and institutions, and had their guaranteed rights, but they could not be the chief builders of the new federal state. Many of the leading Fathers of Confederation, particularly in central Canada, moved out of the provincial sphere into the new national sphere because the opportunities there were larger and the outlook more exciting. Even Joseph Howe ended rather ingloriously in Ottawa, and though he supported the idea at first, confederation knew no more formidable opponent. All this took place without anyone's imagining that it jeopardized the separate schools in Quebec and Ontario, the language rights, or the Quebec Civil Code, all of which were established and accepted at the time the B.N.A. Act became law. Federal and provincial governments were not thought of as competing units, almost sworn enemies, but as complementary institutions all engaged in their allotted tasks for the benefit of the whole people of Canada. Within the wide boundaries of legitimate provincial autonomy there was thought to be ample room for cultural freedom.

It would take too long to trace here the fading of this early Canadian dream towards the end of the nineteenth century. The prolonged economic depression that began in 1873 seemed to prove the failure of the national economic policies,[11] and increasing tension between races was caused by conflicts over schools and language. What a difference it would have made in Canada if the Privy Council had not overruled the unanimous decision of the Supreme Court setting aside the Manitoba School Laws of 1890.[12] We would have avoided the intense bitterness of the racial feeling that preceded the 1896 election. French Canada felt that on the first great test of her rights the B.N.A. Act had failed her. It was of course London, not Ottawa that failed her. These various influences resulted in a great increase in provincial autonomy at the close of the century. The inter-provincial conference of 1887 was the first expression of provincial revolt against federal dominance. It is remarkable how many of the specific requests for constitutional change then made have since been accorded the provinces, chiefly by judicial interpretation.[13] The great western boom in the decade before

[11] *Report of the Royal Commission on Dominion-Provincial Relations*, vol. I, p. 50.

[12] *Winnipeg* v. *Barrett*, 1892 A.C. 445.

[13] I have listed these in *Evolving Canadian Federalism*, ed. A. R. M. Lower, F. R. Scott, *et al.* (Durham: Duke University Press, 1958), pp. 69-70.

World War I brought a revival of federal prestige, seeming to justify the expenditures in railway building, immigration, and land settlement, and the war years 1914-18 added to federal importance by the requirements of national policy and by bringing Canada out into the international arena. But these years also widened the racial gap by reason of the school language issue in Ontario and the conscription issue of 1917, and the centralized emergency powers were swiftly dissipated by constitutional interpretation after the war.

Canada was a very divided country during the 1920's, and men of my generation will remember how much the theme of national unity was the object of our discussion and thought in that decade. Though we may not have seen it clearly at the time, new economic factors were increasing the centrifugal forces in Canada and enlarging provincial authority, for the economic expansion was now, not in railways and land settlement, primarily a federal responsibility, but in developing provincial resources by private capital with the consent of provincial governments, Pulp and paper, lumber, base metals, hydroelectric power, opened new fields for investment, most of it private, much of it American. The era of great corporate expansion had begun. In the law courts, the federal government saw its first important effort at economic regulations, its 1919 Board of Commerce Act and its Combines and Fair Prices Act, struck down,[14] and then lost its jurisdiction over labour relations except for a small number of federal undertakings.[15] The way was cleared for an almost unlimited exploitation of Canadian resources by U.S. capital with the assurance of a minimum of governmental control – far less, certainly, than the same capital would have had to face in the United States itself, where the Inter-State Commerce Commission, the Federal Trade Commission, and the anti-trust laws were in effect.

When the great depression of the 1930's converted even the Conservatives into New Dealers, the federal government made another effort at economic leadership, only to meet a second defeat in the law courts. The Natural Products Marketing Act, the Employment and Social Insurance Act, and the three statutes providing minimum wages, maximum hours, and a weekly day of rest were all held unconstitutional.[16] "The economic

---

[14] *In re* Board of Commerce Act, 1922 1 A.C. 191.
[15] *Toronto Electric Commissioners* v. *Snider*, 1925 A.C. 396.
[16] These decisions are all reported in 1937 A.C., pp. 326-418.

needs of the nation" have had little relevance to our constitutional law, though they have every relevance to our daily lives, our level of employment, and our standard of living.

So far this account may be leaving the impression that the economic situation ought to be much worse in Canada than in fact it is. How have we enjoyed the post World War II prosperity, such as it was? There are two constitutional answers to this; I do not attempt to give economic ones. One is that we did do something about the constitution: we amended it twice so as to give the federal government the power to enact unemployment insurance and old age pension laws. This established Ottawa firmly in the field of social security and added to its freedom in fiscal policy. In the light of present conditions we can see more clearly that while these forms of welfare legislation provide cushions to ease the shock of economic decline, they do not prevent that decline. Some more positive forms of economic leadership and control are going to be necessary unless we want to fold our hands and watch the current hardships, the regional declines, and the growing injustices with total indifference. Something else besides amendment to the B.N.A. Act took place, however, without formal constitutional change but with even greater constitutional significance. This was the growing use of monetary policy, taxation, and planned government spending, as factors in maintaining economic equilibrium. From the time of its economic proposals in 1945, the federal government became committed to a policy of high and stable levels of income and employment. Keynes became a kind of post-natal Father of Confederation.

The emergence of fiscal and monetary policy as economic regulators has become so important a factor today as almost to make us forget the question of legislative jurisdiction. It seems to have by-passed Sections 91 and 92 of the B.N.A. Act. The lawyers are moving out and the economists are moving in. Since Ottawa has the most money, and exclusive control of banking and currency, this fiscal approach restores federal influence in the total governmental picture though no new judgments are forthcoming from the courts to enlarge federal jurisdiction. Ottawa learns to induce where it cannot command, and federal policy is made by bargains with provincial governments. The economic system of course goes on its own way quite apart from this spending power, though greatly affected by it.

Perhaps before handing over entirely to the economists at this point, I may be allowed to keep my foot in the constitutional door for a moment longer. The federal spending power has not gone altogether unchallenged. Indeed, the Tremblay Report challenges it directly as being a violation of the federal principle, especially when the spending is for welfare and educational projects. If the authors of the Tremblay Report had their way, Ottawa would move out of unemployment insurance, old age pensions, family allowances, university and research grants, health insurance, and any other forms of direct subsidy for national welfare or cultural expression. This would indeed be a vast change in our constitutional behaviour. Professor Corry has remarked that it is strange that no one has challenged the spending power in the courts, though he admits it is not likely to be denied at this stage.[17] Actually the Family Allowance Act was challenged on one occasion and was upheld by one judge in the Exchequer Court.[18] The refusal of Quebec universities to take federal grants was a challenge to the spending power, though of a somewhat uncertain kind since these universities first accepted them and then, under what I am convinced was external pressure and not a genuine academic decision, changed their minds.[19]

I wish to put myself on record again as of the opinion that the prerogative right of the Crown to make gifts of any money it possesses is unimpaired in Canada, whether it be the federal Crown or the provincial Crown – assuming, of course, that the legislature votes the appropriation. The reason (stated without argument) is that both aspects of the Crown may dispose

[17] In *Evolving Canadian Federalism*, p. 119.

[18] *Angers* v. *Minister of National Revenue*, 1957 Ex. C.R. 83.

[19] See *Survey of Higher Education, 1952-54* (Dominion Bureau of Statistics, 1957), pp. 9-12, for a brief history of Federal Government University Grants. Premier Lesage, when saying that Quebec universities were free to receive Canada Council grants for buildings, explained that they had failed to obtain them in the past only because of a "caprice" of the former National Union government. See *Montreal Star*, June 1, 1961. The N.C.C.U., of which Quebec universities are members, asked the Massey Commission for *per capita* grants for all students registered in professional faculties, and at its meeting in 1951 passed a unanimous Resolution approving the recommendations of the Massey Report. See *Proceedings of the National Council of Canadian Universities 1951*, p. 73.

gratuitously of their own moneys as they see fit.[20] The first of the federal enumerated powers in the Act of 1867 is the exclusive jurisdiction over the "Public Debt and Property," and money in the Consolidated Revenue Fund is public property. So I believe the federal Crown may decide to invest money in a new industry, like Polymer Corporation, or to subsidize an old one like the coal industry in Nova Scotia, or to buy all butter offered to it at x cents a pound, or to build a War Memorial in France, or a dam in India, or to purchase Old Masters for the National Gallery. It is difficult to see how this country could be governed if this power were to be denied; though this is not the same as saying that every government expenditure is a good one or a wise one. By the same spending power a province may open an office in London or New York, contribute to a *Maison Canadienne* in Paris (though it can only make laws "within the province" according to the wording of the B.N.A. Act), may send students abroad on scholarships, may make gifts of food or money to victims of famine in foreign lands, or may even, as is the case in Quebec, give provincial taxpayers' money to a few selected universities in other provinces.

And while I am in this vein, may I add a word about the concept of welfare in our constitution. There are so many vested interests fighting any extension of public welfare expenditure in Canada, and so much advertising and propaganda against it, that we are in danger of being brainwashed into believing that welfare is an evil word. There can be argument about the quantity and forms of welfare, but it cannot be denied that to serve the public welfare is a proper function of all governments in a democratic state. Not just the provincial, not just the federal, but federal, provincial, and local governments have this duty. Every state worthy of being called free, as well as some that are not, is a form of welfare state today. The Fathers of Confederation were very familiar with the word welfare: both in the Quebec Resolutions and in the London Resolutions the residuary power of the federal parliament was expressed as a power to make laws for the peace, *welfare*, and good government of the

[20] Mr. Barrette when Premier of Quebec shared this view. When asked why he made gifts to educational institutions outside Quebec, he replied, "La province peut faire un don aussi bien qu'un individu" (See *Le Devoir*, April 9, 1960). It is interesting to note that the first Legislature in Quebec in 1868 appropriated $4,000 for "Aid to Distressed Seamen in Nova Scotia." A nice example of the spending power. (See 31 Vict. (Que.) Cap. I, p. 10.)

provinces. "Peace, welfare and good government" are the operative words conferring all jurisdiction to the Legislature in the Act of Union, 1840. No doubt the word had a less inclusive meaning then than now, as had many other words in the constitution, but today's concepts are a logical extension of earlier ones. The Consolidated Statutes of the Province of Canada, 1859, contained laws on Public Health, Inoculation and Vaccination, Emigrants and Quarantine, Charitable and Provident Associations, Private Lunatic Asylums; all these applied to both Upper and Lower Canada, and were over and above the local laws on welfare matters in the two sections of the Province.

Some unknown draftsman changed "welfare" into "order" in the B.N.A. Act so the Section now reads "Peace, Order, and Good Government," but the word was not taken out of the Preamble of the constitution, which still reminds us that "such a Union," that is, a federal Union under the Crown, "would conduce to the welfare of the provinces." Welfare was to be the result of union: how then is the government of the Union not concerned with it? Of course it must be a concern with welfare that is of a different order from that exclusively reserved to provinces, but the federal entry into the field, unless there is a transfer of jurisdiction, leaves provincial jurisdiction intact. The problem of cost is another matter, a practical matter involving concepts of equity, balance, and fair treatment, and particularly bringing to light the important function of Parliament in minimizing the discrepancies in our regional incomes. But this belongs to the politics of federalism more than to the law. That it requires a more co-operative kind of federalism than we have had in the past, and more instruments of co-operation, there can be no doubt. Federal-provincial conferences seem here to stay, and they are likely to play a part in our evolution to which there is no real parallel in United States constitutional behaviour. Let us remember, however, that rightly considered every parliament of Canada is also, in a sense, a federal-provincial conference, since its members represent all sections of the country. The provinces of Canada have two governmental voices, not just one, and Ottawa speaks for Quebec, Ontario, and the rest on all matters within federal competence.

Let us come back to this question of jurisdiction. Some things cannot be done by federal-provincial conferences. They can only be done by federal legislation that is national in scope. There is no escape from this, however much it smacks of centralization. It is just another way of saying that freedom of action for the central government is just as important in a federal state as freedom of action for the component parts. Indeed, in a world moving towards integration, in many respects it is more important. Either certain things are done by an authority with larger jurisdiction than that conferred on provinces, or they are not done at all. The command of the law must bear some relationship to the size of the problems sought to be regulated. We have met this difficulty on the municipal level, where metropolitan government becomes impossible if left to a multitude of separate local municipalities. We have met it on the international level, where state sovereignty continues to hamper efforts at regional and world government. We still find it, and I suppose always shall find it, on the national level.

The point will become clearer if I give some examples of existing deficiencies in the federal power. Canada's capacity to enter into treaty relationships with other states is wholly inadequate to the needs of today. The damaging effect of the I.L.O. Conventions case,[21] which in effect overruled the more liberal interpretation of the Privy Council in the Radio case,[22] have not been overcome. Every time Canada abstains from participating in multilateral conventions aimed at achieving good international standards, because of lack of jurisdiction to implement them, she withholds her influence for peace and co-operation. In internal matters, there is a lack of federal jurisdiction in the fields of marketing legislation, and control of the sale of corporation securities. Provincial jurisdiction over industrial disputes is quite incapable of regulating the situations which can arise when nation-wide employers are dealing with nation-wide unions.[23] Many important aspects of trade and commerce, affecting all provinces, have been held to fall into the provincial jurisdiction over property and civil rights. If we should attempt to exert a wider control over the national economy in peace time the jurisdictional gaps would become very evident.[24] And there is no ultimate power in Canada to amend the constitution itself.

These realities we must keep before us. Adaptation of the

---

[21] 1937 A.C. 326.

[22] 1932 A.C. 304.

[23] See F. R. Scott, "Federal Jurisdiction over Labour Relations – A New Look," *McGill Law Journal* (1960), p. 153.

[24] Some of these are discussed in F. R. Scott, "Social Planning and Federalism" in *Social Purpose for Canada*, ed. Michael Oliver (University of Toronto Press, 1961).

present constitution might come, in part, from judicial interpretation, but this is a lengthy and unsure process. We are confronted again with the need for constitutional amendment. Even if no specific amendments are now being sought, an amendment to give ourselves a complete amending procedure must be secured, or Canada remains in an equivocal position. This is what "repatriation" means in legal terms.

This brings me to my final point. We are now in the process of holding federal-provincial conferences of Attorneys-General, to seek this all-embracing amending formula and the "repatriation" of the constitution. We have to transfer to Canadian legislatures the last vestiges of sovereignty over Canada still remaining in the United Kingdom. When this is done, some body or bodies in Canada will alone make all constitutional changes. But how? This is where we have always failed in the past. Just eleven years ago I read my first paper to this Section of the Society on the topic: "The Redistribution of Imperial Sovereignty." Since then that redistribution has accelerated, and the Mother of Parliaments has been "signing off" its authority over new state after new state. Canada has been left out of this process because we could not agree on the terms on which we would take our freedom. We are like Mr. Melpomenous Jones in Leacock's story, who never could make up his mind to say good-bye; finally after visiting some friends for dinner and being kept on as a house-guest for weeks, he acquired a fatal fever and departed this life murmuring "I think I must go now."

What is happening at the Attorneys-General Conference is mostly confidential and cannot be discussed here. This is itself a fact of some importance. It is our country and our future that is being planned and we – the citizens – should have our chance to be heard at the appropriate time before our governments have taken up fixed positions. Not being able to enlarge upon the suggestions now being considered, I shall content myself with bringing this paper to a conclusion by summarizing my ideas in the form of a series of propositions.

1. The Canadian constitution has not yet recovered from the damaging effects of judicial interpretation in the past. The argument for flexibility in the amending procedure is therefore particularly strong provided it can be achieved without endangering the cultural partnership which is fundamental to our federalism. If we freeze the present distribution of powers the

federal government could be gravely hampered in dealing with future problems.

2. Canada is facing constitutional choices comparable in their importance and their future implications to those which were made a hundred years ago by the Fathers of Confederation. They established a federal system: we must now define its nature.

3. The "repatriation" of the constitution involves replacing the theory of the legal sovereignty of the United Kingdom Parliament, on which the B.N.A. Act now rests, with a new theory. The amending clause will imply that theory.

4. The crux of the problem lies in the degree of provincial consent necessary to effect a transfer of legislative jurisdiction as between Parliament and Legislatures. The compact theory of Confederation, now seemingly uppermost in the present discussions, would require the unanimous consent of provinces for any such change. Such rigidity would I think be fatal to Canadian federalism. The treaty-between-races theory is somewhat more flexible, since it would require the consent of Quebec but not necessarily of all the other provinces. A theory that balanced the need for cultural guarantees with the need for constitutional adaptation to the rapidly changing conditions of the modern world would entrench minority rights without entrenching all other provincial powers in their present form – least of all the whole of "property and civil rights" as those words are presently defined by the courts.

5. Before 1867 it took at least a decade of conferences and discussions before a constitutional solution was found acceptable to a majority of Upper and Lower Canadians and Maritimers. While a decade has passed since the last Federal-Provincial Constitutional Conference of 1950, the interval has been marked, not by intensive discussion, but by the absence of discussion.

6. The nation today is not prepared for the choices it seems to be on the point of making. Any final decisions should be delayed until much wider groups of people have been brought into the picture and invited to participate in the formulation of an amending procedure appropriate to our traditions, our experience, and our present needs.

7. While the present position of Canada *vis-à-vis* the United Kingdom is equivocal and obviously temporary, the dangers of

delay in terminating it are far less than the dangers of too hasty an acceptance of "repatriation" at any price.

8. The continuation of the reserve constituent powers of the United Kingdom Parliament in the amending of the Canadian constitution is no more a limitation on Canadian sovereignty than is the continuation of the position of the Crown in respect of Canada. In both instances the political control of the exercise of the United Kingdom legal powers is in the hands of Canadians. The Crown acts only on the advice of its Canadian ministers, and the United Kingdom Parliament acts only on the advice of the Canadian Parliament.

9. Future conferences on repatriation should include representatives of opposition parties as well as representatives of parties in power. The constitution is for all Canadians and not just for present governments.

Canada is built on a series of paradoxes. East-west versus north-south pulls, central power versus provincial autonomy, economic integration versus cultural dualism – one could extend the list of opposites which must be harmonized and accommodated if we are to remain as a single nation-state in a changing world. Other solutions could be found to the one which the Fathers of Confederation, backed by a majority of the peoples of Canada of both races at the time, chose and thought to be viable. Nationalism is a force as powerful today as ever in the history of mankind, and nationalism in Canada is again a paradox, perhaps the greatest paradox, because it is not a single but a dual nationalism, French-speaking Canada feeling itself to be a nation fully as strongly as the other provinces feel themselves to be a nation. If these understandable and valid forms of nationalism seek their outlet primarily in cultural partnership, on terms of equality, then the political federalism we now possess will not be broken, though it may well have to make further accommodations to internal pressures. If the requirements of cultural dualism are pushed to political extremes, as evidenced in the renewed strength of the separatist movement in Quebec, then of course we shall have failed to maintain the original concept of Confederation and the Union will end in disunion. I am one of those who believe that the original constitution of Canada, changing as it must in face of new demands and new challenges, is still basically adapted to the sum total of our various hopes and aspirations.

The Meaning of Provincial Autonomy

LOUIS-PHILIPPE PIGEON

A proper study of the problem of provincial autonomy requires consideration of some fundamental principles. Laws are the framework of society. Without them, relations between men would be governed by individual brute force. Any order of things means laws in one form or in another. Laws in turn imply an authority empowered to make and to enforce them. Under any form of government the power of this authority over individuals is of necessity very great, and very great also is its influence on their living conditions.

For any given group of humans the constitution of the civil authority by which they are governed is therefore of prime importance. Obviously this will cause any human group possessing special characteristics to desire an authority of its own. A group forming what is sociologically termed a "nation" normally aspires to independence. Small states are apt however to encounter very serious difficulties owing to their inherent military and economic weakness. Instead of precarious military alliances or trade agreements, a federation offers stability and permanency. The federal state is an attempt to reconcile the need of military, political and economic strength, which large units only can offer, with the desire for self-government that is inherent in any human group having distinct collective feelings.

Of course federation necessarily implies that some powers become vested in a central authority. The real problem is the definition of these powers or, its corollary, of the powers remaining in the federated states or provinces.

In the eyes of some men, a federal state is an instrument of unification, in other words, a means of bringing about the gradual disappearance of the segmental differences opposed to complete political unity. In the eyes of others, federation of itself

From: *The Canadian Bar Review*, Volume 29 (1951), pages 1126-35.
By permission of the author and publisher.

implies this complete political unity, the component states or provinces being looked upon as mere administrative entities whose functions should be restricted to the application of general policies defined by the central authority. In the eyes of autonomists, federation implies a division of political authority so that the component states or provinces are free to define their general policy in their own sphere of activity, without being obliged to conform with any pattern set down by the central authority.

In the construction of the British North America Act the courts, and especially the Judicial Committee of the Privy Council, have fairly consistently adopted the autonomist conception of federation:

They [the Federal Government] *maintained that the effect of the statute has been to sever all connections between the Crown and the provinces; to make the government of the Dominion the only government of Her Majesty in North America; and to reduce the provinces to the rank of independent municipal institutions. For these propositions, which contain the sum and substance of the arguments addressed to them in support of this appeal, their Lordships have been unable to find either principle or authority. . . . and a Lieutenant-Governor, when appointed, is as much the representative of Her Majesty for all purposes of provincial government as the Governor-General himself is for all purposes of Dominion government.*[1]

The scheme of theAct passed in 1867 was thus, not to weld the Provinces into one, nor to subordinate Provincial Governments to a central authority, but to establish a central government in which these Provinces should be represented, entrusted with exclusive authority only in affairs in which they had a common interest. Subject to this each Province was to retain its independence and autonomy and to be directly under the Crown as its head.[2]

Their Lordships do not conceive it to be the duty of this Board – it is certainly not their desire – to cut down the provisions of the Act by a narrow and technical construction, but rather to give it a large and liberal interpretation so that the Dominion to a great extent, but within certain fixed limits, may

[1] *Liquidators of the Maritime Bank of Canada* v. *Receiver-General of N.B.*, [1892] A.C. 437, at pp. 441-3.
[2] In re *The Initiative and Referendum Act*, [1919] A.C. 935, at p. 942.

be mistress in her own house, as the Provinces to a great extent, but within certain fixed limits, are mistresses in theirs.[3]

All the arguments advanced against these decisions by numerous writers are based either on the "Peace, Order and good Government" clause or on the so-called "historical construction" of the Act.

In support of the first argument it is contended that the courts have failed to give full effect to the opening words of section 91[4] and that the authority thus conferred on the federal Parliament should be broadly construed.[5] But it is significant that seldom do those who advance this contention quote the complete sentence. They speak of the importance of the grant of legislative authority for the "Peace, Order and good Government of Canada". They point out that such expressions were traditionally used to grant legislative authority; but they pay slight attention to the fact that these pregnant words are immediately followed by the all-important restriction: "in relation to all Matters not coming within the classes of Subjects by this Act assigned exclusively to the Legislatures of the Provinces." If due attention is paid to these words, it becomes impossible to construe the grant of residuary power otherwise than as saving provincial authority instead of overriding it.

---

[3] *"Persons"* case, [1930] A.C. 124, at p. 136.

[4] "It shall be lawful for the Queen, by and with the Advice and Consent of the Senate and House of Commons, to make Laws for the Peace, Order, and good Government of Canada, in relation to all Matters not coming within the Classes of Subjects by this Act assigned exclusively to the Legislatures of the Provinces . . . ."

[5] See, for example, Bora Laskin, " 'Peace, Order and Good Government' Re-examined" (1947), 25 Can. Bar Rev. 1054, at p. 1085, and reprinted in this volume, pp. 66-104: "Some sixty years ago the Judicial Committee said in *Riel* v. *The Queen* that the words 'peace, order and good government' were words 'apt to authorize the utmost discretion of enactment for the attainment of the objects pointed to.' The remark was not made in relation to sections 91 and 92 of the British North America Act and in the context of the Act it is undoubtedly too wide. But in its reference to legislative objects it indicates the type of problem which a court must face in interpreting sections 91 and 92. It is beside the point that the words of the introductory clause are too large and loose for comfortable adjudication. The Judicial Committee has not been reticent about its ability to give content to the large and loose provincial legislative powers in relation to property and civil rights in the province, although it may be noted that it has done so largely in terms of thwarting exercises of federal legislative power, whether for the peace, order and good government of Canada or in relation to the regulation of trade and commerce."

The "historical construction" is a pretended inquiry into the intentions of the framers of the Canadian constitution, otherwise than by a consideration of the meaning of the words used in the final document. The fallacy of this method lies not only in the fact that it runs counter to a fundamental rule of legal interpretation[6] but also in the fact that it is most unreliable. The B.N.A. Act is not the expression of the intention of one man, whose ideas might perhaps be gathered from extrinsic evidence with a reasonable degree of certainty; it is the expression of a compromise between many men holding different and opposed viewpoints. When agreement was reached on a text, are we justified in assuming that agreement was also reached on intentions?

We know that the Fathers of Confederation were far from unanimous in their conception of the proposed federation. Some, like Charles Tupper, held complete unification as their ideal, while others, like E. B. Chandler,[7] favoured a large measure of provincial autonomy. A compromise formula was finally devised to which both groups assented. Does this mean that their conflicting points of view had been reconciled?[8]

Experience in the practice of law shows that it is extremely difficult to visualize all the implications of a complex statute. Taxation statutes, for example, are prepared by specialists and scrutinized by experienced parliamentary counsel. Even then amendments introduced for the express purpose of avoiding unintended and undesired results are far from uncommon. Obviously, the long-term consequences of constitutional enactments are much more difficult of exact appreciation than the immediate consequences of taxation statutes.

6 "The question is, not what may be supposed to have been intended, but what has been said": *Brophy* v. *A.-G. of Manitoba*, [1895] A.C. 202, at p. 216. See also *Ladore* v. *Bennett*, [1939] A.C. 468. This is not a rule of interpretation of statutes but a general rule applicable to all legal documents, such as wills: *Auger* v. *Beaudry*, [1920], A.C. 1010, at p. 1014.

7 See Pope's Confederation Documents, p. 84.

8 There are definite indications that Sir John A. Macdonald had yielded to the desire of the delegates of Lower Canada, who insisted on a definite measure of autonomy. He is reported to have said at the Quebec Conference (Pope's Confederation Documents, p. 86): "New Zealand constitution was a Legislative Union, ours Federal. Emigrants went out under different guarantees. Local charters jarred. In order to guard these, they gave the powers stated to Local Legislatures, but the General Government had power to sweep these away. That is just what we do not want. Lower Canada and the Lower Provinces would not have such a thing."

Another important and often overlooked factor contributing to the difficulty of interpreting the B.N.A. Act is the fact that words actually lose much precision of meaning when used to define broad and fundamental political conceptions. The meaning of words is conventional. In final analysis it rests on generally accepted usage. It is really precise only to the extent that the category of acts or things described by any given word is susceptible of exact and objective definition.

This is the kind of precision which is almost totally lacking in the definitions of legal categories and concepts. They are precise only when aplied to a given existing system of laws. Within this existing framework, such words as civil, criminal, municipal, have a clear and unmistakable meaning. But when the same words are used to define fields of legislative activity, any great degree of precision disappears. This is because, to a certain extent, the distinction between classes of laws is not based on an objective classification of the activities which are their subject-matter, but on the technique used in regulating them.[9] In fact, the same activities are the subject-matter of different classes of laws from different aspects. As an illustration of the many judicial pronouncements in which this is recognized, I should like to quote these words of the late Chief Justice Duff:[10]

The fallacy lies in failing to distinguish between legislation affecting civil rights and legislation "in relation to" civil rights. Most legislation of a repressive character does incidentally or consequentially affect civil rights. But if in its true character it is not legislation "in relation to" the subject matter of "property and civil rights" within the provinces, within the meaning of section 92 of the British North America Act, then that is no objection although it be passed in exercise of the residuary authority conferred by the introductory clause.

On what basis is the "true character" to be ascertained, once it is decided, as it should be, that "civil law" and "criminal law" are not to be confined to the content that they had in 1867?[11]

When the question is critically examined it becomes apparent

[9] If a repressive technique is resorted to, the law is classified as "criminal" or "penal"; if a remedy by private lawsuit is created, the law is classified as "civil."

[10] *Gold Seal Ltd.* v. *A.-G. Alberta* (1921), 62 S.C.R. 424, at p. 460.

[11] *Proprietary Articles Trade Ass.* v. *A.-G. for Canada*, [1931] A.C. 310.

that human activities as a whole are the subject matter of legislation and that these activities are, in our modern society, so inter-related that, if every possible degree of connexity is explored, there is no limit to the permissible extension of any given field of legislation. For instance, in Australia, federal power over "national defence" has, in wartime, been construed as extending to any measure deemed necessary. In Canada, unlimited federal authority for emergency legislation was held to be *implied* in the Constitution:

> *It is proprietary and civil rights in new relations, which they do not present in normal times, that have to be dealt with. . . . In a* sufficiently great *emergency such as that arising out of war, there is implied the power to deal adequately with that emergency for the safety of the Dominion as a whole.*[12]

It is thus seen that a most important distinction rests on the appreciation of a "degree" of necessity. If any degree were held sufficient, federal authority would be practically unlimited. As illustrations of this principle let me consider briefly the jurisprudence of the Supreme Court of the United States on the "Commerce clause" as contrasted with the decisions of the Privy Council and of the Supreme Court of Canada on the federal power to regulate "Trade and Commerce."

In the United States, pre-New-Deal decisions had established the principle that local activities could be regulated by Congress under the commerce clause only if they were "directly" related to "interstate commerce." More recent decisions of the Supreme Court of the United States have brushed aside this distinction,[13] however, with the result that the commerce clause has acquired practically unlimited meaning: "The federal commerce power is as broad as the economic needs of the nation."[14]

In Canada, on the other hand, federal authority over trade and commerce, although unlimited in its terms, was held to be

[12] *Fort Frances Pulp & Power Co.* v. *Manitoba Free Press*, [1923] A.C. 695, at pp. 704-5 (italics added).

[13] "But even if . . . [an] activity be local and though it may not be regarded as commerce, it may still, whatever its nature, be reached by Congress if it exerts a substantial economic effect on interstate commerce, and this irrespective of whether such effect is what might at some earlier time have been defined as 'direct' or 'indirect.' *Per* Mr. Justice Jackson in *Wickard* v. *Filburn* (1942), 317 U.S. 111, at p. 125.

[14] *Per* Mr. Justice Murphy in *American Power and Light Co.* v. *SEC* (1946), 67 S. Ct. 133.

strictly limited to the regulation of interprovincial operations, because to hold otherwise would have deprived provincial legislatures of powers they were clearly intended to possess:

The scope which might be ascribed to head 2, s. 91 (if the natural meaning of the words, divorced from their context, were alone to be considered), has necessarily been limited, in order to preserve from serious curtailment, if not from virtual extinction, the degree of autonomy which, as appears from the scheme of the Act as a whole, the provinces were intended to possess.[15]

I have emphasized the word "degree" in this last quotation because I wish to stress the point that here again, as in the definition of the federal emergency power, it is a question of "degree," not a specific distinction. In my view it is wrong to read the generally accepted definition of legislative autonomy ("that the Dominion to a great extent, but within certain fixed limits, may be mistress in her own house, as the Provinces to a great extent, but within certain fixed limits, are mistresses in theirs"[16]) as implying limits defined with mathematical accuracy. To do so is to conceive political science as an exact science ascertainable in the same manner as the natural sciences.

The government of men is essentially a moral problem. Moral problems are not solved by mathematical formulas but by the exercise of prudent judgment based on fundamental principles of morality. These principles rest on belief in God, and in this sense "Christianity is part and parcel of the law." Moral principles, by their very nature, imply concepts which, in their application to contingencies, cannot be divorced from a certain degree of subjective appreciation, a fact illustrated by the "prudent man" referred to in negligence cases. The proper standard of conduct is not to be ascertained by statistical methods but by a consideration of the "proper" duty to be discharged. What is "proper" is a question to be decided according to conscience, not otherwise.

If anyone doubts the correctness of the statement that words used to describe "degrees" in moral (including legal) questions are of necessity imprecise and open to subjective appreciation, let him consider, on the one hand, the meaning ascribed to the word "gross" in the construction of statutes restricting the right

---

[15] *Per* Duff J. (as he then was) in *Lawson* v. *Interior Tree Fruit Committee*, [1931] S.C.R. 357, at p. 366 (italics added).

[16] *"Persons"* case, [1930] A.C. 124, at p. 136.

of action to "gross negligence" in gratuitous passenger or side-walk accident cases and, on the other, the meaning ascribed to the same adjective in the application of the wartime wages orders restricting wage adjustments to cases of "gross injustice." In the former, anything short of murder or wilful maiming is held excluded; in the latter the slightest inequality is held included.[17]

As a further illustration of the difficulty of precisely defining fundamental legal terms, let us consider the meaning of the word "free." It was discussed by the Privy Council in the construction of the "free trade" provision of the constitution of Australia and the following observations were then made:

"Free" in itself is vague and indeterminate. It must take its colour from the context. Compare, for instance, its use in free speech, free love, free dinner and free trade. Free speech does not mean free speech; it means speech hedged in by all the laws against defamation, blasphemy, sedition and so forth; it means freedom governed by law, as was pointed out in McArthur's *case. Free love, on the contrary, means licence or libertinage, though, even so, there are limitations based on public decency and so forth. Free dinner generally means free of expense, and sometimes a meal open to any one who comes, subject, however, to his condition or behaviour not being objectionable. Free trade means, in ordinary parlance, freedom from tariffs.*[18]

The fundamental idea, the basic truth, expressed in those observations is that freedom is not something absolute. This is strikingly revealed by the practical consequence of the political regime that promises absolute freedom: communism. It yields freedom, but for one man: the dictator. It cannot be otherwise: total emancipation of any one man means total domination over all others. True freedom means freedom under the law. Autonomy is nothing else than freedom under the constitution.

The true concept of autonomy is thus like the true concept of freedom. It implies limitations, but it also implies free movement within the area bounded by the limitations: one no longer enjoys freedom when free to move in one direction only. It should therefore be realized that autonomy means the right of

---

[17] This observation is not meant as a criticism of the decisions; on the contrary it cannot be doubted that they carry out the intent of the enactments.

[18] *James* v. *Commonwealth of Australia*, [1936] A.C. 578, at p. 627.

being different, of acting differently. This is what freedom means for the individual; it is also what it must mean for provincial legislatures and governments. There is no longer any real autonomy for them to the extent that they are actually compelled, economically or otherwise, to act according to a specified pattern. Just as freedom means for the individual the right of choosing his own objective so long as it is not illegal, autonomy means for a province the privilege of defining its own policies.

It must be conceded that autonomy thus understood allows the provinces on occasion to work at cross purposes. But it would be a grave mistake to assume that this is wrong in itself, or that it is necessarily against the national interest. Unfortunately this assumption is all too frequently made and it is also all too frequently the only argument invoked against autonomy (if it can be termed an argument). Here is a typical specimen:

> The most serious specific threat to any orderly kind of future for Canada lies in the nature of our Constitution. The "property and civil rights" clause of section 92 of the British North America Act will make short work of our war-time measures and will very quickly reduce us to the bedlam of provincialism again. Can any sane person believe that the competing authorities, mostly parochial, will give us anything but anarchy leading perhaps to revolution?[19]

It will be noted that autonomy is deprecated here as a mark of insanity, but no other argument is advanced. Obviously the underlying assumption is that diversity in legislation concerning property and civil rights is against national interest. Implicit in this assumption is the belief that uniform legislation enacted by the federal Parliament would be better. Of course uniformity has its advantages, but it also has its disadvantages.

The framing of legislation, as already pointed out, is a political task.[20] Hence it is not an exact science but a matter of prudent judgment, on which even popularly elected men may sometimes go wrong. Why should competition be assumed to be undesirable in this sphere of action, when it proves to be such a

---

[19] From the introduction by A. R. M. Lower to "War and Reconstruction," a pamphlet published in 1943 by the Canadian Institute on Public Affairs.

[20] In the aristotelian sense, not necessarily in the familiar sense of partisan politics.

valuable force in the economic field? It should not be assumed that, in such matters, there is necessarily one right solution, all others being wrong. Human affairs are more complex than that and, very often, several possible courses of action are open among which one may choose. Such is the situation in individual life and such it is in collective action.

This is especially so when the characteristics of individuals or of collectivities are different. Educators have long ago recognized that human beings are not robots and that varying methods and different institutions are necessary to suit varying types of intelligence and differences in character. The same difficulty is met in devising legislation: it is wrong to assume that the same laws are suitable for all peoples. On the contrary, laws have a cultural aspect; hence due consideration should be given in framing them to the character, condition and beliefs of those for whom they are made. Autonomy is designed for the very purpose of meeting this requirement. The French-speaking population of the province of Quebec is obviously the group of Canadian citizens specially interested in it. For them autonomy is linked up with the preservation of their way of life.

Of course, it cannot be denied that the general welfare of a country requires that collective action be made uniform in some important fields, such as defence, tariff, currency. More than that, it must be conceded that the area of uniformity cannot be defined without allowing for extension in emergencies. But the increased need for uniformity in emergencies cannot be relied on as an argument against autonomy in normal times. It is already provided for.

All this means that tests of constitutional validity cannot be rigidly devised. Almost invariably they involve judgment on questions of "degree." The courts have therefore been compelled to rest their decisions touching constitutional issues on broad principles and on a general conception of what the B.N.A. Act intended to secure to the provinces and to the federal authority, respectively, rather than on an impossible technical construction:

Inasmuch as the Act embodies a compromise under which the original Provinces agreed to federate, it is important to keep in mind that the preservation of the rights of minorities was a condition on which such minorities entered into the federation, and the foundation upon which the whole structure was subse-

quently erected. The process of interpretation as the years go on ought not to be allowed to dim or to whittle down the provisions of the original contract upon which the federation was founded, nor is it legitimate that any judicial construction of the provisions of ss. 91 and 92 should impose a new and different contract upon the federating bodies.[21]

On this basis the courts have consistently refused to allow any particular clause of the B.N.A. Act to be construed in a way that would enable the federal Parliament to invade the provincial sphere of action outside of emergencies. "Such a result would appear to undermine the constitutional safeguards of Provincial constitutional autonomy"[22] was the man reason given by Lord Atkin for his refusal to construe section 132 as enabling the federal Parliament to encroach on provincial matters in order to implement labour conventions adhered to by Canada.

The same principle was applied in dealing with provincial legislation. For instance, the Supreme Court of Canada has invalidated an Alberta law interfering with the freedom of the press, because it would have jeopardized the working of federal parliamentary institutions:

Some degree of regulation of newspapers everybody would concede to the provinces. Indeed, there is a very wide field in which the provinces undoubtedly are invested with legislative authority over newspapers; but the limit, in our opinion, is reached when the legislation effects such a curtailment of the exercise of the right of public discussion as substantially to interfere with the working of the parliamentary institutions of Canada as contemplated by the provisions of The British North America Act *and the statutes of the Dominion of Canada.*[23]

Let it be noted that, here again, it is a question of "degree." Undoubtedly the task of construing our constitution would be made lighter for our courts if provincial autonomy could be defined in more specific words, but that hardly appears possible. The great value of the numerous decisions rendered since 1867 lies in the illustrations they afford of the "degree" of autonomy secured to the provinces.

[21] In re *The Regulation and Control of Aeronautics*, [1932] A.C. 54, at p. 70.
[22] *A.-G. for Canada* v. *A.-G. for Ontario (Labour Conventions)*, [1937] A.C. 326, at p. 352.
[23] *Reference re Alberta Statutes*, [1938] S.C.R. 100, at p. 134.

A great volume of criticism has been heaped upon the Privy Council and the Supreme Court on the ground that their decisions rest on a narrow and technical construction of the B.N.A. Act. This contention is ill-founded. The decisions on the whole proceed from a much higher view. As appears from passages I have quoted, they recognize the implicit fluidity of any constitution by allowing for emergencies and by resting distinctions on questions of degree. At the same time they firmly uphold the fundamental principle of provincial autonomy: they staunchly refuse to let our federal constitution be changed gradually, by one device or another, to a legislative union. In doing so they are preserving the essential condition of the Canadian confederation.

Quebec and Canadian Federalism

ALEXANDER BRADY

Canada's federation is distinct from the other two major federations in the English-speaking world in resting upon an alliance of two peoples and two cultures. Other differences exist, but this is fundamental. Since 1867 the dualism of culture has been slowly woven into the political fabric of the nation, although outside Quebec its implications are still not always appreciated or wholly accepted. With the appearance in 1956 of the *Report of the Royal Commission of Inquiry on Constitutional Problems*,[1] English-speaking Canadians have little excuse for misunderstanding the position of their French-speaking compatriots. The Commission was appointed by provincial statute in January, 1953, under the chairmanship of Judge Thomas Tremblay. Its bulky report is never likely to be widely read. It is prolix and sometimes repetitious to the point of tedium; its analysis would have been more telling had it been tidier and more compressed. Yet, despite such flaws, it is a landmark in the literature of federalism: it describes and explains more fully than any other public document the position and anxieties of Quebec in the federal state, and defends the concept of a strict federalism as the essential basis for the success of Canada's national experiment. For the Tremblay Commissioners the issue of Quebec in the federation and the issue of the French in the nation are one and the same. In harmony with their theme they submit numerous recommendations. We cannot, however, assess these or do justice to their premises, without first reviewing briefly the historical position of Quebec in Canadian federalism.

At Confederation the political thinking of leaders in British North America swung between two positions, both empirical.

From: *The Canadian Journal of Economics and Political Science,*
Volume 25 (1959), pages 259-70, published by The University
of Toronto Press. By permission of the author and publisher.

[1] Four vols. (Quebec, 1956). Hereafter called the *Tremblay Report.*

Some of the Fathers had originally feared that the federal principle, especially as exemplified in the neighbouring republic, implied a dispersal of power that would drain the strength, increase the cost, and jeopardize the survival of a new state in North America. Sir John A. Macdonald's first preference, like that of Sir Charles Tupper, was a legislative rather than a federal union. Yet he and his associates quickly yielded to the logic of the fact that the existing colonies enjoyed local autonomy and were unwilling to surrender it.[2] The two Canadas, moreover, possessed a single legislature, but had been compelled by the differences in their cultures to conduct their affairs almost as in a federation. This was the main circumstance which changed Macdonald's mind on the nature of the new state: the French as a minority feared that in legislative union "their institutions and their laws might be assailed, and their ancestral associations, on which they prided themselves, attacked and prejudiced."[3] The French were emphatic in contending for genuine federalism, and those among them who opposed the projected confederation did so because it appeared to offer a provincial autonomy that was shadowy and insufficient. The presence of dual cultures and diverse social values among the people of the St. Lawrence Valley was thus basic in shaping the decision of the Fathers for a federal state.

Since 1867 Quebec has remained consistently attached to a strict federalism as a protector of its own culture and the cultural dualism of Canada. It has been the chief citadel of resistance to centralizing conceptions and homogenizing tendencies. Its position has sometimes been backed by Ontario, which usually however acts independently for reasons of its own. In the first three decades after Confederation Ontario might seem to have been even more emphatic in assailing the centralizing pretensions of Ottawa. Under Oliver Mowat (1872-96) it checkmated the manœuvres of Sir John A. Macdonald, who never wholly subdued his original bias for a legislative union and persistently endeavoured to restrict the role of the provincial legislatures and to exalt that of the national Parliament. But, in Mowat's successive legal contests and triumphs before the Privy Council, Quebec was Ontario's vigilant and reliable ally. Its jurists and politicians were equally keen to elaborate the powers of the provinces under section 92. In Judge T. J. J. Loranger

[2] See, e.g., *Confederation Debates*, p. 29.
[3] *Ibid.*

among others it had a constitutional expert who in the eighties presented with distinguished clarity the provincial case. "If the fedral pretensions prevail," wrote Loranger in 1883, "and if the principle of the provinces' inferiority and dependence of their legislatures with regard to the federal authority is recognized, in less than half a century their absorption will be accomplished and the federal system will give way to the legislative union so rightly feared in our province."[4]

In politics, two Quebec figures in the first half-century of federation especially advanced the provincial cause: Honoré Mercier and Wilfrid Laurier. Both reflected the inflamed feelings of French-Canadian nationalism in the eighties provoked by the sorry events of the Riel Rebellion and its aftermath. Both, and especially Laurier, also responded to the more stable emotions about provincial rights which in greater or lesser degree have inspired all French leaders since 1867. Mercier's principal achievement was his convening an interprovincial conference in 1887 to examine the relations of the provinces with the federal government. Under the chairmanship of Oliver Mowat five provincial premiers there adopted resolutions that challenged and rejected the centralist policies of Macdonald. Although their requests, including a surrender by the federal government of its power to disallow provincial acts, were not acceptable to Ottawa, the case for provincial autonomy received an important impetus from its formal affirmation.

Laurier's leadership of the national Liberals (1887-1919) secured, by quiet persuasion at the highest levels in Ottawa, a sympathy for Quebec's position and for provincial autonomy in general. "The only means of maintaining Confederation," he declared in 1889, "is to recognize that, within its sphere assigned to it by the constitution, each province is as independent of control by the federal Parliament as the latter is from control by the provincial legislatures." This dictum is important, not for its novelty, but for the fact that it influenced Laurier's tactics and policies throughout his career. It was evident in his stand on the Manitoba school question before his electoral triumph in 1896, and in office he never lost a French Canadian's anxiety for the autonomy of the provinces. Admittedly he was aided by the stream of events. In successive decisions from that of Hodge *v.* the Queen in 1883, the Privy Council consolidated and fortified the power of the provincial legislatures, while the growth in

[4] Quoted in *Tremblay Report*, I, 67.

population and industry of Quebec and Ontario enhanced the prestige of their governments and goaded them to seek in the courts that larger legislative competence essential for developing their natural resources. In employing the power of disallowance Laurier and his colleagues sought to pursue a fresh course. They did not consider the power obsolete (although privately Laurier told Blake that it was alien to the federal idea), but generally avoided its use as a corrective of the alleged errors and injustices committed by provincial legislatures, and confined it to cases where the legislation affected federal or imperial interests. No other view, they were convinced, could secure provincial autonomy and local democracy. Laurier's governments between 1896-1911 admittedly disallowed thirty provincial statutes, but of these twenty issued solely from the legislature of British Columbia and affected both Canadian and imperial interests by dealing adversely with the employment and status of Asiatics. Since 1896 only one Quebec act has been disallowed compared with five in the preceding twenty-nine years and only two Ontario acts compared with eight in the earlier period.[5]

Soon after the passing of the Laurier régime, there appeared fresh threats to provincial autonomy, which were mainly related, as they still are, to the issues of finance. On a small scale before the First World War and on a larger scale after it, national governments began to make grants to the provinces on conditions which implied a federal control over their use. This new procedure came from a quickened and wider sense of national interest in the policy-makers at Ottawa, coupled with a desire to circumvent the restrictions imposed on them by the constitution. They were persuaded that, without loss of provincial autonomy, the provinces and the national government might create an *ad hoc* partnership for certain desirable ends with funds jointly contributed. Grants, such as those provided in 1919 to encourage technical education, trespassed on the legislative field of the provinces, but the provincial governments could not resist the temptation to accept virtual supplements to provincial revenue.

From the outset leaders in Quebec viewed this form of federal largesse with disquiet or positive disfavour. Ernest Lapointe, a prominent French-Canadian spokesman in the Liberal Opposition at the close of the First World War, attacked conditional grants. In his view they intruded on provincial jurisdiction and

[5] See G. V. La Forest, *Disallowance and Reservation of Provincial Legislation* (Ottawa, 1955), Appendix A.

were unfair to non-concurring provinces, whose citizens were taxed to benefit those in other provinces.[6] Indirectly but forcibly, a federal government thus exerted coercion in fields where its action was either constitutionally ambiguous or invalid. It practised generosity at the price of provincial autonomy, and employed its own relative affluence to entice and bribe impecunious provinces, whittle away their independence, and generally impair their freedom to manœuvre. In Quebec this argument has ever since rendered doughty service in the polemic of federal-provincial relations.

The inter-war ministries of Mackenzie King, wherein Ernest Lapointe sat as an influential member, were on the whole unsympathetic to conditional grants, although the social and political compulsions of the time involved them in this policy to some degree. In July, 1924, a special committee of the Commons advocated that the federal and provincial governments should share the costs of old age pensions for needy persons over seventy. The Liberals were reluctant to reject a proposal that might win popularity. King himself was deeply interested in policies of social welfare and alert to their importance in political strategy. Hence in 1927 his Government sponsored a scheme whereby it would pay half the cost to every province which agreed to provide old age pensions. The provinces, beginning with British Columbia, made such agreements, and finally in 1936 New Brunswick and Quebec participated, although the Quebec government still viewed old age pensions as an undesirable federal intrusion into the provincial field. It could not, however, continue to ignore the unpalatable fact that if it remained outside the scheme its people would be helping to pay for pensions they were not free to enjoy.

Despite the precedent of old age pensions, the inter-war administrations of Mackenzie King, influenced by their French-Canadian supporters, never displayed enthusiasm for conditional grants. Quebec resented them as the vehicle of a vigorous federal policy. Its leaders had no wish to see the national government in a position to exert pressure on the provinces. Such grants placed it in this position because they implied centralized authority in making decisions by lawmakers and officials in Ottawa, the majority of whom were English Canadians.[7]

---

[6] *House of Commons Debates*, 1919, p. 3794.

[7] For Mackenzie King's concern for the position of the provinces in this matter see *ibid.*, 1931, pp. 1959 ff.

Since 1939 profound changes in Canadian society and ways of thought have involved a heavier subsidization of the provinces. National enactments have multiplied conditional grants until today there are half a hundred different kinds. Some, such as those relating to the reclamation of land and to fisheries, mainly concern specific provinces and regions. Others, such as those in public health and old age assistance, appeal to all the provinces, and enlist the active support of all, including Quebec. This accentuated trend in federal action is traceable to social forces linked with industrialism and nationalism, accelerated by war and the preparation for war. The appetite of a growing industrial people for public services within provincial jurisdiction has sharpened, especially for highways, welfare and health services, and education. Federal governments, of course, might have left the provinces alone to cope with these services as best they could, but they have been persistently pressed by public opinion to feed them with federal funds. In some cases the pressure has been strongest from people in the relatively poor and less favoured areas, but it commonly comes from certain organized interests in all the provinces and especially from the more industrialized regions. The more rapid the pace of urbanization, the more varied and insistent are the demands on the national treasury. On their part federal politicians are loath to miss an opportunity of winning votes by spending money, and now find it easy to justify expenditure on the grounds of a compelling national interest. Since their primary concern is to placate the electors, they must listen to the numerous pressure groups, which often are indifferent to the political and legal facts of federalism and rationalize their own interests in terms of a national interest. Thus the Liberal party, ascendant in Ottawa for the first dozen years after the Second World War, became fired by a stronger nationalism, and rapidly retreated from its former scruples about encroaching on provincial jurisdiction. In successive enactments after 1940 it sponsored abundant grants, conditional and unconditional.

The Tremblay Commission, in surveying this panorama of post-war change, admit with evident sorrow that "a vast network has been spread which binds the provinces to the central government and which, to a certain extent, provides them with the financial means of discharging their legislative functions, but always at the discretion and on the terms of the wealthy and powerful donor."[8] In all this the French Canadians as the chief defenders of traditional federalism face a difficult dilemma. Either they must patiently resign themselves to a course of events that threatens to erode the older federalism, or pursue more resolutely than hitherto the policy of survival by withdrawal. Some fear that they have no choice, and that the decision is made for them by the speed and inexorable strides of an industrialism which transforms their society, exposes them to a stream of influences from outside, and assimilates them in character to English-speaking Canadians. Since 1939 Quebec, with rich mineral resources, abundant water power, and a high birth rate, has shared substantially in the country's material expansion. Its industrial production has multiplied fivefold, and light industries such as textiles have yielded ground to heavy industries such as mining and metallurgy. Industrialism in the province was born long before, but the Second World War accelerated its growth. The drift from farm to factory was quickened. The old rural framework of life, in which for generations the relatively isolated culture of the French Canadians was sustained, is crumbling now that only a fifth of the people live in strictly rural areas. As urban dwellers and industrial workers they undergo much the same experience as labour elsewhere in Canada, respond to the prevalent appetite for social security, and are likely to be no less eager for the services that the federal treasury can ensure. With the progress of industrialism a variety of interests in French-Canadian society, notably organized labour, establish a rapport with like interests in Ontario and other provinces, and become less diffident in dealing with a government in Ottawa. Quebec may still resemble a cultural island within the nation, but an island now with numerous bridges that diminish its isolation.

The Union Nationale party led by Maurice Duplessis has held office in Quebec since 1944, and in the face of these forces has vehemently defended the province's autonomy. It has freely exploited the sentiments of French-Canadian nationalism aroused by the depression of the thirties and the subsequent tensions of the Second World War. Yet it is difficult to determine precisely how much the longevity of M. Duplessis's régime is due to his display of autonomist convictions. Other obvious factors contribute: his smoothly working political machine, his rare art in winning support by dexterous use of patronage, and his gains

[8] *Tremblay Report*, II, 214.

from an electoral distribution of seats that bears little relation to the rapid urbanizing of the population. Despite his strong position, he has found it expedient to accept many conditional grants from Ottawa; others he has brusquely rejected. His criterion for acceptance or rejection is the extent of the threat to the traditional autonomy of the province. Thus he entered into agreements to obtain substantial grants from the federal treasury for health services, including hospital construction, general public health, and the control of tuberculosis and cancer. Although he also accepted the conditions prescribed in 1952 for joint provincial and federal old age assistance for the needy, he rejected the federal subsidies to aid in building the Trans-Canada Highway through Quebec. Even more emphatically he rejected the subsidizing of Quebec universities from federal funds because it touched, not merely traditional provincial jurisdiction, but the sensitive nerves of culture. For him this was an appropriate battle ground. "What counted in Judas' betrayal of Christ," he declared, "was not the sum of thirty pieces of silver but the fact that Judas had betrayed his Master." Acquiescence in such federal action would merely stimulate Ottawa to indulge further in an interference all the more unwarranted in being needless, since the provincial government itself could adequately sustain the colleges of the province, especially if the federal authority left it appropriate fields for direct taxation. This point raises the controversial and basic question of the taxing power, which has occasioned the most prolonged and wordy debates between Ottawa and Quebec.

The modern issue of taxation originated as a by-product of the First World War, when the national government in 1916 resorted to direct taxes on war profits and in the next year on general income. After the war the income tax survived as an important instrument in federal policy, and provoked in Quebec strong protests. "Ottawa," asserted Premier Taschereau in 1920, "has unceremoniously arrogated to itself our own sources of revenue." But the federal income tax was there to stay, and the facts of the depression in the thirties helped to secure its permanence. The depression, however, had contrasting and conflicting effects within the federation. In English-speaking Canada, especially in the west, the current of opinion now ran more strongly than before towards a heavy reliance on Ottawa. The taxing power of the federal government was accepted as an inevitable adjunct to its responsibility. In Quebec, by contrast, the current of opinion ran turbulently in the opposite direction. The harsh tensions of the depression merely exacerbated French Canadian nationalism, raised more urgently the persistent theme of cultural survival, and made the régime of M. Duplessis after 1936 more uncompromising than any previous government in clinging to every element of provincial autonomy. In the economic and social facts of the time Quebec sensed a new and greater menace to the position that it was obligated by long tradition to defend. The Sirois Commission (appointed in August, 1937) was naturally viewed by M. Duplessis as objectionable because it was appointed without prior consultation with the provinces and unilaterally investigated matters that were crucially important to them. His government made explicit to the Commission its opposition to any abridgment of provincial rights, or any significant change in the federal pact unless accepted by all the provinces.

At that time, however, Quebec's position was not isolated. Four other provincial governments also argued before the Sirois Commission against any drastic change, fiscal or otherwise, in the existing distribution of federal power. Only the four then most needy provinces, Manitoba, Saskatchewan, Nova Scotia, and Prince Edward Island, were ready to barter their right to tax for provincial aid. All four proclaimed fidelity to federalism, but, in their precarious financial plight, a secure revenue had more appeal than fiscal liberty. The conference of January, 1941, convened by Ottawa to get agreement for implementing the principal recommendations of the *Sirois Report*, adjourned in failure on the second day because Ontario, British Columbia, and Alberta rejected a revision of the federal system on the terms recommended, and the national Government would consider no others. From September, 1939, to August, 1944, Quebec was ruled by the Liberals under Adélard Godbout, who cautiously did not commit himself. "We are here," he remarked, "to study; we will listen and we are ready to co-operate."

After the Second World War the issue of federal taxation appeared to Quebec in a more ominous light. To meet the urgent necessities of war the federal Government had secured (in 1942) the agreement of all the provinces to vacate in its favour the right to levy personal income and corporation taxes and to accept compensation in annual grants. Here was a means that with provincial consent and without a constitutional amendment might at any time augment the fiscal initiative of

Ottawa, and for many reasons Ottawa was anxious that it should endure into the peace. Public sentiments at the time incessantly pressed the federal Government to do and prepare for countless things. Fears of a post-war depression and haunting memories of unemployment in the thirties were in the air. Conceptions of an economy managed through fiscal controls seeped into the thinking of federal ministers and public servants. The ideas of Maynard Keynes took root in the Department of Finance, and to lend them scope it seemed essential to have federal control over the major and most remunerative taxes. Hence at the Dominion-Provincial Conference on Reconstruction (1945-6) Ottawa submitted to the provinces far-ranging proposals, buttressed by a series of supplementary studies, which among other things would have left to it an exclusive access to personal income and corporation taxes and succession duties, while in return Ottawa provided per capita provincial grants.

Quebec, like some other provinces, viewed these plans of Ottawa as a serious menace to federalism. If they were fully implemented, the major initiative in social policy would irretrievably shift to the national capital, and provincial independence in finance and manœuvrability in policy would drastically diminish. In the words of the Quebec brief the proposals would "exclude the provinces from the most important fields of direct taxation and to that extent deprive them of the exercise of the powers assigned to them by the constitution." Ontario's plea was similar. It denied, moreover, that centralization could provide protection against depression, although it would certainly violate federal principles. Yet neither Quebec nor Ontario outdid in vigorous and eloquent protest the Premier of Nova Scotia, who declared that if the proposals were accepted, "provincial autonomy will be gone. Provincial independence will vanish. Provincial dignity will disappear. The provincial governments will become mere annuitants of Ottawa."

The Conference of 1945-6 dissolved in acrimony and without accomplishment. The wartime agreements, however, ran their course to 1947. In the interval certain fundamental facts in the situation worked inexorably in favour of Ottawa, especially the inequality of the provinces in economic and financial strength and hence their divergence in interpreting the nature of the federal bond. The financially weak or less favoured naturally saw advantages in retaining payments from Ottawa. On principle they were not really averse to rental agreements provided that they got good terms, although for purposes of bargaining they might appear appropriately coy. Their outlook on the federation fundamentally differed from that of Quebec, because they were not preoccupied with the feeling of having to defend through federalism a distinct culture. Consequently they were disposed to take a short-run view of federal matters. The necessities of the day dominated, for under pressure from their electorates they thought primarily of services to which they were committed and must become committed, and of how to secure the revenue necessary to finance them. Even the strong and affluent among the English-speaking provinces do not act very differently, but their strength commonly permits them to take longer views.

This circumstance in the situation makes plain why Ottawa, after failing to obtain agreement for a general scheme, could successfully resort to the tactic of individual agreements on the basis of new formulae. By the beginning of 1948 seven provinces and in 1949 Newfoundland had signed such agreements. Quebec and Ontario then alone remained outside, but in 1952 Ottawa, armed with different formulae, was able to win Ontario and isolate Quebec. The history of these years illustrates how expediency dominates in Canadian federalism. With the rapidly changing society an elaborate process of individual and constant bargaining between the federal and provincial governments is the accepted norm, and the provinces rarely present a united front. On such a basis the federation will continue to operate, for it serves best the short-run interests of Ottawa and all the provinces except Quebec.

The Tremblay Commission, aided by the numerous briefs of organized interests in the province, assess Quebec's place in the federation in the light of history and philosophy. Much of their detailed report, with its wealth of facts, surveys the past and analyses the present in order to underline the special identity of the French community in Canada's evolution, its relation to the federal structure after 1867, and the threats to its survival and the survival of federalism that result from the forces of the twentieth century, especially industrialism, depression, and war.

The historical section of the report is invaluable, and despite a bias on some matters, is likely to be acceptable to scholars outside Quebec. Agreement on facts, however, does not imply agreement on their interpretation. The historical struggle of the French Canadian for cultural survival gives him a special point of view, which the Tremblay Commission express in terms of an appropriate philosophy. This philosophy is a form of Catholic pluralism, emphasizing the necessary freedom for cultural groups to operate and survive, combined with the assumptions of a liberal nationalism. Federal policy, it is argued, should be determined, less by the material conditions and appetites of the society, than by the wholesome impulses towards the freedom of cultural groups and the freedom of the individual to develop his personality in a group. The goals of the Canadian nation should be association not assimilation, diversity not uniformity, the vitality of all the distinct groups in the state and not their standardization. These concepts of liberal Catholic philosophers, such as Jacques Maritain, are readily translated into the traditional French-Canadian attachment to a strict federalism, stressing the full autonomy of the province with its aggregate of usages and traditions. This pluralist philosophy might have found an uncongenial environment in the Quebec of the nineteenth century under its dominant ultramontanism. But in the 1950's it seems to fit comfortably into the French-Canadian heritage.

What kind of offspring in practical recommendations does this marriage of history and philosophy produce? The Tremblay Commission are explicit about what it should produce. They formulate many recommendations, some of which differ greatly in content and purpose from those of the Sirois Commission twenty years ago. They primarily seek to stop the erosion of federalism, threatened by the centralizing pressures of Ottawa especially in finance. They launch what they hope are destructive assaults against the "new federalism" and its apologists, English and French, and single out for criticism the views of a French-Canadian advocate, Maurice Lamontagne, author of *Le Féderalisme canadien*.[9] "To believe and to try to have it believed," they wrote, "that there is respect, in Canada, for the autonomy of the provinces, because they are allowed to exist as mere administrative units to which the central authority will distribute living allowances, is mere self-deception and an attempt to deceive others. It confronts true federalism with mere administrative decentralization which is to be found in any state but

[9] Quebec, 1954.

which does not truly allow autonomy of the regional and local communities."[10]

The Tremblay Commission think of a genuine federal state as one wherein financial and political powers are so apportioned between the federal and unit governments that their self-operating and self-governing functions are unfettered by interferences from one another. "There can be no federalism," they write, "without autonomy of the state's constituent parts, and no sovereignty of the various governments without fiscal and financial autonomy."[11] Such a federal structure must ensure the identity of the whole and the identity of the parts. It implies, not isolation, but close co-operation among the several governments. This general concept of federalism is one to which many modern political theorists would readily subscribe. The inevitable question, however, is, what division of power has most logic in a given situation? Even among genuine liberal pluralists it is far from easy to secure agreement on this thorny issue in view of the speed of economic and social change. The modern industrial economy never stands still, and every major innovation affects profoundly the federal jurisdiction.

The Tremblay Commission naturally enough use a criterion calculated to ensure for a province an authority sufficiently broad to protect its culture. They are confident that the constitution drafted by the Fathers provided this authority, and that in the past the Judicial Committee and the Supreme Court of Canada jealously upheld it. The real threat to the federation in the present generation comes from the centralizing actions of an Ottawa forgetful that federalism implies two orders of government and not one. The national authority has employed various expedients, such as conditional grants, to encroach on provincial jurisdiction. It has freely invoked ancillary powers in the B.N.A. Act, and has used the financial incapacity of the provinces as an excuse for doing countless things, while its own inroads in the field of direct taxation accentuate their incapacity. The Commission are particularly critical of the national government for exercising powers, as in some forms of education, allegedly ancillary to those in section 91. Ottawa may properly legislate for the Indians, the penitentiaries, the armed forces, agriculture, immigration, and radio, but assumes that each of these subjects has an educational aspect that justifies its inter-

[10] *Tremblay Report*, II, 276.
[11] *Ibid.*, III, 294.

vention in the field of education associated with the subject. Judge Tremblay and his colleagues comment caustically on the manner in which the Massey Commission, by what they deem a series of specious arguments, establish a right of the federal government to intervene in certain fields of education and then transfer this right into a duty in the name of the public welfare and spiritual values. They think that the extravagant use of ancillary powers seriously threatens the survival of the federation, and quote with approval Justice Duff's view that the "division of legislative authority is the principle of the British North America Act, and if the doctrine of necessarily incidental powers is to be extended to all cases in which inconvenience arises from such a division, that is the end of the federal character of the Union."[12]

On this premise the Tremblay Commission consider that for the future federal power should be employed, not to displace the provinces, but to establish the conditions, including a sufficient and independent revenue, that would allow them to play the special role assigned to them under the constitution. The provinces need fiscal powers commensurate with their legislative powers, and can secure them only by a logical division of the field of direct taxation between them and the national government. Yet, even with a careful division of the taxing power, some provinces would likely remain unable to obtain revenue sufficient to finance services comparable with those of their wealthier or more industrialized neighbours, and for this situation the Commissioners think that the appropriate remedy is a "financial equalization organism."[13] Instead of leaving solely to Ottawa the major task of combating economic depressions, the provinces should for this purpose be brought into a close co-operative relation with Ottawa and be organized to participate in the anti-cyclic policy according to their capacity and the requirements of their constitutional role.[14] In a period of depression they, like the federal government, should be able to sell bonds to the Bank of Canada. The Commission emphasize the value of a permanent committee of the federal-provincial conferences to secure continuity of co-operation in the interval between conferences, and in addition a permanent council of the provinces, confined exclusively to them, somewhat

[12] *Ibid.*, II, 236.
[13] *Ibid.*, III, 297.
[14] *Ibid.*, III, 299.

on the lines of the Council of State Governments in the United States. One body that they have in mind now already exists in the Federal-Provincial Continuing Committee on Fiscal and Economic Matters.

Such briefly is the main case of the Tremblay Commission for a revitalized federalism. It is both radical and controversial. Its chief argument and proposals are derived from briefs submitted to the Commission, and unquestionably represent important bodies of opinion in the province of Quebec, although not all that province's opinion is necessarily well represented. A convinced federalist elsewhere in Canada could accept the main thesis of the Tremblay Commission that decentralization is desirable to invigorate local autonomy in all the provinces. But the patent fact is that in English-speaking Canada, in the post-war years especially, the current of nationalism has run powerfully in the opposite direction and has been stimulated by the evident insecurities of the national state in the contemporary world. The dangers to Canada's survival as a political entity have among English-speaking Canadians weakened the federal spirit. Moreover there is a growing sense that many problems of social life can best be settled nationally and that social progress demands national standards. Hence the pressure of special interests for action from Ottawa has increased rather than diminished.With its larger and more flexible source of income Ottawa can most effectively achieve what these special interests want. Federal politicians, moreover, with the indispensable help of the national treasury, never cease to angle for votes by promising many things and doing many things. The very nature of democracy is contributory to this end. Here are nationalizing forces, which at present are not easy to control in order to guarantee the complete integrity of the federal system.

Yet federalism in Canada has not suffered a final eclipse. It is not on the road to dissolution. Many of the provinces constitute immense territories with abundant resources, and already have grown into populous and prosperous communities which are destined to become more populous and more self-confident. They will increasingly require all the legislative and administrative powers that they now possess to achieve effective regional planning and development. Consequently their political leaders will be anxious to erect defences against the continued seepage of power and initiative to Ottawa. Much of the distinctiveness in Canada's nationality in the future must derive from the recognition of its cultural dualism, and the more this fact is appreciated the more sensitive will be the concern for federalism. In the meantime Quebec's devotion to the federal idea has served a national purpose; it has helped to lessen the danger of excessive centralization in Ottawa and the equal danger of a rigid framework advantageous to Ottawa. Rigid arrangements acceptable today may be intolerable tomorrow. Flexibility is a prime condition for a healthy federalism, and paradoxically Quebec by its unbending position has been its guarantor.

I. THE JUDICIAL COMMITTEE OF
THE PRIVY COUNCIL

The History of The Judicial
Committee of the Privy Council

VISCOUNT SANKEY, LORD CHANCELLOR

. . . It will be convenient to summarize in the briefest terms
the nature of the appeal from Dominion or Colonial courts to
His Majesty in Council. The position of this Board, the Judicial
Committee of the Privy Council, in relation to such appeals may
first be indicated. The Judicial Committee is a statutory body
established in 1833 by an Act of 3 & 4 Will. 4, c. 41, entitled an
Act for the better Administration of Justice in His Majesty's
Privy Council. It contains (*inter alia*) the following recital:
"And whereas, from the decisions of various courts of judicature
in the East Indies, and in the plantations, and colonies and other
dominions of His Majesty abroad, an appeal lies to His Majesty
in Council." The Act then provides for the formation of a
Committee of His Majesty's Privy Council, to be styled the
Judicial Committee of the Privy Council, and enacts that "all
appeals or complaints in the nature of appeals whatever, which
either by virtue of this Act or of any law, statute or custom may

From: *British Coal Corporation* v. *The King* [1935] A.C. 500, pages
510-12.

be brought before His Majesty in Council" from the order of any Court or judge should thereafter be referred by His Majesty to, and heard by, the Judicial Committee, as established by the Act, who should make a report or recommendation to His Majesty in Council for his decision thereon, the nature of such report or recommendation being always stated in open court. The Act contained a great number of provisions for the conduct of appeals. It is clear that the Committee is regarded in the Act as a judicial body or Court, though all it can do is to report or recommend to His Majesty in Council, by whom alone the Order in Council which is made to give effect to the report of the Committee is made.

But according to constitutional convention it is unknown and unthinkable that His Majesty in Council should not give effect to the report of the Judicial Committee, who are thus in truth an appellate Court of law, to which by the statute of 1833 all appeals within their purview are referred.

A later Act, the Judicial Committee Act, 1844, must next be mentioned. Apart from certain changes in procedure, the main effect of that Act was to authorize Her Majesty to provide, by Order or Orders in Council made for that purpose, for the admission of any appeals to Her Majesty in Council from judgments or orders of any Court of justice within any British Colony or possession abroad even though such Court might not be a Court of Error: this followed a recital that by the laws in force in certain of Her Majesty's Colonies no appeal could be brought save only from Courts of Error or of Appeal and that it was expedient to provide that Her Majesty in Council should be authorized to admit such appeals. In effect therefore Her Majesty in Council was thus empowered to override a Colonial law limiting or excluding appeals to Her Majesty in Council from any colonial Court.

In this way the functions of the Judicial Committee as a Court of law were established. The practice had grown up that the colonies under the authority either of Orders in Council or of Acts of Parliament should provide for appeals as of right from their Courts to the King in Council and should fix the conditions on which such appeals should be permitted. But outside these limits there had always been reserved a discretion to the King in Council to grant special leave to appeal from a colonial Court irrespective of the limitations fixed by the colonial law: this discretion to grant special leave to appeal was in practice described as the prerogative right: it was indeed a residuum of the Royal prerogative of the sovereign as the fountain of justice. In early days it was to the King that any subject who had failed to get justice in the King's Court brought his petition for redress. As time went on, such petitions were brought to the King in Parliament (which was the origin of the modern judicial functions of the House of Lords) or to the King in his Chancery (from which flowed the jurisdiction of the Court of Chancery). But this was so only in causes which had been dealt with in English Courts: from the Courts of the Channel Islands and later from the Courts of the Plantations or Colonies the petition went to the King in Council, and this continued to be the practice after the jurisdiction of the Privy Council in English common law cases had been abolished. It was this appellate jurisdiction (along with other jurisdictions such as in Admiralty or Ecclesiastical Causes) which was affirmed and regulated by Parliament in the Privy Council Acts of 1833 and 1844. Although in form the appeal was still to the King in Council, it was so in form only and became in truth an appeal to the Judicial Committee, which as such exercised as a Court of law in reality, though not in name, the residual prerogative of the King in Council. No doubt it was the order of the King in Council which gave effect to their reports, but that order was in no sense other than in form either the King's personal order or the order of the general body of the Privy Council.

"Peace, Order and Good Government" Re-examined

BORA LASKIN

I

It is not good husbandry to plow tilled land and it may be equally a display of folly to venture on a re-examination of the judicially determined content of the introductory clause of section 91 of the British North America Act. That clause has been the favourite "whipping-boy" of most of the articles and comments on Canadian constitutional law[1] and justification for another inquiry into it might, understandably, be required to rest on some substantial ground. But if the amount of literature on Canadian constitutional law is a reflection of the interest which the subject holds for the legal profession, no one who dares to write on it need offer any apology, regardless of the weight of his contribution. Even if extenuation is necessary, there is at least this to be said : (1) the opinion of the Privy Council in *Attorney-General of Ontario* v. *Attorney-General of Canada* (*Reference re Privy Council Appeals*),[2] making it possible for the Parliament of Canada to vest final and exclusive appellate jurisdiction in respect of all Canadian causes in the Supreme Court of Canada, is an invitation to review our constitutional position; and (2) the opinions of the Privy Council in the *Canada Temperance Fede-*

From: *The Canadian Bar Review*, Volume 25 (1947), pages 1054-87. By permission of the author and publisher.

[1] See: Kennedy, The Interpretation of the British North America Act (1943), 8 Camb. L. J. 146; MacDonald, Judicial Interpretation of the Canadian Constitution (1936), 1 Univ. of Tor. L. J. 260; Tuck, Canada and the Judicial Committee of the Privy Council (1941), 4 Univ. of Tor. L. J. 33; Richard, Peace, Order and Good Government (1940), 18 Can. Bar Rev. 243; Jennings, Constitutional Interpretation – The Experience of Canada (1937) 51 Harv. L. Rev. 1; O'Connor, Report to the Senate on the B.N.A. Act (1939), Annex 1, pp 52-78.

[2] [1947] 1 D.L.R. 801.

ration case[3] and in the *Japanese Canadians Deportation* case[4] contain propositions bearing on the introductory words of section 91 which, on one view, neutralize much of what had been said by the Judicial Committee on the matter in the past twenty-five years and, on another view, merely add to the confusing course of judicial pronouncements on the "peace, order and good government" clause.

There are several high points in the judicial history of this clause which may well serve as focal points for any thorough consideration of its content. I nominate as members of this select company (1) *The Dominion Insurance Act* reference,[5] (2) the *Snider* case,[6] (3) the *Natural Products Marketing Act* reference[7] and (4) the *Canada Temperance Federation* case. The *Local Prohibition* case[8] must, of course, be included in this group, but in some respects its stature is of retrospective magnitude just as that of the *Russell* case[9] (also a "must" for the group) is, from a certain point of view, of retrospective insignificance.

The dominant judicial personalities in the history of the introductory clause of section 91 appear to be Viscount Haldane on the Judicial Committee and, on the Supreme Court of Canada, its former Chief Justice, Sir Lyman Duff. While the practice of the Privy Council to give but a single, ostensibly unanimous, opinion has hidden from view any possible dissenter, the freedom of the members of the Supreme Court to express their individual opinions produced an opponent to the Haldane-Duff viewpoint in the person of Sir Lyman's predecessor, the late Chief Justice Anglin.[10] Viscount Haldane's views on the distribution of legislative power under the British North America Act were not uninfluenced by his long apprenticeship,

[3] *Attorney-General of Ontario* v. *Canada Temperance Federation*, [1946] 2 D.L.R. 1.
[4] *Co-Operative Committee on Japanese Canadians* v. *Attorney-General of Canada*, [1947] 1 D.L.R. 577.
[5] *Attorney-General of Canada* v. *Attorney-General of Alberta*, [1916] 1 A.C. 588.
[6] *Toronto Electric Commissioners* v. *Snider*, [1925] A.C. 396
[7] *Reference re Natural Products Marketing Act*, [1936] S.C.R. 398, affirmed [1937] A.C. 377 (*sub nom. Attorney-General of British Columbia* v. *Attorney-General of Canada*).
[8] *Attorney-General of Ontario* v. *Attorney-General of Canada*, [1896] A.C. 348.
[9] *Russell* v. *The Queen* (1882), 7 App. Cas. 829.
[10] See *In re Board of Commerce Act, etc.* (1920), 60 S.C.R. 456; *The King* v. *Eastern Terminal Elevator Co.*, [1925] S.C.R. 434.

when at the Bar, as counsel for the provinces in at least ten cases, although this may be discounted by several appearances as counsel for the Dominion.[11] Sir Lyman's views on the "peace, order and good government" clause were not solely the result of the compulsion of Privy Council decisions. The "locus classicus" accolade bestowed by the Privy Council[12] on his judgment in the *Natural Products Marketing Act* reference[13]

[11] As counsel for the provinces: *St. Catherines Milling & Lumber Co. v. The Queen* (1888), 14 App. Cas. 46; *Attorney-General of Ontario v. Attorney-General of Canada*, [1894] A.C. 189; *Brophy v. Attorney-General of Manitoba*, [1895] A.C. 202; *Attorney-General of Ontario v. Attorney-General of Canada*, [1896] A.C. 348; *Attorney-General of Canada v. Attorney-General of Ontario*, [1897] A.C. 199; *Brewers & Maltsters' Association of Ontario v. Attorney-General of Ontario*, [1897] A.C. 231; *C.P.R. v. Notre Dame de Bonsecours*, [1899] A.C. 367; *Union Colliery v. Bryden*, [1899] A.C. 580; *Madden and Attorney-General of British Columbia v. Fort Sheppard Ry.*, [1899] A.C. 626; *Attorney-General of Manitoba v. Manitoba Licence Holders' Association*, [1902] A.C. 73. As counsel for the Dominion: *Attorney-General of Canada v. Attorney-General of Ontario*, [1898] A.C. 248; *Attorney-General of Canada v. Attorney-General of Ontario*, [1898] A.C. 700.

I do not discount the influence of Lord Watson, especially that stemming from his opinion in the *Local Prohibition* case; but so far as the introductory clause of section 91 is concerned, it was Viscount Haldane that gave it its particular character. It should be nóted, however, that Viscount Haldane magnanimously has credited Lord Watson for the form of the British North America Act under judicial interpretation. In an article on the Privy Council in (1922), 1 Camb. L. J. 143, at p. 150, Viscount Haldane says:

"Particularly [Lord Watson] rendered an enormous service to the Empire and to the Dominion of Canada by developing the Dominion Constitution. At one time, after the British North America Act of 1867 was passed, the conception took hold of the Canadian Courts that what was intended was to make the Dominion the centre of government in Canada, so that its statutes and its position should be superior to the statutes and position of the Provincial Legislatures. That went so far that there arose a great fight; and as the result of a long series of decisions Lord Watson put clothing upon the bones of the Constitution, and so covered them over with living flesh that the Constitution of Canada took a new form. The Provinces were recognized as of equal authority co-ordinate with the Dominion, and a long series of decisions were given by him which solved many problems and produced a new contentment in Canada with the Constitution they had got in 1867. It is difficult to say what the extent of the debt was that Canada owes to Lord Watson, and there is no part of the Empire where his memory is held in more reverence in legal circles."

[12] In *Attorney-General of Canada v. Attorney-General of Ontario*, [1937] A.C. 326.

[13] [1936] S.C.R. 398.

may, in part, have been merely a self-serving tribute to a skilful and faithful exposition of its own course of decision but Sir Lyman showed, as clearly as the *Board of Commerce* case,[14] that he had embarked on that course as much by his own choice as by the dictates of *stare decisis*.

Even on the most generous view of the Privy Council's labours in constitutional interpretation on behalf of the Canadian people, one must find them false to their own oft-declared purpose of discussing each question as it arose and refusing to lay down principles which might later be applied to unforeseen circumstances.[15] Unnecessary, if not also innocuous, dicta in various cases became precious formulae for the decisions in later cases. One can readily admit that any judge may yield to a well-nigh irresistible urge to go beyond what is strictly necessary for his decision, and he ought not to be blamed if his successors treat his dicta as binding upon them. The power of members of an ultimate court to bind their successors (something which the "sovereign" legislature does not admit in relation to its successors) is perhaps peculiar to the judicial function of the House of Lords. The Judicial Committee has, in words at least, declared that it is not absolutely bound by its own decisions,[16] but it has hastened to qualify this by the statement that "on constitutional questions it must be seldom indeed that the Board would depart from a previous decision which it may be assumed will have been acted upon both by governments and subjects."[17] It is unfortunate that this type of hindsight could not have been matched by an equal degree of foresight as to the possible consequences, for succeeding generations of Canadians, of introducing generalities into cases where they had no place.

It would be too much of a threshing of old straw to review at length those Privy Council opinions which resulted in (1) separating the introductory words of section 91 from the declaratory enumerations in that section, and (2) reducing the introductory clause to a position supplementary to the declaratory enumerations. It is sufficient for the purposes of this article merely to state these results, while pointing out that in terms

---

[14] (1920), 60 S.C.R. 456.

[15] E.g., *Citizens Insurance Co.* v. *Parsons* (1881), 7 App. Cas. 96. In the *Manitoba Licence Holders' Association* case, [1902] A.C. 73, the Board referred in this connection to "the advice often quoted but not perhaps always followed".

[16] E.g., *Tooth* v. *Power*, [1891] A.C. 284.

[17] *Canada Temperance Federation* case, *supra*, note 3, at p. 6.

(1) the introductory clause constitutes the Dominion's sole grant of legislative power, and (2) the enumerations are merely illustrations of what is included in the power to make laws for the peace, order and good government of Canada.[18] The righteous indignation of many writers who have commented on this inverted interpretation of the introductory clause is understandable, but I believe that there has been an exaggerated belabouring of this judicial rearrangement of the terms of section 91; and its over-emphasis (as in the case of the O'Connor Report) has distracted attention from a more fruitful point of attack, namely, the lame and artificial application of the "aspect" doctrine to the introductory clause of section 91.[19] Any discussion of the scope of federal legislative power cannot, of course, be divorced from a consideration of the opening words of section 91 as being an original or a supplementary grant of authority. But a sufficient appreciation of "aspect" could have surmounted even the "supplementary" view which the Privy Council espoused. My understanding of the group of Canadian "new deal" cases indicates this to be so.[20]

The *Russell* case was the first occasion upon which the Judicial Committee was invited to sustain Dominion legislation under the introductory words of section 91. It rose to the invitation in an opinion in which it initially characterized the impugned legislation, the Canada Temperance Act. The emphasis in this characterization was laid not so much on the subject matter of the Canada Temperance Act as on the purpose to which it was directed. As later cases put it, the Privy Council ascertained the pith and substance of the legislation so as to discover its "aspect" because that was the cardinal inquiry in assessing its validity under sections 91 and 92 of the British North America Act.[21] The approach from the standpoint of

[18] The subject is canvassed in the O'Connor Report, *supra*, note 1, and in Kennedy, *op. cit.*, *supra*, note 1.

[19] The "aspect" doctrine is laid down in *Hodge* v. *The Queen* (1883), 9 App. Cas. 117, in these words: "Subjects which in one aspect and for one purpose fall within Section 92 may in another aspect and for another purpose fall within Section 91."

[20] These cases involved decisions on a group of ten federal enactments among which were the Natural Products Marketing Act, 1934, the Employment and Social Insurance Act, 1935, and three statutes implementing international labour conventions. The cases are discussed in MacDonald, The Canadian Constitution Seventy Years After (1937), 15 Can. Bar Rev. 401.

[21] E.g., *Attorney-General for Ontario* v. *Reciprocal Insurers*, [1924] A.C. 328.

"aspect" rather than "subject matter" has depended on giving
due weight to the phrase "in relation to matters" which recurs
in sections 91 and 92 and which precedes the reference and
listing in those sections of "classes of subjects." In those cases
(and there are a number)[22] where the Privy Council has talked
of "subject matter" rather than of "aspect," it has been guilty,
if I may paraphrase a sentence of Mr. Justice Duff (as he then
was), of a failure to distinguish between legislation "in relation
to" and legislation "affecting."[23] No such failure is evident in
the *Russell* case, because throughout its opinion in that case the
Judicial Committee measured its characterization of the legislation against a number of classes of subjects enumerated in
section 92 as well as against the grant of legislative power to the
Dominion in section 91.

The consideration which moved the Privy Council to uphold
the Canada Temperance Act as a valid exercise of power to
legislate for the peace, order and good government of Canada
may best be underlined in the Board's own words. Thus, "the
primary matter dealt with" was "one relating to public order
and safety"; the "declared object of Parliament in passing the
Act is that there should be uniform legislation in all the provinces respecting the traffic in intoxicating liquors with a view
to promote temperance in the Dominion"; "Parliament deals
with the subject as one of general concern to the Dominion upon
which uniformity of legislation is desirable, and the Parliament
alone can so deal with it"; there is no ground or pretence for
saying that the evil or vice struck at . . . is local or exists only in
one province"; "the present legislation is clearly meant to apply
a remedy to an evil which is assumed to exist throughout the
Dominion."[24] The feature of these statements is their suggested
connection with data which would support the existence of a
temperance problem on a national scale. Such an approach
infuses some realism into the "aspect" doctrine, permitting it
to reflect the social facts of Canadian life.

The Privy Council in the *Russell* case spoke of the Canada
Temperance Act as "legislation meant to apply a remedy to an
evil which is assumed to exist throughout the Dominion."
Assumed by whom? The answer must be that the Parliament of

[22] E.g., *Board of Commerce* case, [1922] 1 A.C. 191; *Dominion Insur-
     ance Act* reference, [1916] 1 A.C. 588.
[23] *Gold Seal Ltd.* v. *Attorney-General of Alberta* (1921), 62 S.C.R. 424,
     at p. 460.
[24] 7 App. Cas. 829, at pp. 841-2.

Canada made the assumption and that the Judicial Committee was prepared to respect it. One could wish for a recital of the specific facts on which the assumption was made or given credence. But it is at least important that the judgment of the Parliament of Canada was persuasive for the Judicial Committee. While this is perhaps nothing more than the application of a doctrine of "presumption of constitutionality" its import is a far-reaching one if we remember that the *Russell* case was decided in a period when the use of extrinsic aids in interpretation was extremely narrow.[25] About forty years later, in the *Board of Commerce* case, the Judicial Committee in invalidating certain federal anti-profiteering legislation recited that "it can therefore be only under necessity in highly exceptional circumstances, such as cannot be assumed to exist in the present case, that the liberty of the inhabitants of the Provinces may be restricted by the Parliament of Canada and that the Dominion can intervene in the interests of Canada as a whole in questions such as the present one."[26] The Board is now unwilling to make any assumption in favour of the validity of Dominion legislation for the peace, order and good government of Canada; and, what is more, we are left without any discussion by the Judicial Committee of the factual considerations which underlay the enactment of the rejected federal legislation. It may be as unwise for a court to make assumptions in favour of legislative power as against it, when it can easily call for factual material by which it can reach a conclusion on reasonable grounds. But given a decided judicial attitude against resort to extrinsic aids in interpretation, an assumption in favour of constitutionality offers a court a way of reconciling its enormous power of judicial review with the great responsibilities that rest upon Canada's democratically-elected legislatures to satisfy the social wants of a free people. As I shall attempt to show, Viscount Haldane, during the period when he was spokesman for the Privy Council, gave his decisions in terms of cold abstract logic, purporting to find its points of reference within the four corners of the B.N.A. Act, and uninformed and unnourished by any facts of Canadian living which might have afforded a rational basis for his constitutional determinations. The fact that extrinsic aids have been resorted to more freely in the last two decades has seemingly had no effect upon the rigid abstractions with which Canadian constitutional interpretation was surrounded at the close of Viscount Haldane's period of Judicial Committee service.

Honest men may well disagree on whether available data do or do not justify legislation of a particular character and on whether the reasonable inference from such data supports a federal "aspect" in such legislation. But a sense of unreality is the result of constitutional interpretation which has an anchorage only in the mind and unsupported predilections of the judge, whose task it is (as in the case of the British North America Act) to determine from time to time the reach of the governmental functions of the Dominion and the Provinces respectively.

The course of decision respecting the meaning and content of the introductory clause of section 91 suggests that it can conveniently be discussed under three heads: (1) its relation to the so-called "trenching" and "ancillary" doctrines; (2) its position as an "emergency" power; and (3) its position as a "residuary" power.

II

The so-called "trenching" doctrine, the origin of which is usually ascribed to *Tennant* v. *Union Bank of Canada*[27] is, at bottom, merely a bit of embroidery on the "aspect" doctrine. Unfortunately it has become, in the hands of some judicial potters, a kind of clay used to stop up alleged over-extensions of federal power to legislate for the peace, order and good government of Canada. There is a disarming charm about the trenching doctrine when, in Privy Council terms, it champions the paramountcy of federal legislation enacted under the enumerated classes of subjects listed in section 91. But, on closer examination, it becomes merely an apology to the provincial legislatures for any validation of Dominion legislation. Its use to explain a privileged encroachment on provincial legislative authority is purely gratuitous because once a court is satisfied that impugned legislation carries a federal "aspect," no invasion of provincial legislative authority exists.

A similar conclusion must be the result of any close examination of the operation of the so-called ancillary doctrine or the

[27] [1894] A.C. 31.

doctrine of "necessarily incidental," the origin of which is usually ascribed to *Attorney-General of Ontario* v. *Attorney-General of Canada*[28] (*Voluntary Assignments* case). To say that the Dominion in legislating in relation to a matter coming within an enumerated class of subject in section 91 can also enact provisions which are necessarily incidental to effective legislation under the enumerated class is a tortuous method of explaining the "aspect" doctrine. It has the effect, however, not only of bisecting Dominion legislation but of enlarging the area of exercise of provincial legislative power. The latter result (in the absence of conflicting Dominion legislation) is perhaps not particularly objectionable but the former makes a travesty of the "aspect" doctrine. Legislation, as the Judicial Committee has itself said from time to time, must be considered as a whole and its aspect ascertained in the light of all its provisions.[29] To make what can only be an artificial distinction between those provisions of a federal enactment which are strictly in a federal aspect and those necessarily incidental to the effective operation of the legislation, is to trifle with legislative objectives and with the draftsman's efforts to realize them. Even so close and critical a student of constitutional law as Dean MacDonald accepts the reality of a distinction between the aspect and ancillary doctrines, though it may be that he does so more in terms of resignation than of conviction. He puts the difference in this way:

The distinction between the "aspect" and "ancillary" doctrines is that under the former the provision in question is validly within the scope of an enumerated Dominion power, the only peculiarity being that, from some other aspect or for some other purpose, similar legislation might also be enacted by a province; while, under the latter doctrine, the provision in question is invalid per se *as being legislation within an exclusive provincial head but in its particular context it derives validity because of*

---

28 [1894] A.C. 189. And see *Attorney-General of Canada* v. *Attorney-General of British Columbia*, [1930] A.C. 111 (*Fish Canneries* case) where the Judicial Committee summed up in four propositions its approach to the distribution of legislative power under sections 91 and 92. The second proposition, although hewing to the "no trenching" line in relation to the Dominion's general power, is more consistent with the "aspect" doctrine than with any notion of emergency.

29 E.g., *Great West Saddlery Co.* v. *The King*, [1921] 2 A.C. 91.

its necessity to effective legislation under an admitted Dominion head.[30]

To me this is a distinction without a difference, a super-refined and unnecessary embellishment of the aspect doctrine which can only divert attention from the need for close and careful consideration of the problem of aspect.

There was nothing in the *Russell* case to indicate any notion of "trenching" or of the idea of "necessarily incidental"; nor did these ideas appear in the *Hodge* case[31] which, in upholding the validity of the Ontario Liquor Licence Act, proceeded simply on the "aspect" approach. Not until the *Local Prohibition* case is there a suggestion that the "trenching" and "ancillary" doctrines (which had been enunciated in the meantime) might operate to confine the exercise of federal power to legislate for the peace, order and good government of Canada. The matter is mentioned in a queer isolated sentence in the *Manitoba Licence Holders' Association* case.[32] In *Montreal* v. *Montreal Street Railway*[33] the Judicial Committee woodenly repeats (and with an error which is also perpetuated by Chief Justice Duff in the *Natural Products Marketing Act* reference) statements in the *Local Prohibition* case.[34] In the *Dominion Insurance Act* reference in 1916, Viscount Haldane in a sweeping statement, unsupported by citation of authority but clearly resting on his understanding of the *Local Prohibition* case (in which he was one of counsel for the province) puts the matter in terms of finality:

It must be taken to be now settled that the general authority to make laws for the peace, order, and good government of Canada, which the initial part of s. 91 of the British North America Act confers, does not, unless the subject-matter of legislation falls within some one of the enumerated heads which follow, enable the Dominion Parliament to trench on the subject-matters entrusted to the provincial Legislatures by the

---

[30] *Supra*, note 1, at p. 274, footnote 52.

[31] (1883), 9 App. Cas. 117.

[32] [1902] A.C. 73.

[33] [1912] A.C. 333.

[34] Lord Atkinson in the *Montreal Street Ry.* case, in stating certain propositions in the words of the *Local Prohibition* case, says: ". . . The exception contained in s. 91 near its end was not meant to derogate from the legislative authority given to provincial Legislatures by *the 16th subsection* of s. 92," etc. Lord Watson in the *Local Prohibition* case said the "16" subsections of s. 92, not the 16th.

enumeration in s. 92. There is only one case, outside the heads
enumerated in s. 91, in which the Dominion Parliament can
legislate effectively as regards a province, and that is where the
subject-matter lies outside all of the subject-matters enumera-
tively entrusted to the province under s. 92.[35]

It is my submission that the above statement is unwarranted
not only in its finality but in its pose as a clear reflection of
antecedent interpretation.

The *Local Prohibition* case involved a reference to the
Supreme Court of Canada in which that court held unanimously
that a provincial legislature has no legislative jurisdiction to
prohibit the manufacture of intoxicating liquor within the
province, and held by a majority that a provincial legislature
has no legislative jurisdiction to prohibit the sale within the
province of intoxicating liquor.[36] In reversing the Supreme
Court, the Judicial Committee stated that a province could,
in the absence of conflicting legislation by the Parliament of
Canada, prohibit the manufacture of intoxicating liquor in the
province if the manufacture were so carried on as to make its
prohibition a merely local matter; and that the province could
prohibit the sale of intoxicating liquor in so far as there was no
conflict "with the paramount law of Canada." Lord Watson
stated:

> *If the prohibitions of the Canada Temperance Act had been*
> *made imperative throughout the Dominion, their Lordships*
> *might have been constrained by previous authority to hold that*
> *the jurisdiction of the Legislature of Ontario . . . had been*
> *superseded.*[37]

This then would indicate that with respect to the actual issues
before it, the Judicial Committee recognized the paramountcy
of federal legislation over provincial legislation in a situation
where in the absence of Dominion legislation the province might
competently legislate; in other words, even accepting the artificial "trenching" doctrine, the Dominion could "trench" in the
exercise of legislative authority for the peace, order, and good
government of Canada.

A long dictum in the *Local Prohibition* case seems, however,

35 [1916] 1 A.C. 588, at p. 595.
36 (1894), 24 S.C.R. 170.
37 [1896] A.C. 348, at p. 369.

at variance with this position, and it is important to set this dictum out in full, as follows:

The general authority given to the Canadian Parliament by the introductory enactments of s. 91 is "to make laws for the peace, order, and good government of Canada, in relation to all matters not coming within the classes of subjects by this Act assigned exclusively to the legislatures of the provinces"; and it is declared, but not so as to restrict the generality of these words, that the exclusive authority of the Canadian Parliament extends to all matters coming within the classes of subjects which are enumerated in the clause. There may, therefore, be matters not included in the enumeration, upon which the Parliament of Canada has power to legislate, because they concern the peace, order, and good government of the Dominion. But to those matters which are not specified among the enumerated subjects of legislation, the exception from s. 92, which is enacted by the concluding words of s. 91, has no application; and, in legislating with regard to such matters, the Dominion Parliament has no authority to encroach upon any class of subjects which is exclusively assigned to provincial legislatures by s. 92. These enactments appear to their Lordships to indicate that the exercise of legislative power by the Parliament of Canada, in regard to all matters not enumerated in s. 91, ought to be strictly confined to such matters as are unquestionably of Canadian interest and importance, and ought not to trench upon provincial legislation with respect to any of the classes of subjects enumerated in s. 92.[38]

It may be observed, with respect to this long passage, that it is the source of Viscount Haldane's positive assertion in the *Dominion Insurance Act* reference, already quoted. In so far as it applies the concluding clause of section 91 to all the enumerations of section 92 and not only to the 16th enumeration, it has been the subject of competent criticism elsewhere;[39] and it can

[38] *Ibid.*, at p. 360.
[39] *Supra*, note 18. The concluding clause of s. 91 reads as follows: "And any matter coming within any of the classes of subjects enumerated in this section shall not be deemed to come within the class of matters of a local or private nature comprised in the enumeration of the classes of subjects by this Act assigned exclusively to the Legislatures of the Provinces." Jennings, *op. cit.*, *supra*, note 1, at p. 4 accepts the view finally taken by the Judicial Committee in the *Local Prohibition* case that the concluding clause of s. 91 refers to all 16 heads of s. 92 and not merely to s. 92 (16).

hardly be gainsaid that if the concluding clause of section 91 is necessary (as the Privy Council holds) to justify the exclusiveness of the Dominion enumerations as against the whole of section 92, this means that the classes of subjects in section 92 are the dominant ones save to the extent necessary to give scope to those enumerated in section 91. The legerdemain displayed by the Privy Council in dealing with the concluding clause of section 91 gives the surprising result that only the matters within the enumerations of section 91 are deemed to be outside of section 92, whereas any careful reading of sections 91 and 92 indicates that only the matters in section 92 are excluded from Dominion power under section 91 and that the content of the classes of subjects in section 92 is, moreover, cut down by the enumerations in section 91.

The passage previously quoted, in so far as it enjoins the Dominion, when exercising power to legislate for the peace, order, and good government of Canada, from trenching "upon provincial legislation with respect to any of the classes of subjects enumerated in Section 92," conflicts with what was actually decided in the case. Reconciliation of the contradiction is possible only if we ignore the language of the dictum and re-interpret it in terms of the "aspect" doctrine. On such a view, the pieces of an otherwise insoluble puzzle fall into place because there must be a ready acceptance of the proposition that power to legislate for the peace, order, and good government of Canada relates to matters which are "unquestionably of Canadian interest and importance."

I referred earlier to a "queer isolated sentence" in the *Manitoba Licence Holders* case. That case is the counterpart for Manitoba of the *Hodge* case and the *Local Prohibition* case, and it repeats what was said in the latter case that "it is not incompetent for a provincial legislature to pass a [liquor] measure . . . provided the subject is dealt with as a matter 'of a merely local nature' in the province and the [provincial] Act itself *is not repugnant to any Act of the Parliament of Canada.*"[40] Lord Macnaghten speaking for the Privy Council assigned the provincial enactment to section 92 (16) rather than section 92 (13), purporting to apply what he conceived to be the Board's opinion in the *Local Prohibition* case. He goes on, however, to say this: "Indeed, if the case is to be regarded as dealing with matters within the class of subjects enumerated

[40] [1902] A.C. 73, at p. 78.

in No. 13 [of section 92] it might be questionable whether the
Dominion Legislature could have authority to interfere with
the exclusive jurisdiction of the province in the matter."[41] This
sentence, a sort of biologic sport in the context of the whole
opinion, appears to be an attempt to reconcile practically the
actual results in the *Local Prohibition* and the *Manitoba Licence
Holders* cases with the long dictum from the *Local Prohibition*
case quoted earlier. Besides wearing a strange look in preferring
a dictum to the actual ratio, the sentence drives a wedge between
section 92 (16) and the other enumerations of section 92. This
seems the more remarkable when one considers how, in relation
to the concluding clause of section 91, the Judicial Committee
in the *Local Prohibition* case went out of its way to oppose *all*
the enumerations of section 92 to those in section 91. It said,
in that connection, that "all the matters enumerated in the
sixteen heads of Section 92 [were] from a provincial point of
view of a local or private nature."[42] The suggestion of the
Manitoba Licence Holders case goes beyond merely segregating
section 92 (16) from the other enumerations in section 92 and
making it alone subservient to the federal power to legislate for
the peace, order, and good government of Canada. Its necessary
consequence is further to reduce the effectiveness of the peace,
order and good government clause, because by giving that clause
a hollow paramountcy over section 92 (16) (a sort of provincial
residuary clause)[43] it can the more easily be dismissed in relation to other more effective enumerations of section 92 such as
No. 13. It is significant in this connection that only in respect of
liquor legislation has this dubious preference been accorded to
the federal power, so that it represents a whittling down of the
"aspect" doctrine as applied in *Russell* v. *The Queen* and *Hodge*
v. *The Queen*. Viscount Haldane lends support to this conclusion because in the *Dominion Insurance Act* reference he refers
to the aspect doctrine as "a principle which is now well
established but [which] none the less ought to be applied only
with great caution."[44] His statement in that case, already quoted,
on the subordination of the peace, order, and good government
clause to the enumerations in section 92 shows the extent to
which he ignores the aspect doctrine. He speaks there of

[41] *Ibid.*
[42] [1896] A.C. 348, at p. 359.
[43] See, Note (1946), 24 Can. Bar Rev. 223.
[44] [1916] 1 A.C. 588, at p. 596.

"subject matter of legislation" and of "subject-matters entrusted to the provincial legislatures"; and further on in his opinion in the case he refers to the *Russell* case as one where "the Court considered that the particular subject-matter in question lay outside the provincial powers." It is clear, of course, that the particular subject-matter was within provincial powers in a local aspect and outside such powers only where the purpose of the legislation was such as to give it a federal "aspect."

A great deal has been made, both by Sir Lyman Duff[45] and by Viscount Haldane,[46] of the unreported McCarthy Act decision of the Judicial Committee. There the Board, without giving reasons, invalidated the Dominion Liquor License Act, 1883, affirming, in so doing, the opinion of the Supreme Court of Canada.[47] It is important to note that this decision followed decisions of the Judicial Committee upholding the Canada Temperance Act and the Ontario Liquor License Act. An examination of the Dominion Liquor License Act reveals it to have been a purely local licensing statute, contemplating decentralized administration through district Boards of License Commissioners. The whole tenor of the Act indicated that it was dealing with the liquor traffic as a purely local problem in local licence districts. It is hardly a matter of surprise that the Supreme Court of Canada should have invalidated the enactment; but even so, the majority of the court saved those parts of the enactment relating to the carrying into effect of the provisions of the Canada Temperance Act. It is difficult hence to understand why Viscount Haldane in the *Snider* case should have felt that it was hard to reconcile the *Russell* case with the *McCarthy Act* decision; or why he so artfully says, "as to this last decision it is not without significance that the strong Board which delivered it abstained from giving any reasons for their conclusions."[48] For, if the *McCarthy Act* case affirms anything, it affirms the application of the aspect doctrine already referred to in the *Hodge* case.

There is, of course, a constant temptation to apportion legis-

---

[45] In the *Board of Commerce* case (1920), 60 S.C.R. 456, at pp. 509, 511; and in the *Natural Products Marketing Act* reference, [1936] S.C.R. 398, at pp. 409, 411.

[46] In the *Snider* case, [1925] A.C. 396. See also another reference in the *Dominion Insurance Act* reference, [1916] 1 A.C. 588, at p. 596, which states the result accurately.

[47] See schedule to 1885 (Can.), c. 74.

[48] [1925] A.C. 396, at p. 411.

lative power under the B.N.A. Act according to subject-matter of legislation, to read sections 91 and 92 as if they distribute fields of law-making instead of legislative power directed to various purposes, whether those purposes be related to the peace, order and good government of Canada or to matters within enumerated classes of subjects. To yield to this temptation involves ignoring the qualitative and quantitative character of a particular legislative problem. Moreover, having regard to the course of decision which reduced the peace, order and good government clause to a supplementary position and having regard to the use made of the "trenching" and "ancillary" doctrines with respect to that clause, constitutional interpretation becomes a mechanical process in which the substantial inquiry in connection with the validity of federal legislation for the peace, order and good government of Canada is whether the subject-matter of the legislation is part of "property and civil rights in the province" within section 92(13).

III

There can surely be nothing more remarkable in judicial annals than the Privy Council's treatment of the peace, order and good government clause from the *Russell* case in 1882 to the *Japanese Canadians Deportation* case in 1946. Beginning with the *Board of Commerce* case in 1921 and carrying through the *Fort Frances* case[49] and culminating in the *Snider* case in 1925, Viscount Haldane laboriously built a doctrine of "emergency" around the clause, only to have Viscount Simon puncture the doctrine in no uncertain fashion in the *Canada Temperance Federation* case in 1946. But at the close of 1946 the Judicial Committee, speaking through Lord Wright in the *Japanese Canadians Deportation* case, reverted to the language of emergency with a strange detachment and a seemingly innocent unconcern which expressed itself in an omission to mention the *Canada Temperance Federation* case decided earlier in the same year.

The germ of the "emergency" character of the introductory clause is attributed to two sentences in Lord Watson's opinion in the *Local Prohibition* case, reading as follows:

Their Lordships do not doubt that some matters, in their origin

[49] *Fort Frances Pulp & Power Co.* v. *Manitoba Free Press*, [1923] A.C. 695.

local and provincial, might attain such dimensions as to affect the body politic of the Dominion, and to justify the Canadian Parliament in passing laws for their regulation or abolition in the interest of the Dominion. But great caution must be observed in distinguishing between that which is local and provincial, and therefore within the jurisdiction of the provincial legislatures, and that which has ceased to be merely local or provincial, and has become matter of national concern, in such sense as to bring it within the jurisdiction of the Parliament of Canada.[50]

It is well to note that these sentences are more consistent with an appreciation of the aspect doctrine than of any doctrine of power in extraordinary circumstances. *Ex facie*, they make allowance for a social and economic development of Canada which might transform local problems into national ones, so that they might require federal rather than provincial solutions. When Chief Justice Duff comes to deal with these two sentences in his judgment in the *Natural Products Marketing Act* reference, not only does he drain them of any vitality but he makes them ridiculous.

The learned Chief Justice begins by warning that the two sentences must be read in their context, and this admits of no contradiction. He refers to them as being "in . . . carefully guarded language"; and he continues as follows:

It has been assumed, apparently, that they lay down a rule of construction the effect of which is that all matters comprised in any one of the enumerated sub-divisions of section 92 may attain "such dimensions as to . . . cease to be merely local or provincial" and become in some other aspect of them matters relating to the "peace, order and good government of Canada" and subject to the legislative jurisdiction of the Parliament of Canada.

---

[50] [1896] A.C. 348, at p. 361. In the *Labour Conventions* case, [1937] A.C. 326, at p. 353, the Judicial Committee said of Lord Watson's two sentences: "They laid down no principle of constitutional law, and were cautious words intended to safeguard possible eventualities which no one at the time had any interest or desire to define." This seems a little incongruous when the Judicial Committee proceeds in its next sentence to approve Chief Justice Duff's analysis of the introductory clause of section 91 in the *Natural Products Marketing Act* reference, an analysis which certainly treated the two sentences as expressing a principle of constitutional law. That it is difficult to understand its application is another matter.

The difficulty of applying such a rule to matters falling within the first subdivision, for example, of section 92, which relates to the amendment of the provincial constitutions "notwithstanding anything in this Act," must be very great. On the face of the language of the statute, the authority seems to be intended to be absolute. In other words, it seems to be very clearly stated that matters comprised within the subject matter of the constitution of the province "except as regards the office of Lieutenant-Governor" are matters local and provincial, and that they are not matters which can be comprised in any of the classes of subjects of section 91.

Then the decision in . . . Montreal Park and Island Railway v. City of Montreal *seems to be final upon the point that local works and undertakings, subject to the exceptions contained in subdivision no. 10 of section 92 and matters comprised within that description, are matters local and provincial within the meaning of section 92 and excepted from the general authority given by the introductory enactment of section 91.*

The same might be said of the solemnization of marriage in the province. Marriage and divorce are given without qualification to the Dominion under subdivision 26 of section 91, but the effect of section 92 (12), it has been held, is to exclude from the Dominion jurisdiction in relation to marriage and divorce the subject of solemnization of marriage in the province. It is very difficult to conceive the possibility of solemnization of marriage, in the face of this plain declaration by the legislature, assuming aspects which would bring it within the general authority of the Dominion in relation to peace, order and good government, in such fashion, for example, as to enable the Dominion to prohibit or to deprive of legal effect a religious ceremony of marriage. The like might be said of no. 2, Taxation within the Province; the Borrowing of Monies on the Sole Credit of the Province; Municipal Institutions in the Province; and the Administration of Justice, including the constitution of the Courts and Procedure in Civil Matters in the Courts.[51]

This, with respect, merely sets up a man of straw in order that he may easily be knocked down. The term "matters" has no meaning apart from legislative issues which may call for the exercise of legislative powers. Those issues depend not on artificial presuppositions but on the existence of facts and

[51] [1936] S.C.R. 398, at p. 418.

circumstances which give rise to some social pressure for legislation. There is no difficulty hence in understanding that the
"some matters" in Lord Watson's two sentences could well
relate to issues finding concrete support for federal treatment
and that they do not necessarily comprehend the abstractions in
which Chief Justice Duff seeks to envelop them.

The learned Chief Justice's conclusions as to the meaning of
the two sentences are as follows:

> As we have said, Lord Watson's language is carefully
> guarded. He does not say that every matter which attains such
> dimensions as to affect the body politic of the Dominion falls
> thereby within the introductory matter of section 91. But he said
> that "some matters" may attain such dimensions as to affect
> the body politic of the Dominion and, as we think the sentence
> ought to be read having regard to the context, in such manner
> and degree as may "justify the Canadian Parliament in passing
> laws for their regulation or abolition. . . ." So, in the second
> sentence, he is not dealing with all matters of "national concern"
> in the broadest sense of those words, but only those which are
> matter of national concern "in such sense" as to bring them
> within the jurisdiction of the Parliament of Canada.[52]

This statement involves a *circulus inextricabilis*. On the Chief
Justice's analysis, only "some matters" which attain such dimensions as to affect the body politic of the Dominion fall within
federal power. To the question, What are those matters?, the
answer given by the Chief Justice seems to be that they are
matters of national concern in such sense as to bring them
within federal jurisdiction. Surely this is merely turning the
phrase "some matters" in upon itself and amounts to a definition
in the terms of the phrase to be defined. It is well to mention at
this point that the Judicial Committee in the *Labour Conventions* case said of the judgment of Chief Justice Duff that "[it]
will, it is to be hoped, form the *locus classicus* of the law on this
point and preclude further disputes"; and again, that "they
consider that the law is finally settled by the current of cases
cited by the Chief Justice on the principles declared by him."[53]
There is certainly a strange and hollow sound to these words
when one considers that Viscount Simon in the *Canada Temperance Federation* case categorically rejected any notion of

[52] *Ibid.*, at p. 419.
[53] [1937] A.C. 326, at p. 353.

"emergency" in an opinion which did not bother to mention either Chief Justice Duff's *locus classicus* or the approbation given it by the Privy Council.

It is in the *Board of Commerce* case that the notion of emergency appears in recognizable form. The federal legislation impugned in that case was clearly of a far-reaching character, but nowhere in their opinions in the case do the Supreme Court or Privy Council challenge the necessity for stringent legislation. Admittedly, this is no argument upon which to support a federal exercise of power – or any provincial exercise of power for that matter. But if the necessity for restrictive legislation rests on the existence of a condition which is not local or provincial but general, and the legislation enacted to cope with it is predicated on the generality of the evil to be struck at, a federal "aspect" may well be found in such legislation. There may, of course, be a difference of opinion as to what inferences may legitimately be drawn from facts in evidence and as to whether any questioned legislation is fairly based on reasonable inferences from proved facts. That, however, is part of the necessary travail of constitutional adjudication unless the adjudication proceeds without a firm basis in the facts and circumstances surrounding the question to be determined.

The Supreme Court in the *Board of Commerce* case was divided on the question of the validity of the federal legislation there considered. Mr. Justice Anglin, for half the court, was of opinion that it was a valid exercise of legislative authority in relation to the regulation of trade and commerce and, moreover, that it was supportable as legislation for the peace, order and good government of Canada. In this latter connection he said:

Effective control and regulation of prices so as to meet and overcome in any one province what is generally recognized to be an evil – "profiteering" – an evil so prevalent and so insidious that in the opinion of many persons it threatens to-day the moral and social well-being of the Dominion – may thus necessitate investigation, inquiry and control in other provinces. It may be necessary to deal with the prices and the profits of the growers or other producers of raw material, the manufacturers, the middlemen and the retailers. No one provincial legislature could legislate so as to cope effectively with such a matter and concurrent legislation of all the provinces interested is fraught with so many difficulties in its enactment and in its administration and enforcement that to deal with the situation at all adequately by that means is, in my opinion, quite impracticable.

Viewed in this light it would seem that the impugned statutory provisions may be supported, without bringing them under any of the enumerative heads of s. 91, as laws made for the peace, order and good government of Canada in relation to matters not coming within any of the classes of subjects assigned exclusively to the legislatures of the provinces, since, in so far as they deal with property and civil rights, they do so in an aspect which is not "from a provincial point of view local or private" and therefore not exclusively under provincial control.[54]

On the other hand, Duff J. held the legislation to be invalid, and it is instructive to note his reasoning. Thus he says:

There is no case of which I am aware in which a Dominion statute not referable to one of the classes of legislation included in the enumerated heads of sec. 91 and being of such a character that from a provincial point of view, it should be considered legislation dealing with "property and civil rights," has been held competent to the Dominion under the introductory clause.[55]

It is a matter of surprise that such a generalization should be based on but a single decision, namely, the *Dominion Insurance Act* reference – especially when it can be countered by the *Russell* case. If we exclude the "company" cases,[56] these were the only cases up to the time of the *Board of Commerce* case in which the Judicial Committee was called on to sustain federal legislation under the introductory clause of section 91. And the "company" cases can by no stretch of the imagination qualify for inclusion under that clause if as a condition thereof "it is essential that the matter dealt with shall be one of unquestioned Canadian interest and importance as distinguished from matters merely local in one of the provinces."[57]

There is no suggestion of "emergency" in the passage quoted from Duff J.'s judgment but rather a playing up of the provincial power under section 92 (13). The *Russell* case is dismissed

---

[54] (1920), 60 S.C.R. 456, at p. 467.

[55] *Ibid.*, at p. 508.

[56] There was also, of course, the *McCarthy Act* decision in 1885 where no reasons were given. As to the "company" cases, see *John Deere Plow Co. Ltd.* v. *Wharton*, [1915] A.C. 330.

[57] (1920), 60 S.C.R. 456, at p. 506, *per* Duff J.

with the statement that "it must be remembered that *Russell's* case was in great part an unargued case."[58] This is, of course, a barb (repeated again by Sir Lyman in his judgment in the *National Products Marketing Act* reference[59]) directed to the admission, made by Mr. Benjamin as counsel for the appellant in the *Russell* case, that if the Canada Temperance Act had been made imperative throughout Canada without local option it would have been valid. There is certainly nothing in the *Russell* case to indicate that this admission was fatal; and since the Act was in fact a local option statute it might have been good tactics to make an admission which was relevant to something not before the court. Presumably, Mr. Justice Duff is pointing out that counsel failed to make an argument which might have produced a different result in the *Russell* case. This does not lead anywhere because it should be equally possible to overturn other decisions in the same way. And treated as a plea against the too rigid application of *stare decisis* to constitutional decisions, the argument of Mr. Justice Duff apparently defeats the purpose he has in making it.

Mr. Justice Duff comes to actual grips with the problem in the *Board of Commerce* case in a passage which delineates in terms more reasonable than abstract the objections to easy enlargement of the content of the introductory words of section 91. It is as follows:

The scarcity of necessaries of life, the high cost of them, the evils of excessive profit taking, are matters affecting nearly every individual in the community and affecting the inhabitants of every locality and every province collectively as well as the Dominion as a whole. The legislative remedy attempted by section 18 is one of many remedies which might be suggested. One could conceive, for example, a proposal that there should be a general restriction of credits, and that the business of money lending should be regulated by a commission appointed by the Dominion Government with powers conferred by Parliament. Measures to increase production might conceivably be proposed and to that end nationalization of certain industries and even compulsory allotment of labour. In truth if this legislation can be sustained under the residuary clause, it is not easy to put a limit to the extent to which Parliament through the instrumen-

---

[58] *Ibid.*, at p. 507.
[59] [1936] S.C.R. 398, at p. 420.

tality of commissions (having a large discretion in assigning the limits of their own jurisdiction, see sec. 16), may from time to time in the vicissitudes of national trade, times of high prices, times of stagnation and low prices and so on, supersede the authority of the provincial legislatures. I am not convinced that it is a proper application of the reasoning to be found in the judgments on the subject of the drink legislation, to draw from it conclusions which would justify Parliament in any conceivable circumstance forcing upon a province a system of nationalization of industry.[60]

The argument which Duff J. makes, for all its plausibility, is directed to a question which was not before the court. The legislation in the *Board of Commerce* case established a board empowered to prohibit the formation and operation of combines and the making of unfair profits, to prevent the accumulation of (defined) necessaries of life beyond reasonable amounts and to require the sale of any surplus at fair prices. The issue of nationalization raised by the learned justice almost appears as an attempt to parade the horrors which might ensue from an enlargement of the content of the "peace, order and good government" clause. We may note that he omits to tell us whether nationalization would be more acceptable in provincial garb. But whether the issue be nationalization or anti-profiteering and anti-combine legislation, the "aspect" approach cannot admit of denial of legislative power "in any conceivable circumstance." The British North America Act does not enshrine, in its distribution of legislative power, any particular economic theory, although it does express some economic policy, as for example, in section 121 which provides for free entry into each province of products of any sister province.[61] It is understandable judicial technique to worry about the next case, but the judge in a constitutional case cannot justifiably fix the sights so far ahead as to detach himself completely from his immediate surroundings. And no more should he loll about in the past if that would also place him in an unreal environment.

When the *Board of Commerce* case reached the Privy Council the notion of the "extraordinary" or "abnormal" character of federal power under the opening words of section 91 makes

[60] (1920), 60 S.C.R. 456, at p. 512.
[61] Section 121 reads as follows: "All articles of the growth, produce or manufacture of any one of the provinces shall, from and after the union, be admitted free into each of the other provinces."

its appearance in the argument of provincial counsel; and in the opinion of Viscount Haldane this idea is given countenance by his reference to the facts that the impugned legislation was (1) passed after the conclusion of the war of 1914-18,[62] and (2) was not fashioned as a temporary control measure. Undoubtedly these facts may be relevant in determining whether the aspect of the legislation falls within the introductory words of section 91; but to fasten on them to the exclusion of the actual circumstances and conditions which induced the legislation seems to be arbitrary. Yet that is what Viscount Haldane does as the following passage reveals:

The first question to be answered is whether the Dominion Parliament could validly enact such a law. Their Lordships observe that the law is not one enacted to meet special conditions in wartime. It was passed in 1919, after peace had been declared, and it is not confined to any temporary purpose, but is to continue without limit in time, and to apply throughout Canada. No doubt the initial words of s. 91 of the British North America Act confer on the Parliament of Canada power to deal with subjects which concern the Dominion generally, provided that they are not withheld from the powers of that Parliament to legislate, by any of the express heads in s. 92, untrammelled by the enumeration of special heads in s. 91. It may well be that the subjects of undue combination and hoarding are matters in which the Dominion has a great practical interest. In special circumstances, such as those of a great war, such an interest might conceivably become of such paramount and overriding importance as to amount to what lies outside the heads in s. 92, and is not covered by them. The decision in Russell v. The Queen *appears to recognize this as constitutionally possible, even in time of peace; but it is quite another matter to say that under normal circumstances general Canadian policy can justify interference, on such a scale as the statutes in controversy involve, with the property and civil rights of the inhabitants of the Provinces. It is to the Legislatures of the Provinces that the regulation and restriction of their civil rights have in general been exclusively confided, and as to these the Provincial Legislatures possess quasi-sovereign authority.*[63]

[62] It was enacted, however, before the Treaty of Versailles became effective.

[63] [1922] 1 A.C. 191, at p. 197.

Having rebuffed the Dominion in any "normal" resort to the power to legislate for the peace, order and good government of Canada, Viscount Haldane proceeds to place the power on an "abnormal" level, as follows:

It has already been observed that circumstances are conceivable, such as those of war or famine, when the peace, order and good Government of the Dominion might be imperilled under conditions so exceptional that they require legislation of a character in reality beyond anything provided for by the enumerated heads in either s. 92 or s. 91 itself. Such a case, if it were to arise, would have to be considered closely before the conclusion could properly be reached that it was one which could not be treated as falling under any of the heads enumerated. Still, it is a conceivable case, and although great caution is required in referring to it, even in general terms, it ought not, in the view their Lordships take of the British North America Act, read as a whole, to be excluded from what is possible. For throughout the provisions of that Act there is apparent the recognition that subjects which would normally belong exclusively to a specifically assigned class of subject may, under different circumstances and in another aspect, assume a further significance. Such an aspect may conceivably become of paramount importance, and of dimensions that give rise to other aspects. This is a principle which, although recognized in earlier decisions, such as that of Russell *v.* The Queen, *both here and in the Courts of Canada, has always been applied with reluctance, and its recognition as relevant can be justified only after scrutiny sufficient to render it clear that the circumstances are abnormal. In the case before them, however important it may seem to the Parliament of Canada that some such policy as that adopted in the two Acts in question should be made general throughout Canada, their Lordships do not find any evidence that the standard of necessity referred to has been reached, or that the attainment of the end sought is practicable, in view of the distribution of legislative powers enacted by the Constitution Act, without the co-operation of the Provincial Legislatures.*[64]

It is of some significance that Viscout Haldane makes no reference to Lord Watson's opinion in the *Local Prohibition* case; and it may hence be justifiably said that the "emergency"

[64] *Ibid.,* at p. 200.

colouring given to the introductory clause of section 91 was a product of Viscount Haldane's craftsmanship. War, after all, was a serious matter and Viscount Haldane, as a former British War Minister, could be counted on to appreciate the wide sweep of authority that must be confided in a central authority during a time of war. Presumably, the problems of peacetime living were capable of decentralized treatment regardless of their proportions. But, that he should have sought to support his doctrine on the basis of the *Russell* case, which involved a local option statute, merely emphasizes its sham quality. It may be noted that the suggestion for co-operation between the Dominion and provincial legislatures to attain ends denied to federal legislation alone was not original with Viscount Haldane but was made earlier by Mr. Justice Duff.[65] As is well known, the co-operation theory, which was miraculously put to a concrete test in respect to the marketing of natural products, was despatched in its first encounter with the Privy Council.[66]

The *Board of Commerce* case, in retrospect, was a companion case to *Fort Frances Pulp and Power Co.* v. *Manitoba Free Press*, and both were merely a dress rehearsal for *Toronto Electric Commissioners* v. *Snider*. The *Fort Frances* case involved a federal statute which, although enacted after the cessation of hostilities in the war of 1914-18, provided for the continuation, until the proclamation of peace, of newsprint controls which had been inaugurated under the War Measures Act. Here was an enactment which met the *Board of Commerce* case test of a temporary statute strictly related to a condition of war and Viscount Haldane had no trouble in pulling himself up by his own bootstraps and finding the statute to be valid.

In so doing, however, he overextended himself even in relation to the *Board of Commerce* case. In the first place, he speaks of implied powers arising in time of war. This naturally makes one wonder why, if in time of war the Dominion can rely on implied powers, it should have been necessary to fit the "peace, order and good government" clause into an emergency jacket. As a constitutional "Houdini," Lord Watson succeeded merely

---

[65] (1920), 60 S.C.R. 456, at p. 506.
[66] *Attorney-General of Canada* v. *Attorney-General of British Columbia*, [1937] A.C. 377. Nevertheless, the Judicial Committee in this case still advised the Dominion and provinces to try co-operation (p. 389). See Royal Commission on Dominion-Provincial Relations (1940), Appendix 7, Difficulties of Divided Jurisdiction, by J. A. Corry, chap. 2.

in reducing the clause to a supplementary position; Viscount
Haldane's magic is strong enough to make it disappear altogether and to make it reappear as a spirit. In the second place,
it is clear that practical considerations are unimportant for
Viscount Haldane in respect to his co-operation theory. The
tensions in a federal state which make legislative co-operation
practically impossible in normal times are ignored by him. A
time of war is, practically speaking, the only sure guarantee of
effective co-operation; but the exercise of legislative power in
wartime, says Viscount Haldane, "is not one that can be reliably
provided for by depending on collective action of the Legislatures of the individual Provinces agreeing for the purpose."[67]

In the *Snider* case, Viscount Haldane reaches his apotheosis.
It is there that he tries to bury the *Russell* case which he had
used as a springboard for his "emergency" doctrine in the *Board
of Commerce* case. The passage in his opinion in which he
explains the decision in the *Russell* case as predicated on in-
temperance being at the time "a menace to the national life of
Canada," requiring intervention by the federal Parliament "to
protect the nation from disaster," is well known and has been
well heaped with the ridicule it deserves.[68] It is a typical "Haldane" touch to find in the *Snider* case the statement that "it is
plain from the decision in the *Board of Commerce* case that the
evil of profiteering could not have been so invoked, for provincial powers, if exercised, were adequate to it."[69] Here is the
arbiter *sans peur et sans reproche* ready to solve any problem by
a prepared formula, invariable in its compounds, regardless of
the matter to be solved; not for him any stress or doubts such as
have agitated the minds and hearts of great constitutional judges
in other federal countries. He has fashioned the Procrustean
bed; let the constitution, the British North America Act, lie
on it.

The *Snider* case affords a typical example of a legislative
problem which had undergone a change in character with the
passing of years but which was met by the Judicial Committee
with the inflexible concepts that are often the product of a neat
mind, unwilling in the interests of some sort of formal logic to
disarrange thought patterns that had been nicely fitted together.

---

[67] [1923] A.C. 695, at p. 704.
[68] *Cf.* Anglin C. J. in *The King* v. *Eastern Terminal Elevator Co.*,
[1925] S.C.R. 434, at p. 438; Kennedy, *op. cit., supra*, note 1.
[69] [1925] A.C. 396, at pp. 412-13.

The Industrial Disputes Investigation Act, 1907, as amended, introduced a scheme for conciliation of labour disputes which involved the mandatory postponement of strikes or lockouts pending the termination of conciliation efforts. A number of serious work stoppages preceding and following the enactment of the statute had indicated and buttressed the need for legislative establishment of federal machinery of conciliation. All the factors that weighed so heavily with the Judicial Committee in the *Russell* case were evident in the *Snider* case: there was the need for public order in industrial relations, there was generality, there was uniformity, there was the attempt "to remedy an evil which [was] assumed to exist throughout the Dominion." The genuineness of the legislation in these respects was reflected in the reach of its provisions, which covered employers "employing ten or more persons and owning or operating any mining property, agency of transportation or communication, or public service utility, including . . . railways, . . . steamships, telegraph and telephone lines, gas, electric light, water and power works."[70] The Appellate Division of the Supreme Court of Ontario, with only one of its five members dissenting, found the Act to be valid as an exercise of federal legislative power in relation to the regulation of trade and commerce and in relation to the criminal law.[71] Certainly that seemed to be a substantial enough ground of decision, at least in relation to most, if not all, of the industries covered by the Act. Viscount Haldane had, however, disabled himself by previous opinions from finding any support for the legislation in the "trade and commerce" clause.[72] And in dealing with it as an exercise of the "criminal law" power, part of his reasoning makes for despair, as where he says:

> *It is not necessary to investigate or determine whether a strike is* per se *a crime according to the law of England in 1792. A great deal has been said on the subject and contrary opinions expressed. Let it be assumed that it was. It certainly was so only on the ground of conspiracy. But there is no conspiracy involved in a lock-out; and the statute under discussion deals with lock-outs* pari ratione *as with strikes. It would be impossible, even if it were desirable, to separate the provisions as to*

---

[70] 1907 (Can.), c. 20, s. 2 (c).

[71] (1924), 55 O.L.R. 454, Hodgins J. A. dissenting.

[72] By his opinions in the *Dominion Insurance Act* reference and in the *Board of Commerce* case.

strikes from those as to lock-outs, so as to make the one fall under the criminal law while the other remained outside it; and, therefore, in their Lordships' opinion this argument also fails.[73]

It could not, of course, have been very surprising to find Viscount Haldane rejecting the contention that the Industrial Disputes Investigation Act was an exercise of power to legislate for the peace, order and good government of Canada. One is inclined to agree in this result but only because adequate power to regulate industrial relations (at least in respect of industries having an impact beyond the province of their location) ought to be found in the "trade and commerce" power. Recent judgments by the British Columbia Court of Appeal in *Reference re Hours of Work Act to C.P.R. Hotel Employees*[74] and by Bigelow J. of the Saskatchewan Supreme Court in *C.P.R. and C.P. Express Co.* v. *Attorney-General of Saskatchewan*[75] may well mark the development of a tendency to this view.

What makes the *Snider* case significant is the revealed impotence of the "peace, order and good government" power in the face of the wide sweep given to section 92 (13). Viscount Haldane does not treat the phrase "property and civil rights in the province" in the context of the British North America Act as a class of subject for the exertion of provincial legislative power, but rather as relating to attributes of the citizenry of the Dominion which are beyond the reach of Dominion legislation wherever any portion of them can be the subject of provincial legislation. It is this unusual conception of section 92 (13) which has produced the paralysis in the Dominion power to legislate for the peace, order and good government of Canada, a paralysis so forcibly exposed to Canadian view in the group of "new deal" cases decided by the Judicial Committee early in 1937. How else can one explain the following barren comment by Viscount Haldane in the *Snider* case: "It does not appear that there is anything in the Dominion Act which could not have been enacted by the Legislature of Ontario, excepting one provision. The field for the operation of the Act was made the whole of Canada."[76]

[73] [1925] A.C. 396, at p. 409.
[74] [1947] 2 D.L.R. 723.
[75] [1947] 4 D.L.R. 329.
[76] [1925] A.C. 396, at pp. 403-4. This notion was expressed by Duff J. much earlier in *In re Sections 4 and 70 of the Canadian Insurance Act, 1910* (1913), 48 S.C.R. 260.

The Haldane conception of section 92 (13) in association with his "emergency" doctrine stands responsible for the striking down of the Dominion legislation involved in the *Employment and Social Insurance Act* reference.[77] The Act provided for compulsory unemployment insurance, to be administered by a commission and supported by contributions from employer, employee and government; and it was enacted in the midst of an unemployment crisis and with a view to forestalling for the future the degree of distress which then existed. It is interesting that Duff C.J., whose analysis of the introductory clause of section 91 in the *Natural Products Marketing Act* reference made it impossible for the Supreme Court to uphold the Employment and Social Insurance Act under that clause, was prepared to find the Act valid as an exercise of legislative power in relation to the public debt and property (section 91(1)) and the raising of money by any mode or system of taxation (section 91(3)).[78] There would certainly seem to be a greater heterodoxy involved in attempting to uphold it under these powers than if it were supported as an exercise of authority to legislate for the peace, order and good government of Canada.

The Judicial Committee, when the case came before it, affirmed the invalidity of the Act in a short opinion, almost shocking in its casualness unless one remembers that the "emergency" fixation settled the fate of the Act so far as the introductory clause of section 91 was concerned and that the "insurance" cases likewise were a premonition of its doom as an encroachment on provincial power under section 92(13). On both heads, the Privy Council gives us the now monotonous formulae of earlier cases: "It is sufficient to say that the present Act does not purport to deal with any special emergency"; "It is an Act whose operation is intended to be permanent"; "this Act is an insurance Act affecting the civil rights of employers and employees in each Province."[79] Not even a pretence at analysis, no effort expended to give explicit consideration to the effects of years of national unemployment in the 1930's, to the need for legislating preventively as well as curatively; the "law" on the subject was beyond recall or redefinition. The whole sorry story of the Judicial Committee's decisions in the Canadian "new deal"

---

[77] *Attorney-General of Canada* v. *Attorney-General of Ontario*, [1937] A.C. 355.

[78] [1936] S.C.R. 427. Duff and Davis JJ. dissented from the holding that the act was invalid.

[79] [1937] A.C. 355, at p. 367.

cases was discussed in a special number of this Review in 1937.[80] In the perspective of the past decade, its performance in those cases is surely a monument to judicial rigidity and to a complacence which admits of no respectable explanation unless it be that the blinders fashioned by Viscount Haldane's opinions permitted no deviation from the course on which he set Canadian constitutional interpretation. This is far from convincing, but it serves to explain why the social, factual considerations in the "new deal" legislation were largely irrelevant. To admit their relevancy would make it impossible to maintain a mythical consistency predicated on a fixed notion of the meaning of "property and civil rights in the province."

Viscount Simon's opinion in the *Canada Temperance Federation* case may be likened to the removal of shutters from a house which has been kept dark for many years. From one point of view, namely in its affirmation of the *Russell* case and of the validity of essentially the same statute as was there involved, it is nothing more than an echo of the *Russell* case, perhaps doomed to the same isolation; and, unfortunately, the "emergency" language of the *Japanese Canadians Deportation* case threatens this consequence. Again, it is difficult to say what deduction may properly be drawn from Viscount Simon's failure to mention the "new deal" cases. Does this leave the authority of Duff C.J.'s *locus classicus* unimpaired or is this seemingly intentional ignoring of that judgment a prelude to re-invigoration of the "peace, order and good government" clause? If language means anything, the second alternative must be favoured; because Viscount Simon goes much further than is strictly necessary in deflating the *Snider* case not only in its appraisal of the *Russell* case but also in its actual approach to the "peace, order and good government" clause. Thus Viscount Simon expresses himself as follows:

The first observation which their Lordships would make on this explanation of Russell's *case is that the British North America Act nowhere gives power to the Dominion Parliament to legislate in matters which are properly to be regarded as exclusively within the competence of the Provincial Legislatures, merely because of the existence of an emergency. Secondly, they can find nothing in the judgment of the Board in 1882 which suggests that it proceeded on the ground of emergency;*

[80] (1937), 15 Can. Bar Rev. 393-507.

there was certainly no evidence before that Board that one existed. The Act of 1878 was a permanent, not a temporary, Act and no objection was raised to it on that account. In their Lordships' opinion, the true test must be found in the real subject matter of the legislation: if it is such that it goes beyond local or provincial concern or interests and must from its inherent nature be the concern of the Dominion as a whole (as for example in the Aeronautics *case [1932] A.C. 54 and the* Radio *case [1932] A.C. 304) then it will fall within the competence of the Dominion Parliament as a matter affecting the peace, order and good government of Canada, though it may in another aspect touch upon matters specially reserved to the Provincial Legislatures. War and pestilence, no doubt, are instances; so too may be the drink or drug traffic, or the carrying of arms. In* Russell v. The Queen *Sir Montague Smith gave as an instance of valid Dominion legislation a law which prohibited or restricted the sale or exposure of cattle having a contagious disease. Nor is the validity of the legislation, when due to its inherent nature, affected because there may still be room for enactments by a provincial legislature dealing with an aspect of the same subject in so far as it specially affects that province.*

It is to be noticed that the Board in Snider's *case nowhere said that* Russell v. Reg. *was wrongly decided. What it did was to put forward an explanation of what it considered was the ground of the decision, but in their Lordships' opinion the explanation is too narrowly expressed. True it is that an emergency may be the occasion which calls for the legislation, but it is the nature of the legislation itself, and not the existence of emergency, that must determine whether it is valid or not.*[81]

And further:

Moreover, if the subject matter of the legislation is such that it comes within the province of the Dominion Parliament that legislature must, as it seems to their Lordships, have power to re-enact provisions with the object of preventing a recurrence of a state of affairs which was deemed to necessitate the earlier statute. To legislate for prevention appears to be on the same basis as legislation for cure. A pestilence has been given as an example of a subject so affecting, or which might so affect, the whole Dominion that it would justify legislation by the Parliament of Canada as a matter concerning the order and good

[81] [1946] 2 D.L.R. 1, at p. 5.

government of the Dominion. It would seem to follow that if the Parliament could legislate when there was an actual epidemic it could do so to prevent one occurring and also to prevent it happening again.[82]

These words contain expressions of opinion such as have not been heard from the Judicial Committee since 1882. And brave as they are, must they not be diluted in the light of a further statement by Viscount Simon that "their Lordships have no intention, in deciding the present appeal, of embarking on a fresh disquisition as to relations between sections 91 and 92 of the British North America Act, which have been expounded in so many reported cases"?[83] One can also be disturbed in this respect by Viscount Simon's reference in the first of his quoted passages to the requirement that the subject-matter of legislation go beyond local or provincial concern or interests and from its *inherent nature* be the concern of the Dominion, as a whole. Does this contemplate some fixed category of Dominion objects of legislation, or are we, at long last, to be able to judge the validity of legislation in the context of our society and its contemporary problems?

A bold judiciary can find in Viscount Simon's opinion all the material necessary for "a fresh disquisition as to the relations between sections 91 and 92" and, that being so, it was unnecessary for that learned judge to embark on it himself.

No doubt some persons will be disquieted by Viscount Simon's view that an emergency may be the occasion for legislation but that it is the nature of the legislation and not the existence of the emergency which will determine its validity. This raises the question whether the emergency may be not only the occasion but also the justification for the legislation. If it is the justification for the legislation what happens when the emergency ceases? Should the court be able to invalidate legislation the *raison d'être* of which rests on the existence of a state of war, for example? In the *Fort Frances* case Viscount Haldane suggested that such legislation may become *ultra vires* but that "very clear evidence that the crisis had wholly passed away would be required."[84] The *Japanese Canadians Deportation* case reiterates the "emergency" language of the *Fort Frances* case but adds something new in the following statement:

[82] *Ibid.*, at p. 7.
[83] *Ibid.*, at p. 6.
[84] [1923] A. C. 695, at p. 706

> *Again if it be clear that an* emergency has not arisen *or no longer exists, there can be no justification for the exercise or continued exercise of the exceptional powers. . . . But very clear evidence that an emergency has not arisen or that the emergency no longer exists is required to justify the judiciary even though the question is one of* ultra vires, *in overruling the decision of the Parliament of the Dominion that exceptional measures were required or were still required.*[85]

This passage expresses the view, seemingly contrary to what is indicated in the *Board of Commerce* case, that some kind of presumption exists in favour of the validity of Dominion legislation where the legislation is predicated on an emergency. It goes beyond the *Fort Frances* case which went only the length of saying that, accepting the existence of an emergency and of legislation valid for that reason, the court will defer to some extent to the opinion of the federal authorities that the emergency is still operative and hence that the legislation is still valid.

It should be noted that Lord Wright in the *Japanese Canadians Deportation* case does not mention the *Canada Temperance Federation* case and one can properly speculate on how the opinions in the two cases fit together. It is clear that the *Fort Frances* case viewed the introductory clause of section 91 as conferring only an emergency power; and the *Japanese Canadians Deportation* case suggests the same thing. Viscount Simon, however, indicates a scope for the clause beyond conditions of emergency. In so far, however, as an emergency is both the occasion and justification for federal legislation, a question of *ultra vires*, in the sense of the *Japanese Canadians Deportation* case, may well arise once the emergency is gone or if, in fact, no emergency existed. Nevertheless, legislation may be validly enacted under the "peace, order and good government" clause which needs no justification of emergency; and there is no room here for any subsequent declaration of invalidity. The opportunity certainly offered itself in the *Canada Temperance Federation* case but *stare decisis* bulked large in the Judicial Committee's affirmation of the validity of the Canada Temperance Act.

---

[85] [1947] 1 D.L.R. 577, at p. 585.

IV

The Judicial Committee has admitted some scope for invocation of the introductory clause of section 91 as a "residuary" power. In the terms of its own formulae of interpretation, the Board has recognized valid exertions of legislative power under the opening words of section 91 in relation to (1) the incorporation of companies with Dominion objects,[86] and (2) radio communication.[87] These are illustrations of a "residuary power of legislation beyond those powers that are specifically distributed by the two sections [91 and 92]."[88] The *Aeronautics* case reflected a little confusion in the minds of the Judicial Committee as to the "emergency" and "residuary" features of the introductory clause. In that case it stated that "aerial navigation is a class of subject which has attained such dimensions as to affect the body politic of the Dominion."[89] Certainly there was no emergency in the *Snider* case sense although it could reasonably be said, using Privy Council language, that aerial navigation did not come within a provincial class of subject or within a Dominion enumeration so that it must be within the Dominion's residuary power. In the *Labour Conventions* case, however, the Judicial Committee retrospectively assigned the legislation in the *Aeronautics* case to section 132 of the British North America Act.[90] On an "aspect" view it would seem, clearly enough, that the legislation fell within the scope of the "peace, order and good government" clause, if not also within the "trade and commerce" power.

In its application of the introductory clause of section 91 to cover federal incorporation of companies, the Judicial Committee has sounded a few notes that seem dissonant when one recalls its tune in relation to that clause generally. Thus we are told that the clause confers an exclusive power; and further, that "the effect of the concluding words of s. 91 is to make the exercise of this capacity of the Dominion Parliament prevail in case of conflict over the exercise by the Provincial legislatures

[86] *Great West Saddlery Co.* v. *The King,* [1921] 2 A.C. 91.
[87] *In re Regulation and Control of Radio Communication in Canada,* [1932] A.C. 304.
[88] *In re Initiative and Referendum Act,* [1919] A.C. 935, at p. 943.
[89] [1932] A.C. 54, at p. 77.
[90] [1937] A.C. 326, at p. 351.

of their capacities under the enumerated heads of s. 92."[91]
There is no sign here that the Dominion Parliament cannot
"trench" when acting under the introductory clause of section
91. And we are also introduced to the notion, novel in the light
of the Judicial Committee's prior interpretations, that the concluding words of section 91 secure the paramountcy of legislation under the introductory clause over legislation under the
enumerations in section 92. This means, of course, that the
Dominion's power under the introductory clause is covered by
the phrase "classes of subjects enumerated in this section" in the
concluding clause of section 91. It is a significant reading of
section 91 but one which Viscount Haldane did not resort to in
the *Board of Commerce* case or in the *Fort Frances* case or in
the *Snider* case. It is a reading which is in line with the aspect
doctrine and it is hardly required if the introductory clause of
section 91 is deemed to confer effective federal legislative power
only in the residuary sense suggested by the Privy Council in
the "company" cases. It does become important, however, if
the introductory clause is given a content compatible with the
approach indicated in the *Russell* case.

V

The vicissitudes of the "peace, order and good government"
clause, the Dominion's general legislative power, indicate that
the Judicial Committee sought to give it a fixed content in terms
of subject-matter of legislation. Thus, it might be read (at least
before 1946) as empowering the Parliament of Canada to make
laws for the emergencies of war, famine or pestilence, for the
incorporation of companies with Dominion objects and for the
regulation of radio communication. This nightmarish association of subjects is distinguished by the same sort of affinity
that has characterized the Judicial Committee's numerous pronouncements on the Dominion's general power. It is quite a
price to pay for realizing Lord Watson's wish, as expressed in
the *Local Prohibition* case, to secure the autonomy of the
provinces.[92]

---

[91] [1921] 2 A.C. 91, at p. 115. *Cf.* Scott, The Consequences of the Privy
Council Decisions (1937), 15 Can. Bar Rev. 485, at pp. 488-9 where
he says: "The concluding paragraph of sec. 91 was obviously intended
to apply to every subject specified in 91, including the general power
of the residuary clause . . . . "

[92] [1896] A.C. 348, at p. 361.

But has provincial autonomy been secured? In terms of positive ability to meet economic and social problems of inter-provincial scope, the answer is no. A destructive negative autonomy exists, however, which has as a corollary that the citizens of a province are citizens of the Dominion for certain limited purposes only. This does not, of course, herald the break-up of our federal system. The individual provinces have a considerable stake in federation, beyond the mere maintenance of autonomy, and the plenary federal taxing power in its rather rough way gives the people of all the provinces some sense of a Canadian community. Our international commitments have, of course, the same effect.

Some sixty years ago the Judicial Committee said in *Riel* v. *The Queen* that the words "peace, order and good government" were words "apt to authorize the utmost discretion of enact-ment for the attainment of the objects pointed to."[93] The re-mark was not made in relation to sections 91 and 92 of the British North America Act and in the context of the Act it is undoubtedly too wide. But in its reference to legislative objects it indicates the type of problem which a court must face in interpreting sections 91 and 92. It is beside the point that the words of the introductory clause are too large and loose for comfortable adjudication. The Judicial Committee has not been reticent about its ability to give content to the large and loose provincial legislative power in relation to property and civil rights in the province, although it may be noted that it has done so largely in terms of thwarting exercises of federal legislative power, whether for the peace, order and good government of Canada or in relation to the regulation of trade and commerce.

It has been said that the Judicial Committee's course of in-terpretation has been perhaps the inevitable result of its perhaps inevitable choice to treat the British North America Act as a statute rather than as a constitution.[94] My examination of the cases dealing with the Dominion's general power does not indicate any inevitability in the making of particular decisions; if anything, it indicates conscious and deliberate choice of a

---

[93] (1885), 10 App. Cas. 675, at p. 678. This was said in relation to the British North America Act, 1871 (Imp.), c. 28, giving the Dominion power in s. 4 "to make provision for the administration, peace, order and good government of any territory not for the time being included in any province."

[94] Jennings, *op. cit., supra*, note 1. See also Kennedy, The British North America Act: Past and Future (1937), 15 Can. Bar Rev. 393.

policy which required, for its advancement, manipulations which can only with difficulty be represented as ordinary judicial techniques. But since these decisions are with us, willy-nilly, can we expect for the future that an ultimate court, whether it be the Judicial Committee or the Supreme Court, will depart from them? Able commentators feel that this is asking too much of the judiciary and that we must, if we seek a change in our constitutional interpretation, seek a change in our constitution.[95] One is justified, however, in being as optimistic for the prospect of a change in interpretation as for the prospect of a change in the constitution. At least, one can point to a beginning in the erosion of the old decisions by the opinion in the *Canada Temperance Federation* case; and one can point as well to the "constitution" approach to the British North America Act expressed by Viscount Jowitt in the *Privy Council Appeals* reference.

It is clearly preferable that the constitution be kept fluid through judicial interpretation than through repeated amendment, and the "aspect" doctrine is a ready tool for the purpose. It would be rash indeed to state that the inertia of *stare decisis* can easily be overcome with respect to the accumulated body of Privy Council doctrine. But, viewing this as a consummation devoutly to be wished, its practical realization would seem to involve at least the following steps: (1) enactment of federal legislation to vest in the Supreme Court of Canada ultimate judicial power; (2) full exercise by members of the court of the privilege of writing separate opinions; and (3) care by the federal government to bring before the court, in its initial exercise of ultimate power, legislation drafted with the utmost possible skill and not having any subject-matter connection or similarity to prior legislation invalidated by the Privy Council. This is worth a fair trial with a Canadian court operating in a Canadian climate of opinion; and amendment as a postulated alternative may not be without effect in the matter.

Undoubtedly, many will say that this would amount to a clear attempt to subvert the court. On the contrary, it would represent an attempt in a federal context to appeal to those sentiments in existing constitutional doctrine which express principles of growth. The present-day common-law lawyer is prone to forget that his forbears made the same appeal in trying

---

[95] Kennedy, *op. cit., supra*, note 94; MacDonald, The Canadian Constitution Seventy Years After (1937), 15 Can. Bar Rev. 401.

to keep the common law flexible, and that he himself does this today notwithstanding the encrustation of *stare decisis*. Our constitutional case law offers enough choices for fresh beginnings to enable a court to mark out a new trail without doing violence to judicial techniques. It may be true that "Judges are not the most competent people to determine high matters of state."[96] But their tradition of impartiality and a security of tenure which mirrors their independence are offsetting compensations. We are saddled in any event with judicial review so long as our federal system subsists. We ought not to forego the opportunity of trying to place it on the higher level of constitutional interpretation as opposed to keeping it on the lower level of statutory interpretation. Limiting judicial techniques are operative at both levels, as even the judgments of the Supreme Court of the United States reveal. We can always seek final refuge in amendment.

[96] Jennings, *op. cit., supra*, note 1, at p. 39.

Some Privy Counsel

F. R. SCOTT

"Emergency, emergency," I cried, "give us emergency,
This shall be the doctrine of our salvation.
Are we not surrounded by emergencies?
The rent of a house, the cost of food, pensions and health, the
  unemployed,
These are lasting emergencies, tragic for me."
Yet ever the answer was property and civil rights,
And my peacetime troubles were counted as nothing.
"At least you have an unoccupied field," I urged,
"Or something ancillary for a man with four children?
Surely my insecurity and want affect the body politic?"
But back came the echo of property and civil rights.
I was told to wrap my sorrows in water-tight compartments.
"Please, please," I entreated, "look at my problem.
I and my brothers, regardless of race, are afflicted.
Our welfare hangs on remote policies, distant decisions,
Planning of trade, guaranteed prices, high employment –
Can provincial fractions deal with this complex whole?
Surely such questions are now supra-national!"
But the judges fidgeted over their digests
And blew me away with the canons of construction.
"This is intolerable," I shouted, "this is one country;
Two flourishing cultures, but joined in one nation.
I demand peace, order and good government.
This you must admit is the aim of Confederation!"
But firmly and sternly I was pushed to a corner
And covered with the wet blanket of provincial autonomy.
Stifling under the burden I raised my hands to Heaven
And called out with my last and expiring breath
"At least you cannot deny I have a new aspect?
I cite in my aid the fresh approach of Lord Simon!"
But all I could hear was the old sing-song,
This time in Latin, muttering *stare decisis*.

From: *The Canadian Bar Review*, Volume 28 (1950), page 780. By
permission of the author and publisher.

The Establishment of The Supreme Court of Canada

FRANK MACKINNON

The British North America Act gave to the Parliament of Canada the power to provide for "the Constitution, Maintenance and Organization of a General Court of Appeal for Canada, and for the Establishment of any additional Courts for the better Administration of the Laws of Canada."[1] Eight years after Confederation this power resulted in the establishment of the Supreme Court, an event which not only introduced a new institution, but also stirred up imperial sensibilities and a series of constitutional controversies. The creation of the Supreme Court was one thing; fitting it into the Canadian scene was quite another.

The necessity for such a court had been discussed at the various pre-Confederation conferences. It was evident to the Fathers that the diversities of the elements which they hoped to unite in a nation were reflected in the existing legal organizations. In the English-speaking provinces, the common law of England was the basis of the legal structure, whereas in Canada East the English criminal law and French civil law functioned jointly. The statutory law differed from province to province. The right of appeal to the Judicial Committee of the Privy Council existed in all.

Then, too, the nature of the Canadian federation and its distribution of power demanded a national judiciary which would

From: *The Canadian Historical Review*, Volume 27 (1946), pages 258-74, published by The University of Toronto Press. By permission of the author and publisher.

[1] British North America Act, 1867, Section 101.

fit into the framework of constitutional government along with the executive and the legislature. In England, where constitutional power rested entirely in Parliament, the determination and interpretation of its own jurisdiction was the prerogative of that supreme body. But in Canada, legislative functions were to be divided between two classes of legislature, and therefore constitutional controversies were almost inevitable. An overall legal authority was necessary to interpret the enactments of the various legislatures where disputes arose with respect to the power of the legislatures to pass such enactments. For this function, the creation of a supreme court was imperative.

To the champions of Confederation, therefore, a unifying legal force seemed necessary and, in the words of Sir John Macdonald, ". . . it was thought wise and expedient to put into the constitution a power to the General Legislature, that, if after full consideration they think it advisable to establish a General Court of Appeal from all the Superior Courts of all the provinces, they may do so."[2] Sir George E. Cartier went further at Quebec and dreamed of a distinguished court of a definitely federal character which would play a vital part in the proposed union:

Accordingly, when we have lived some years under the Federal regime, the urgent need of such a Court of Appeal with jurisdiction in such matters will be felt, and, if it is created, it will be fit that its jurisdiction should extend to civil causes which might arise in the several Confederate Provinces, because it will necessarily be composed of the most eminent judges in the different provinces, of the jurists whose reputation stands highest, of men, in short, profoundly skilled in the jurisprudence of each of the provinces which they will respectively represent.[3]

As in the case of many of the legislative powers conferred by the British North America Act, Section 101 was implemented

[2] *Debates of the Parliament of Canada on the Confederation of British North America* (Quebec, 1865), 41.

[3] *Ibid*. 576. Cartier's views regarding the establishment of the Court and the appeals to the Judicial Committee of the Privy Council are significant: "I think that it is important not to establish it until a certain number of years shall have elapsed from the establishment of Confederation and to make it consist of judges from the several provinces. . . . I do hold, and the spirit of the conference at Quebec indicated, that the appeal to the judicial committee of Her Majesty's Privy Council must always exist, even if the court in question is established" (*ibid*.).

with considerable difficulty. Macdonald foresaw this and commenced the proceedings with caution. On May 21, 1869 he introduced in the House of Commons a "Bill for the establishment of a Supreme Court of Canada." This court was to be composed of one Chief Justice and six judges who were to hold office on good behaviour and be removable only upon the address of the Senate and House of Commons. It was to be the Dominion's highest court, but was not to be considered as doing away with the existing right of appeal to the Judicial Committee of the Privy Council in England.[4] This bill, on which there was no second reading, was, as Macdonald later explained, "rather more for the purpose of suggestion and consideration than for a final measure which the Government hoped to become law."[5] Copies of it were sent to the judges throughout the Dominion for their opinions.[6]

By the following session, the criticisms offered had been carefully considered by the government, and a new bill was introduced on March 18, 1870. On this occasion, the Prime Minister stressed two of the more controversial aspects of the new court – the federal, and the imperial. While it was not to be a cast iron rule that every province should have a representative on the court, the Chief Justice and six judges were to be chosen as far as possible in a representative manner from the benches and bars of the various provinces. In respect of appeals to the Privy Council, Sir John indicated that the government was anxious to maintain them, for "we had no power to deprive a British subject of the right of going to the foot of the Throne for redress" and as long as the appeals remained, "our courts will be obliged to look up to the decisions of the great Courts of England as an authority."[7] As on the previous occasion, the bill was withdrawn by Sir George Cartier on May 11.[8]

Several difficulties caused the government to abandon these two measures. Some critics thought the new court an unnecessary addition to an already adequate judicial system. Many were worried one way or the other by the question of the abolition of appeals. But the chief trouble was the hostility of Quebec to the

---

[4] Clipping from *Ottawa Times*, 1869 in "Parliamentary Debates, Canada, 1869," scrapbook in Library of Parliament, 75.

[5] *Dominion Parliamentary Debates*, 1870, 523.

[6] The replies are contained in volume 159 of the Macdonald Papers in the Public Archives of Canada.

[7] *Dominion Parliamentary Debates*, 1870, 528.

[8] *Ibid.*, 1,567.

proposed court and to the possibility that it might infringe on provincial rights and legislative powers. Macdonald indicated this in the House of Commons a few years later when he declared: "The difficulties connected with the establishing a court satisfactory to the Province of Quebec was one of the great reasons that made me hesitate so long in presenting a measure for the establishment of a Supreme Court which I twice submitted to the Parliament of Canada, and that hesitation induced me to postpone pressing the measure while I held the office of Minister of Justice."[9] Nevertheless, Sir John planned the introduction of a third bill in 1873 but its presentation was prevented by his defeat of that year.

In 1875 the Honourable Télesphore Fournier, Minister of Justice in the Mackenzie Government, introduced a bill for the establishment of a "Supreme Court and a Court of Exchequer for the Dominion of Canada," a bill which had been described by the Speech from the Throne as "essential to our system of jurisprudence and to the settlement of constitutional questions."[10] M. Fournier explained that the inclusion of a "Court of Exchequer" in this bill was designed to avoid giving the Supreme Court an original jurisdiction by creating two courts, one of appellate jurisdiction, and another a tribunal of the first instance composed of the same members.[11]

No mention was made in the bill of appeals to the Judicial Committee of the Privy Council. But the minister frankly acknowledged that, while no obstacle had been placed in the way of such appeals, which remained optional, "he wished to see the practice put an end to altogether." He added that he "would like very well to see a clause introduced declaring that the right of appeal to the Privy Council existed no longer" for the right of appeal had many disadvantages and "had been considerably abused in the Province of Quebec by wealthy men and wealthy corporations to force suitors to compromise in cases in which they had succeeded in all the tribunals of the country."[12]

The minister stressed the role of the proposed court as a constitutional arbitrator "which would settle the extent of the powers of local legislatures when these powers were in dis-

[9] *Canada, House of Commons Debates*, 1880, 240

[10] *Ibid.*, 1875, 3.

[11] *Ibid.*, 285.

[12] *Ibid.*, 286.

pute."[13] He added that the bill "had for its sole object the harmonious working of our young constitution."[14] Thus Fournier looked upon the court not so much as an addition to the judicial framework of Canada, but rather as an instrument for strengthening her federal weaknesses. This feeling, which had been voiced by Cartier, and was now accentuated by Fournier, helped to take the Supreme Court question somewhat out of the judicial sphere and bring it, to its own disadvantage, into the arena of political considerations, a situation which was to be aggravated by subsequent events.

Sir John Macdonald, on behalf of the Opposition, supported the proposed legislation, which was very similar to his own of some years before, though he took exception to the views of the Minister of Justice on the matter of the appeals. "It would," he said, "be severing one of the links between this country and the mother country if the right of appeal were cut off ruthlessly."[15]

But despite the support of the leaders on both sides of the House, the bill received much criticism during the debate which followed its introduction. The Honourable David Mills objected to the feature which gave the court appellate jurisdiction, not only with regard to the administration of Dominion laws, but also over matters of local concern in the provinces. He deplored the tendency to treat the question as though Canada were a legislative union, and expressed his opinion that the court should be empowered to consider only cases arising under federal legislative jurisdiction. Fournier's reply to this was that "the whole spirit of the Confederation Act was to give the Court of Appeal jurisdiction over provincial as well as Dominion laws."[16] The chief criticism was that the bill did not compel the bringing of cases from the provincial courts to the Supreme Court, but left to the litigants the option of carrying them direct to the Privy Council. This arrangement prompted one member, Aemilius Irving of Hamilton, to say that he "could not imagine a more dismal spectacle than would be afforded by six melancholy men living in this city endeavouring to catch an appeal case, which, but for this Act, would have gone to England. They would become rusty and relapse perhaps into a state of barbarism."[17] This criticism was answered by the suggestion that the Supreme Court was not designed as an intermediate or alternative step, but as a final phase in litigation.

The most significant feature of the debate was the adoption of two of the dozen amendments which were moved. One, introduced by Mr. Irving, read as follows: "The judgment of the Supreme Court shall in all cases be final and conclusive, and no error or appeal shall be brought from any judgment or order of the Supreme Court to any court of appeal established by the parliament of Great Britain and Ireland, to which appeals or petitions to Her Majesty in Council may be ordered to be heard, saving any right which Her Majesty may be graciously pleased to exercise as her royal prerogative."[18] This amendment, which had obviously been invited by the Minister of Justice in his introductory speech, had as its declared purposes to decrease the number of appeals and to reduce the costs of litigation.

This immediately brought Sir John Macdonald to his feet declaring that "this amendment was the first step toward the severance of the Dominion from the mother country" and that its adoption would defeat the measure. If he had known that the amendment was to be proposed he would not have given his co-operation, because he believed that with the amendment the bill would be "abortive" and that "within six months it would be thrown aside in disgrace." Despite his strong stand, however, the amendment was adopted by a vote of 112 to 40. Sir John then added a final thrust: "Great as would be the benefit of a Supreme Court to the Dominion, it would not compensate for the injury that would be inflicted on the country in wounding the loyal sentiment of the people, and the feeling of uncertainty it would excite in England as to whether there was not an impatience in this country of even the semblance of Imperial authority."[19]

The other amendment which was adopted involved the principle of sectional representation on the court. One of the Quebec members, Toussaint Laflamme of Jacques Cartier, moved that two of the judges "shall be taken from the judges of the Superior Court or Court of Queen's Bench, or from amongst the barristers or advocates of the province of Quebec." The purpose was to ensure "the good and sound interpretation of the

---

[18] *Ibid.*, 976.
[19] *Ibid.*, 980-1.

laws of that province."[20] This one was followed closely by
another moving that "at least one of the judges of the Court
shall be selected from the bench and bar in British Columbia."[21]
This was lost because of the feeling on both sides of the House
that the representative principle was not of the same importance to the other provinces as it was to Quebec.

The bill was passed on April 8, 1875, with the appeal amendment embodied in it as Clause 47. On the third reading of the
bill in the Senate on April 6 a motion that Clause 47 be struck
out resulted in a tie vote and was lost only on the casting vote
of the Speaker.

Sir John Macdonald had predicted that the Supreme Court
Act would be disallowed or threatened with disallowance in
England because of the objection of the imperial authorities to
the appeals clause. He was right. The government was informed
through Lord Carnarvon, the Colonial Secretary, that disallowance was almost inevitable in view of the strenuous objection of
the Lord Chancellor and the law officers of the Crown to the
principle involved in the appeals clause. At the same time it was
pointed out that Clause 47 did not in reality limit the right of
appeal because the sovereign prerogative was paramount and
because the Judicial Committee of the Privy Council was not
a "Court of Appeal established by the Parliament of Great
Britain." Mackenzie and Blake, the latter having replaced
Fournier as Minister of Justice, argued the matter with the
imperial authorities both by correspondence and by personal
visits to England. This controversy, which nearly wrecked the
Supreme Court Bill, can be reviewed here only briefly, though
it is one of the interesting episodes in Canadian constitutional
history, and also affords an excellent illustration of Canada's
imperial relations during the eighteen-seventies.[22]

[20] *Ibid.*, 970.
[21] *Ibid.*, 974.
[22] The significant official correspondence is contained in a forty-page
manuscript entitled "Correspondence Confidentially Printed for the
Use of the Privy Council," P.A.C., Laurier Papers, vol. 280, C.C.5.
The negotiations with respect to Clause 47 are dealt with in the
following : "Some Data Relating to the Appeal to the Privy Council," by L. A. Cannon, K.C. (*Canadian Bar Review*, October, 1925,
455); "Edward Blake and the Supreme Court Act," by F. H. Underhill (*Canadian Historical Review*, September, 1938, 245). Older but
less complete treatments of the subject are included in "The Supreme
Court of Canada," by Robert Cassels (*Green Bag*, Boston, 1890, II,
241); and in "The Supreme Court of Canada," by Donald MacMaster
(*Canada, An Encyclopedia of the Country*, Toronto, 1900, VI, 332).

The Colonial Office objected to Clause 47 for three types of reasons – those concerning the actual decision of cases, those arising from the nature of Canadian federalism, and those involving the imperial connexion.

The first of these was weak and served merely to support the other two. Carnarvon thought that British residents who held rights, investments, or property in Canada should be protected by the appeal. Edward Blake haughtily replied that this "practically presumes that British subjects and foreigners would not receive justice at the hands of the Canadian Judges while it affirms that the Canadians would receive justice at the hands of the British Court."[23] Carnarvon considered that the appeals helped to maintain the uniformity of the law of England in the provinces. Blake replied that the law already differed among the provinces and the provincial legislatures were continuing to alter it. In any event, the Canadian Minister of Justice emphasized that any advantages of the appeals from the standpoint of litigation were more than outweighed by the disadvantages, particularly delay and excessive costs.

More significant were the objections to Clause 47 which were based on federalism. The imperial view on this was expressed in a Colonial Office memorandum:

The Dominion of Canada has recently been erected on a federal basis, including several provinces. Questions of great nicety must arise under such a constitution between the federal and provincial legislatures and judicatures. These are precisely questions upon which the decisions of a Court of Final Appeal, not included within the Confederation, would be most impartial and valuable. Again, in Canada strong divisions of race, religion, and party are known to exist. The policy and duty of the British Government, and especially of the Last Court of Appeal has been to secure absolute impartiality to the rights or claims of the minority of the population. Laws passed by a strong political majority, and administered by Judges and Courts appointed by the representatives of the same majority, are less likely to ensure an entire respect for the rights of all classes than the decisions of a perfectly impartial and independent tribunal.[24]

Blake's reply was pungent and to the point:

[23] "Correspondence for the Privy Council," 34.
[24] *Ibid.,* 14.

> *. . . nor can I conceive anything calculated more deeply to wound the feelings of Canadians than an insinuation that impartial decisions are not to be expected from their Judges. With reference to the alleged value of decision of a Court "not included in the Confederation," I would observe that with the practical operation of the Federal Constitution of Canada, with the customs and system which may have grown out of its working with many of the elements which have been found most valuable if not absolutely necessary to a sound decision in that class of cases, a Court composed of English Judges cannot possibly be thoroughly acquainted.*[25]

The biggest issue involved in the question of appeals concerned the imperial connexion, or, more specifically, the principle of enhancing Canada's status by the removal of appeals to an English tribunal. This principle was in line with Blake's policy of keeping the Colonial Office reminded of responsible government and of diminishing the appearance of colonial governance by making the Governor-General responsible to his ministers rather than to himself or the British government.

Lord Carnarvon questioned the expediency of permitting, through such means as Clause 47, any doubt as to the stability of Canada's ties with the mother country. Here he drew for support upon the parliamentary utterance of Sir John Macdonald on the subject. Moreover, he considered the clause to be an infringement on Her Majesty's royal prerogative, for "the Supreme Appellate authority of the Empire or the realm is unquestionably one of the highest functions and duties of sovereignty."[26] The Canadian Minister of Justice replied boldly that "the Parliament of Canada, which is composed of the Queen, the Senate and the House of Commons, has power to abolish any prerogative of the Crown affecting the Canadian people within the range of subjects on which that Parliament is authorized to legislate."[27] After all, he added, "the Canadian Judges are Her Majesty's Judges just as much as Her Judicial Officers who reside in England."[28] With respect to the "redress from the throne" argument, he could not see why colonial subjects needed it, when British subjects at home did not possess it. But in one sharp sentence Blake summed up his viewpoint:

[25] *Ibid.*, 31.
[26] *Ibid.*, 13.
[27] *Ibid.*, 22.
[28] *Ibid.*, 24.

"I must say that the general tenor of these and other observations which attribute to the Crown, through this appeal, a power so vast, vague and undefined, is ill calculated to reconcile the mind to its continuance, and rather brings back to our recollection, the fact that the power, whatever it be, is but a relic of the ancient, odious, and abolished judicial powers assumed by the Privy Council and its committees, including the Court of Star Chamber.[29]

It seems clear from a reading of the correspondence that the real issue behind the appeals controversy was political rather than legal. The Colonial Office, which in the later eighteen-sixties welcomed Canada's nation-building efforts as relieving it from an unwanted burden, was now in the seventies swinging in the other direction. The Canadian government did not like this change; and both sides used the appeals issue to express themselves.

It would be a mistake, however, to consider the matter solely as a struggle between an ambitious Canadian government seeking national autonomy and a recalcitrant Colonial Office relentlessly maintaining the old ties. The inescapable fact is that Canadians themselves were not agreed on the appeals question; nor were they ready to place their entire confidence in the new

[29] *Ibid.*, 25.

It is significant that the distinguished British jurist Lord Haldane held a similar view of the royal prerogative. In the course of the debate on the Australian Commonwealth Bill he said: "The expression of which in these debates we have heard much 'the Queen's prerogative' is a mere technical phrase and should be put aside." Quoted by John S. Ewart, who was of the same opinion, in "Judicial Appeals to the Privy Council: The Case for Discontinuing Appeals" (*Queen's Quarterly*, 1930, 457).

The political background of the prerogative is clearly revealed by the Judicial Committee itself in 1875 with respect to the demand of the Australian colonies for the abolition of appeals: ". . . this power has been exercised for centuries over all the dependencies of the Empire by the Sovereign of the Mother Country sitting in Council. By this institution, common to all parts of the Empire beyond the seas, all matters requiring a judicial solution may be brought to the cognizance of one court in which all have a voice. To abandon this controlling power and abandon each colony and dependency to a separate Court of Appeal of its own would obviously destroy one of the most important ties connecting all parts of the Empire in common obedience to the courts of law; and to renounce *the last and most essential mode of exercising the authority of the Crown over its possessions abroad*" (italics mine). This statement is quoted and discussed by John S. Ewart in the *Kingdom of Canada and Other Essays* (Toronto, 1908), 228-9.

Supreme Court. Sir John Macdonald and his colleagues had strongly opposed the appeals clause, and the clause had barely passed the Senate. It was not even evident that the Liberals were united on the subject. These facts were clear to the Colonial Office and were quite sufficient to encourage a reluctance to agree to a step about which there was so much doubt in Canada itself. More significant still was the ambiguity of the appeals clause. It was so worded that it could not have abolished the appeals, a consideration which could hardly have escaped the Canadian Department of Justice. Such an important change surely required a clearer wording. One might wonder if the ambiguity were an evidence of hesitancy resulting from lack of agreement. Or perhaps the clause might have been designed as a constitutional barometer to test the prevailing opinions on both sides of the Atlantic with respect to the imperial connexion. At all events, it is evident that the general uncertainty in Canada combined effectively with the reluctance of the British government to prevent the abolition of the appeals.

Meanwhile, the Supreme Court was sitting on the sidelines, appointed and ready to function, but waiting for the result of the issue. At length an arrangement was made in the summer of 1876 by which the Supreme Court Act would be left to its operation in view of the fact that Clause 47 did not really affect the right of appeal. At the same time the Canadian government was advised by Lord Carnarvon to arrange for the regulation of appeals in order to prevent their abuse. The Mackenzie administration then commenced to plan legislation which would abolish the appeals, but the complexities of the problem and the growing difficulties which the government had to face in other quarters caused the shelving of the issue. It was obvious that any real change in the number of appeals would have to come through the usefulness of the Supreme Court itself and through the trust and respect of the Canadian people for their highest tribunal.

Much has been said in this connexion about the efforts of Edward Blake to abolish the appeals and make the Supreme Court truly "supreme." His work had a peculiar and surprising epilogue. Despite his defence of the independence of Canadian judges and his scoffing at the necessity for appeals to an outside tribunal, many years later, when he was a member of the British House of Commons, he spoke as follows on the second reading of the Commonwealth of Australia Constitution Bill:

I speak from experience; because I know that in the country whence I come, while a different set of circumstances obtains and there are different provisions, there is yet a written federal constitution; and it was found with us that where bitter controversies had been excited, where political passions had been engendered, where considerable disputations had prevailed, where men eminent in power and politics had ranged themselves on opposite sides, it was no disadvantage, but a great advantage to have an opportunity of appealing to an external tribunal such as the Judicial Committee, for the interpretation of the Constitution on such matters.[30]

This statement is a revealing commentary on the Supreme Court and Canadian federalism, and on Blake himself.

Thus from the beginning the "supremacy" of the Supreme Court was overshadowed by the right of appeal to the Privy Council in view of the inability of the Mackenzie Government to secure its abolition. Although the right of appeal directly from the Court to the Privy Council was to be limited, it remained in the case of judgments of the courts of last resort in the provinces. The losing parties in the provincial courts were to have the option of proceeding either to the Supreme Court or directly to the Privy Council. The Supreme Court was therefore "supreme" only in cases which were taken to it, and even then its "supremacy" was subject to the royal prerogative. In the event of an appeal from the Court to the Privy Council, it was the duty of the latter to advise the Sovereign on the exercise of the prerogative. The extent to which the royal prerogative would be advised, at first uncertain, was later described by Lord Fitzgerald who declared that "Their Lordships are not prepared to advise Her Majesty to exercise her prerogative by admitting an appeal to Her Majesty in Council from the Supreme Court of the Dominion save where the case is of gravity, involving matters of public interest, or some important questions of law, or affecting property of considerable amount, or where the case is otherwise of some public importance of a very substantial character."[31] Hence the authority of the Supreme Court would be final only in relatively unimportant cases.

[30] *England, House of Commons Debates*, 4th series, vol. 83, May 21, 1900, 774.
[31] *Prince* v. *Gagnon*, L. R. 8 App. Cas., 103. Two earlier cases also stressed the importance aspect of appeal cases: *Johnston* v. *St. Andrew's Church*, L. R. 3 App. Cas., 159; and *Valin* v. *Langlois*, L. R. 5 App. Cas., 115.

Meanwhile the government had appointed the Court on October 8, 1875. Such an opportunity for political patronage attracted many of Mackenzie's followers and the Prime Minister was besieged with petitions for appointment. But Mackenzie expressed himself as determined to put the Supreme Court beyond the pale of political preferment. To Lieutenant-Governor Archibald of Nova Scotia who had asked for a seat on the Court he wrote: "I may say, however, that no political considerations will influence the government in making these or any other judicial appointments. In regard to appointments for the Bench, legal fitness and personal character will alone be considered."[32] To John Charlton who had sought a favour for a friend he indicated that ". . . in the matter of judicial appointments I must be guided by legal authorities rather than by political influences. While very desirous of always meeting the wishes of our political supporters . . . I have invariably told them that I could not make appointments to the Bench an ordinary matter of patronage."[33]

The six persons appointed by Mackenzie, in collaboration with Edward Blake, to be the first judges of the Supreme Court were widely known. The first Chief Justice, Sir William Buell Richards, had been Attorney-General of Upper Canada and Chief Justice of Ontario. Sir William Johnstone Ritchie, who succeeded Richards, had been Chief Justice of New Brunswick. Sir Samuel Henry Strong, who later became the third head of the Court, had sat on the Court of Errors and Appeal for Ontario. The Honourable Télesphore Fournier had a special interest in the Court, for, as Minister of Justice, he had introduced the bill for its establishment into the House of Commons. The Honourable Jean Thomas Taschereau had been on the Quebec bench for many years. Nova Scotia was represented by the Honourable William Alexander Henry who had been Solicitor-General and Attorney-General in the provincial government. Although the Prime Minister considered that he had chosen a worthy personnel for the Court he did not escape charges of political patronage and it was not long before the judges were subjected to constant criticism.

The Court got off to a bad start. It held its initial sitting on January 11, 1876, and called its first case in the following June, although it was not until August of that year that Lord Carnar-

[32] P. A. C., Mackenzie Letterbook, 1874-5, vol. IV, 307.
[33] Ibid., 288.

von advised the Governor-General that the Supreme Court Act would not be disallowed. Thus the status of the Court was by no means certain during its first few months, a fact which placed it in an awkward situation and helped to postpone public confidence. Meanwhile its critics became more numerous as delays in proceedings, personal deficiencies of the judges, and the superior influence of the Judicial Committee of the Privy Council showed clearly that a judicial tribunal must be respected to be useful. Repeated objections were levelled from the start until finally, within three years of its establishment, an active campaign was commenced against the Court in Parliament.

On April 21, 1879, a bill to abolish the Court was introduced by Mr. Joseph Keeler, member for Northumberland East (Ontario) who branded it as "entirely unnecessary and useless." Both the Government and the Opposition treated the introduction of this bill as a practical joke and the first reading ended in a debate on procedure. But on February 19 of the following year, another bill with the same purpose was introduced and carried to second reading by Mr. Keeler. This time a lively debate took place on the merits and weaknesses of the Court. The critics decried the expense to the taxpayers of maintaining the Court; some declared that the cost to the litigants in appearing before it barred the poor from justice. Much objection was levelled at the decisions and the delay in rendering them. The possibility of the invasion of provincial rights was continually brought up. Political influence was also charged, for some branded the Court as a refuge for the political supporters of the late administration. The *Canadian Law Journal* thus summed up the criticism, parliamentary and otherwise: "The Court has so far been a failure, partly owing to the inherent difficulties of our confederation, partly to the fact that the best talent has not always for some reason or other been taken advantage of, and partly owing to the difficulties and infirmities of a personal nature which we do not care to enlarge upon."[34] Even a prominent member of the Government, Sir Hector Langevin, Minister of Public Works, announced: "I myself have never had reason to entertain great love for the Supreme Court.[35]

During the debate in the House, the Government and Opposition leaders rallied to the support of the Court. Both groups had sponsored its establishment and were anxious to give it a

[34] *Canadian Law Journal*, XVIII, 1882, 88.
[35] *Canada, House of Commons Debates*, 1880, 265.

fair trial. Some considered that Parliament should not permit criticism of the Court, while the Honourable Alexander Mackenzie said, and Mr. Mills agreed, that it might as well be proposed to repeal the B.N.A. Act as to abolish the Supreme Court.[36] But Macdonald thought that if it could not stand investigation, the Court would not deserve public confidence. Sir John expressed the Government's attitude:

I must admit that I do not think there is any advantage to be gained in shutting our eyes to the fact that the Court, by some accident or misfortune, has not obtained that confidence which such a tribunal ought to have succeeded in obtaining. . . . But it is a new court, a court established early in our history as a Dominion. . . . I have no doubt that, as the Court grows older, the people of the country will become more accustomed to consider it as one of the tribunals of which they should be proud, and of which they would not willingly be deprived.[37]

For the Opposition, Edward Blake declared that the Canadian constitution would be unworkable without a national court to settle problems which would be inevitably arising thereunder. He indicated that it was an anomaly for persons to declare that, while Canadians had the right to make their own laws, there could not be found in Canada men capable of judging by what laws she should be governed. He stressed the fact that the experience and modes of thought of the British judges were not conducive to the proper interpretation of Canadian conditions and legislation which had their roots in an entirely different constitutional system. He added: "Now a constitution like ours, complicated and delicate in its adjustments, requires for its interpretation that measure of learning, experience and practice which those who live under it, who work it, and who are practically engaged in its operation are all their lives acquiring. I deny that it can be well expounded by men whose whole lives have

[36] An interesting debate took place at this point on the question of whether giving a member an opportunity of having his bill discussed was tantamount to the adoption of its principle. Alexander Mackenzie thought it was and made every effort to prevent discussion of the abolition bill. Sir John Macdonald thought that it was the right and duty of Parliament to debate such matters whether or not it agreed with them. After all, said Macdonald, Parliament created the Court and it was therefore quite proper for Parliament to review the Court's position.

[37] *Canada; House of Commons Debates,* 1880, 239.

been passed, not merely in another, but in an opposite sphere of practice; and these men must come to the consideration of these topics at the greatest disadvantage and from the wrong point of view."[38]

The government took note of the criticism and announced its intention of meeting the objections which were raised. The bill then received the six months' hoist by a vote of 148 to 29.

Meanwhile, the situation behind the scenes at the Court itself indicated clearly that there was room for improvement. Justices Strong and Gwynne had no respect for the judgments of Justice Henry or for the leadership of Chief Justice Ritchie. In a letter to the Prime Minister, Strong described Henry's deliverances as "long, windy, incoherent masses of verbiage, interspersed with ungrammatical expressions, slang and the veriest legal platitudes inappropriately applied," and advised that "nothing but his [Henry's] removal from it can save the unfortunate Court." He added that "I am not sure that the change if effected will make the Court efficient for the Chief seems to think of anything rather than his judicial work and is never ready with his judgments."[39]

During the next four years, the position of the Court improved as its opponents tired of criticizing it and as confidence in it increased. Auguste Landry, member for Montmagny, introduced several bills for the abolition of the Court though it was not until 1885 that one of his bills reached second reading. By that time, however, the abolition question was almost a dead issue. Though pressed to do so, Sir John Macdonald did not make any changes in the personnel of the Court, and left the judges to solve their own difficulties. Considerable improvement was brought about by changes in procedure with respect to hearing cases and delivering judgments, and the general speeding up of the routine work of the Court. The separation of the Supreme and Exchequer Courts in 1887 was an added reform which had frequently been demanded. By 1885 Louis Davies, who pleaded frequently before the Court and who was later to become Chief Justice of Canada, was able to say in the House of Commons that "It must be evident from the vast preponderance of opinion of Hon. members in the House, that the opinion of the bars in the several Provinces is in favour of

[38] *Ibid.*, 253.
[39] P. A. C., Macdonald Papers, 1888-9, no. 329, Strong to Macdonald, February 9, 1880.

the Court continuing as it is. It is quite evident the Court has given great satisfaction to the majority of the provinces."[40]

The early years of the Supreme Court of Canada, as we have seen, were extremely troublesome for the Court and its sponsors. Cradled in doubt and opposition, the tribunal took well over a decade to win the confidence of Canadian lawyers and public men. Under the circumstances, the Court could not have been regarded as a success in the early years. As Bacon says in his essay *On Judicature*: "The place of Justice is a hallowed place; and therefore not only the Bench but the foot-pace and precincts, and purprise thereof ought to be preserved without scandal and corruption; for certainly, 'Grapes (as the Scripture saith) will not be gathered of thorns or thistles,' neither can Justice yield her fruit with sweetness amongst the briers and brambles of catching and polling Clerks and Ministers."

The general weakness of the Court was a lack of respect characterized by ridicule, distrust, or, in many cases, cold indifference. More specifically, however, it was hampered by several obstacles, the chief of which was the right of appeal to the Judicial Committee of the Privy Council. It was difficult to regard the Supreme Court as "supreme" when there existed recourse to a higher tribunal, and for this reason many regarded the Court as being a needless step in the judicial process and held with Professor Diccy that the Judicial Committee was "the true Supreme Court of the Dominion."[41] This situation not only lessened the prestige of the Court, but affected its interpretation of the law. Since the Court had to be guided by the decisions of the higher authority, it was not completely free to develop a body of principles of its own. These weaknesses were obvious from the beginning, and the government sponsoring the Court made every effort to remove them. But, unfortunately for the Court, the appeals question was bound up with the imperial tie and with the lack of agreement among Canadians regarding abolition. Political considerations, therefore, triumphed over the judicial.

Again, the Court was regarded with mistrust by those concerned with provincial rights. Because it was the creation of the federal Parliament, many felt that the Court should not be given power over provincial matters. Quebec critics in particular resented the fact that cases which had been judged in Quebec

[40] *Canada, House of Commons Debates*, 1885, 162.
[41] A. V. Dicey, *Law of the Constitution* (9th ed., London, 1939), 168.

courts should be reviewed by the Supreme Court of which only two judges were from Quebec. They were suspicious of judicial review generally and objected to Sir John Macdonald's opinion that the Court was "calculated to decide all questions within its jurisdiction coming before it, whether it may be in regard to the construction of the constitution, as to what the constitution is, or in regard to any other matters arising out of constitutional questions."[42] But the Quebec critics were not sure which they liked better, the Supreme Court or the Judicial Committee. In proposing the abolition of appeals, M. Fournier had said that the appeals privilege had been abused in Quebec,[43] and there was much dissatisfaction in Quebec over the Judicial Committee's decision of 1874 in the Guibord case,[44] and its opinion with respect to the New Brunswick Common School Act of 1871.[45] But a similar dissatisfaction with the Supreme Court's decision was felt in the Charlevoix controverted elections case of 1876.[46] The subject was therefore pro and con. Whether provincial and minority rights were influenced one way or the other by the establishment of the Supreme Court was never clearly shown, but the fact remains that the Court itself suffered much in prestige by the resulting suspicion.[47]

These and other attacks mentioned above helped to undermine confidence in the Supreme Court during its early years, and the Court itself, as we have seen, gave cause for opposition and ridicule. Nevertheless, it is to the credit of both the Mackenzie and Macdonald administrations and of the judges themselves, that many of the Court's inner weaknesses were remedied quietly and behind the scenes.

The Fathers of Confederation agreed that Canada needed a Supreme Court and provided the power for setting it up. The task was not easy. Canadians permitted themselves the luxury of criticizing, ridiculing, and obstructing their Court, so that its way was hard and the burden heavy. But it is to be noted that,

---

[42] *Canada, House of Commons Debates*, 1880, 240.

[43] For the period March 10, 1870 to March 10, 1875 there were only fifteen appeals from the English-speaking provinces, while during the five-year period 1871-5, there were thirty-eight prosecuted from Quebec alone. See "Correspondence for the Privy Council," Blake to Carnarvon, June 29, 1877, 19.

[44] L. R. 1874, vol. 6, 157.

[45] *Mather* v. *Town of Portland*, 2 Cartwright, 486.

[46] *Brassard et al* v. *Langevin*, 1 S.C.R., 145.

[47] See also F. R. Scott, "The Privy Council and Minority Rights" (*Queen's Quarterly, autumn*, 1930).

while the Court encountered many hardships at the beginning, it enjoyed the support of the leaders of both parties in Parliament. Macdonald agreed with Mackenzie, Fournier, and Blake on the importance of the Court. These men had great hopes for it and stood by it through its years of difficulty. Probably this fact alone saved it from destruction and helped it forward to a respected place in Canadian life.

The Supreme Court of Canada:
A Final Court of and for Canadians

BORA LASKIN

INTRODUCTION

In 1894 a judge of the Supreme Court of Canada, later to be its first French-Canadian Chief Justice, lamented that "constitutional questions cannot be finally determined in this Court. They never have been and can never be under the present system."[1] The system of which he spoke has now come to an end. It was a system under which Canadian judicial dependence on Imperial authority was of a piece with Canadian subservience in both the legislative and executive areas of government. And just as the action of Imperial legislative and executive organs was necessary to bring that subservience to a proper constitutional termination,[2] so was the action of another Imperial organ, the Judicial Committee of the Privy Council, necessary to bring to a close judicial dependency.[3] A colony may outgrow but it does not escape its origins without revolution. Constitutional change in Canada has been far from revolutionary. It has been piecemeal, protracted, and accomplished with propriety. Even today, one badge of colonialism remains – the formal amendment of the British North America Act by the Parliament of Great Britain. It will disappear, of course, as soon as representatives of the Dominion and provincial governments can agree on formulas and procedures for amendment by Canadian action

From: *The Canadian Bar Review*, Volume 29 (1951), pages 1038-1042, and 1057-1076. By permission of the author and publisher.

[1] Taschereau J. in *A.-G. Can.* v. *A.-G. Ont.* (1894), 23 S.C.R. 458, at p. 472.
[2] See Reports of Imperial Conferences of 1926 and 1930; Statute of Westminster, 1931 (Imp.), c. 4.
[3] *A.-G. Ont.* v. *A.-G. Can.*, [1947] A. C. 127.

alone.[4] But the matter is not beset by urgency: *solvitur ambulando*.

As of December 23rd, 1949, the Supreme Court of Canada has become a significant part of the machinery of Canadian self-government.[5] The purpose of this article is to focus attention on a tribunal which for seventy-five years has had an uncertain role in the development of Canadian law. Where its governing statute gave no appeal, the judgments of provincial appellate courts necessarily prevailed, subject only to review by the Privy Council. Where an appeal lay, the Supreme Court might be by-passed in favour of a direct appeal to the Privy Council. Even if a Supreme Court appeal was taken, a further appeal to the Privy Council by the latter's leave was a continuing possibility.[6]

The Supreme Court of Canada, unlike the Supreme Court of the United States and the High Court of Australia, is not a constitutional court in the sense of having its existence and its jurisdiction guaranteed by fundamental law.[7] Its being, as well as its organization and jurisdiction, has depended on the exercise by the Dominion Parliament of the legislative power conferred by section 101 of the British North America Act. Nevertheless, constitutional considerations have dogged the Supreme Court since its establishment in 1875.[8] They nearly stifled it at birth and gave it an uneasy infancy.[9] It was, in fact, an intermediate appellate court which could neither compel resort to its facilities nor control further appeals from its decisions.

[4] Proceedings of Constitutional Conference of Federal and Provincial Governments, 1950; Proceedings of Constitutional Conference of Federal and Provincial Governments (second session), 1950.

[5] Supreme Court Act amendment of 1949 (Can. 2nd sess.), c. 37.

[6] The Privy Council had stated from time to time (e.g. in *In re Initiative and Referendum Act*, [1919] A. C. 935, at p. 939) that it preferred to have the opinion of the Supreme Court in cases on appeal.

[7] See U.S. Constitution, article III, sections 1 and 2. S. 1 declares that "the judicial power of the United States shall be vested in one supreme court . . ."; s. 2 deals with jurisdiction. And see Commonwealth of Australia Constitution Act, 1900 (Imp.), c. 12, ss. 71 and 73. By s. 71, "the judicial power of the Commonwealth shall be vested in a federal supreme court, to be called the High Court of Australia . . ."; s. 73 deals with jurisdiction. On the other hand, s. 101 of the B.N.A. Act declares merely that "the Parliament of Canada may . . . provide for the constitution, maintenance and organization of a general court of appeal for Canada . . .".

[8] Supreme Court Act, 1875 (Can.), c. 11. The Act was proclaimed on September 17th, 1875.

[9] See MacKinnon, The Establishment of the Supreme Court of Canada (1946), 27 Can. Hist. Rev. 258.

Legal and sentimental ties between Great Britain and Canada involved the Court in controversy about appeals to the Privy Council even before its first panel of judges was appointed.[10] Its federal origin and auspices roused suspicion of what the Court might do in attenuating provincial interests. The Court's slow beginning, and friction among some of its judges, prompted a number of attempts to secure its abolition.[11] Yet its initial organization and its survival appear today to have been an inevitable concomitant of Canadian nationhood.

How far the intermediate position of the Court tended to its obscurity is difficult to estimate. I do not refer to any obscurity in a professional legal sense. The Court made itself felt whenever the opportunity offered. But it is clear that the Court has not hitherto been regarded by the public at large as a potent element in Canadian self-government. Perhaps this is a role which a national tribunal can essay only if it has ultimate judicial authority. But the legal profession cannot escape some of the responsibility for public neglect of the Court. It is a fact that hardly anything has been written about its doctrine, and only recently has there been any professional curiosity manifested about its jurisdiction.[12] It has had nine chief justices (inclusive of the present incumbent of that office) and none has yet been the subject of any published biography. Indeed, neither the Court itself nor (with a few exceptions) its judges have been subjected to appraisal in any book or article.[13] It is a pity that this has been so because the Court has had able and devoted men on its roster and, wherever *stare decisis* has left it relatively

---

[10] The story is told in a collection of official correspondence entitled "Correspondence confidentially printed for the use of the Privy Council respecting the Supreme and Exchequer Court of Canada." It covers the period from October 6th, 1875, to August 29th, 1876. The controversy centred around a clause of the Supreme Court bill, introduced by way of amendment, making the Court the final appellate authority. It was apparently not immediately realized that the Dominion could not then abolish the appeal to the Privy Council by grace. When this became clear, the threat of disallowance disappeared. See Underhill: Edward Blake, the Supreme Court Act and the Appeal to the Privy Council (1938), 19 Can. Hist. Rev. 245; Cannon, Some Data relating to the Appeal to the Privy Council (1925), 3 Can. Bar Rev. 455.

[11] See *op. cit., supra*, footnote 9.

[12] Cf. W. Glen How, The Too Limited Jurisdiction of the Supreme Court (1947), 25 Can. Bar Rev. 573.

[13] See, for example, E. R. Cameron, Sir Louis Davies (1924), 2 Can. Bar Rev. 305.

free, it has given adequate proof of responsible utterances.[14]

It is an easy prophecy that professional and non-professional apathy will disappear now that the Supreme Court has become the final court in all Canadian causes. The membership of the Court, its pronouncements, its administrative organization for the despatch of business, are now matters of grave import for lawyers and non-lawyers alike. This would be so even if Canada were not wrestling with problems of federalism. The problems, challenging enough when they were faced by the Privy Council which did not have to live with its own solutions, are even more challenging to a court which must experience them as well as help to decide what to do about them.

SUPREME COURT MEMBERSHIP

Inclusive of the present complement of judges, forty-two persons have served on the Supreme Court of Canada. It is worthy of notice that more than half of these appointees came to the Court with previous judicial experience in provincial courts. Worthy of note, too, is that three appointees had been federal ministers of justice and two had been deputy ministers in the department of justice. Five other appointees had served as provincial attorneys-general. On its establishment in 1875 the Court was composed of six judges, of whom two had to be from Quebec.[15] It remained a six-judge court until 1927 when provision was made for a seventh judge.[16] At the close of 1949, with the abolition of appeals to the Privy Council, the Court became a nine-judge tribunal.[17]

Whether one regards it as inevitable or not, it is a fact that membership on the Court has from the beginning been affected by sectional and religious considerations in the same way as has

---

[14] See *infra* the reference to the Supreme Court's constitutional doctrine.
[15] The first panel of judges was appointed on October 8th, 1875. There was no separate Exchequer Court until 1887 (Can.), c. 16, and until that time the judges of the Supreme Court also constituted the Exchequer Court.

   It should be noted that while Parliament agreed that two of the judges should come from Quebec (s. 4 of the Act of 1875), it rejected a proposal requiring that one of the judges should be from British Columbia: see footnote 9, *supra*.
[16] 1927 (Can.), c. 38.
[17] 1949 (Can. 2nd sess.), c. 37. This amendment also restored the one-third proportion of Quebec appointees which had been reduced when a seventh judge was added in 1927.

the composition of all federal cabinets since Confederation.[18] The French-Canadian and English-Canadian components of the population, the Protestant and Roman Catholic persuasion of most of the citizenry, the sectional (and provincial) pressure for representation in central organs of government, were factors to which appointments to the Court gave expression. Until the turn of the century, the Supreme Court was an all-eastern affair. Chief Justice Killam of Manitoba, the first appointment from the western provinces, joined the Court on August 8th, 1903, but he resigned within two years to become head of the Board of Railway Commissioners. The next western appointee was Mr. Justice Duff of British Columbia, who assumed his office on September 27th, 1906, and retired after a memorable and distinguished career extending over thirty-seven years, the last ten to eleven of which he served as Chief Justice. The new province of Newfoundland aside, there have been one or more appointees from every province save Alberta. In truth, however, and for reasons unique to Canadian federalism, the Court has always been numerically dominated by Ontario and Quebec appointees. If precedent in judicial appointments means anything – and it has governed for a long time already – there will be only three places in the present nine-judge court to distribute among eight provinces. On a basis of existing proportions of population, this division is not particularly outrageous. But population ratios are not the only factors to be considered. The present statutory requirement of three appointees from Quebec means that it is Ontario that will have to forego its traditional equality with Quebec to permit a larger selection of Supreme Court judges from outside the two central provinces. One may well cavil at concessions to political federalism in the selection of persons to staff a final court of appeal which is supposed to represent high professional competence and, I hope, mature social understanding. It is not, of course, demonstrable that a purely merit system of appointments would or could raise the calibre of Supreme Court judges. But the greater freedom of choice which such a system permits should reasonably conduce to such a result. Be that as it may, Canadian practice in appointments has been to assume that merit is equally served in the recognition of sectional and religious qualifications. It is a practice that is not likely to change.

[18] Cf. Rogers, Federal Influences on the Canadian Cabinet (1933), 11 Can. Bar Rev. 103.

[Editor's Note. Pages 1042 to 1057 of the original essay are omitted here, along with the relevant footnotes numbered 21 to 85 inclusive. The omitted portions are not directly concerned with The Supreme Court as the final appellate tribunal on federal constitutional issues. Rather the omitted portions deal with the internal organization of the Court for the despatch of business and the general jurisdictional rules for admitting appeals of all types.]

THE CONSTITUTIONAL DOCTRINE OF THE COURT

It is beyond the scope of this article to appraise the Supreme Court's decisions, during the seventy-five years of its existence, in the various branches of law which they cover. Something deserves to be said, however, about its work in constitutional interpretation since it is this work, which is beyond simple legislative change, that will hereafter mark the Court as at least a co-ordinate branch of government with the legislature and the executive. A preliminary issue may be posed. Is it worthwhile or useful to review decisions of a court which have hitherto had no conclusive impact on constitutional law? Must not the Supreme Court, in the new role which it now enjoys, start off with the Privy Council decisions? I propose to say more about this problem further on in this article. For the moment, it will suffice to say that it is not only the actual Privy Council decisions themselves with which the Supreme Court must reckon: there is also the important inquiry into the attitude which animated the Privy Council in coming to its particular conclusions. It is hardly credible that the Supreme Court will seek to walk in the shadow of the Privy Council, asking itself not only what Privy Council decisions are controlling but striving to reflect the Privy Council's approach to problems of interpretation. Such a final court would be merely a judicial "zombie," without soul or character.

Any estimate of the Supreme Court's constitutional doctrine must be related to the period during which it had not yet felt the authoritative effect of the Privy Council's views. There were, in fact, two such periods. One, ending with the *Local Prohibition* case in 1896,[86] was concerned with fixing the relationship between sections 91 and 92, adjusting the powers conferred on

[86] *A.-G. Ont.* v.*A.-G. Can.*, [1896] A.C. 348.

the Dominion to those conferred on the provinces. The second period, ending with the *Board of Commerce* case in 1921[87] (or, perhaps, with the *Snider* case in 1925[88]), involved elaboration of the content of the respective powers in the relationship in which they had previously been fixed. Essentially, this was a matter of weighing, on the federal side, the peace, order and good government clause and the trade and commerce clause against the property and civil rights clause on the provincial side.

The Supreme Court of Canada which decided *Severn* v. *The Queen* in 1878,[89] *Valin* v. *Langlois* in 1879,[90] *Fredericton* v. *The Queen*[91] and *Citizens Insurance Co.* v. *Parsons* in 1880,[92] was composed of judges for whom Confederation was a personal experience with an evident meaning. This was certainly not the case with the Privy Council. The latter could not be expected to display the sensitivity for the British North America Act that is found in the early pronouncements of the Supreme Court. The disagreements among members of the Supreme Court in its early days were on the question whether the provinces could be permitted to enact legislation which might prove obstructive to a prospective federal programme. Those of the judges who would have permitted local legislation had no doubt that federal legislation, if enacted to meet a national problem on a national level, must prevail. The judges who denied provincial power were unwilling to permit local experiments even in the absence of federal legislation. This is a far cry, indeed, from the Privy Council philosophy, which was the antithesis of the Supreme Court's approach, subordinating the central power to local autonomy without regard to the size or quality of problems which were susceptible of uniform treatment through national legislation.

The first judgment of the Supreme Court of Canada on a constitutional point, *Severn* v. *The Queen*, exhibited an appreciation of comparative federal constitutional law in its references to decisions of the Supreme Court of the United States. Of especial interest, for comparative purposes today, is the comment on the commerce power in the United States as reflected in

[87] *In re Board of Commerce Act*, [1922] 1 A.C. 191.
[88] *Toronto Electric Commissioners* v. *Snider*, [1925] A.C. 396.
[89] 2 S.C.R. 70.
[90] 3 S.C.R. 1.
[91] 3 S.C.R. 505.
[92] 4 S.C.R. 215.

Gibbons v. *Ogden*,[93] and the conviction that the Dominion's power under section 91(2) of the B.N.A. Act was much broader. "Our constitution," said Fournier J., "does not acknowledge as in the United States, a division of power as to commerce."[94] Strong J., who dissented in the *Severn* case in favour of sustaining provincial legislation, was equally emphatic: "That the regulation of trade and commerce in the provinces, domestic and internal as well as foreign and external, is by the B.N.A. Act exclusively conferred upon the Parliament of the Dominion, calls for no demonstration, for the language of the Act is explicit."[95] It remained for the Privy Council to give an ironic response. Not only did it deny, in *Bank of Toronto* v. *Lambe*,[96] the relevance of American decisions, but it purported, earlier in *Citizens Insurance Co.* v. *Parsons*,[97] to find support for its interpretation of the Dominion's commerce power in the Act of Union of England and Scotland of 1707. It is an easy inference that an Imperial judicial tribunal, dealing with a colonial constitution formally promulgated by Imperial authority, would tend to interpret it in imperial terms. In one of its last independent utterances, a member of the Supreme Court in *In re Prohibitory Liquors Laws* sought to remind the country, and perhaps the Privy Council too, that the B.N.A. Act was a Canadian instrument fashioned by and for Canadians. Said Mr. Justice Sedgewick: "In other words, it must be viewed from a Canadian standpoint. Although an Imperial Act, to interpret it correctly reference may be had to the phraseology and nomenclature of pre-confederation Canadian legislation and jurisprudence, as well as to the history of the union movement and to the condition, sentiment and surroundings of the Canadian people at the time. In the British North America Act it was in a technical sense only that the Imperial Parliament spoke; it was there that in a real and substantial sense the Canadian people spoke, and it is to their language, as they understood it, that effect must be given."[98] Gwynne J. in the same case also reminded the Privy Council that if any comparative constitu-

---

[93] (1824), 9 Wheat. 1.

[94] 2 S.C.R. 70, at p. 121.

[95] *Ibid.*, at p. 104. See also Henry J. (at p. 138): "Every constituent of trade and commerce and the subject of indirect taxation is . . . withdrawn from the . . . local legislatures."

[96] (1887), 12 App. Cas. 575.

[97] (1881), 7 App. Cas. 96.

[98] 24 S.C.R. 170, at p. 231.

tional doctrine was represented in the distribution of legislative power in the B.N.A. Act, it was more properly related to United States experience than to that of Great Britain.

It is a notable feature of the Supreme Court's early decisions that there was no separation of the federal general power under section 91 of the B.N.A. Act from the specific enumerations which illustrated its reach.[99] The latter were given their full effect as qualifying the scope of provincial heads of power. This interpretation had an interesting application – in the light of later Privy Council views – in *Severn* v. *The Queen*. Here, a manufacturer of liquor, licensed under Dominion excise legislation, was charged under an Ontario statute with selling liquor by wholesale without a provincial licence. A majority of the Supreme Court invalidated the provincial Act. Two of the six-judge court dissented on the ground that the provincial licensing power – section 92(9) of the B.N.A. Act – should be permitted to operate in relation to sale when the Dominion had confined its licensing control to manufacture. Fournier J., of the majority, answered this argument as follows: "The power to authorize the manufacture of an article must necessarily imply, as does the right to import, the right to sell."[100] The members of the majority were concerned about provincial interference with Dominion revenues. The Privy Council discounted the *Severn* case in *Bank of Toronto* v. *Lambe* and destroyed its effect with finality in *A.-G. Man.* v. *Manitoba License Holders Association*,[101] where it was held (reversing the Manitoba Court of Appeal) that it was no answer to provincial legislation that it interfered with the sources of Dominion revenues. Recently, the Ontario Court of Appeal in *Rex* v. *Pee-Kay Smallwares Ltd.* applied the *Manitoba License Holders* case to a prosecution

---

[99] As is well known, this was the result reached by the Privy Council in *A.-G. Ont.* v. *A.-G. Can.*, [1896] A. C. 348. Compare, however, the statement by Ritchie C.J. in *Valin* v. *Langlois* (1879), 3 S.C.R. 1, at p. 14: "In determining the question of ultra vires, too little consideration has, I think, been given to the constitution of the Dominion, by which the legislative power of the local assemblies is limited and confined to the subjects specifically assigned to them while all other legislative powers, including what is specifically assigned to the Dominion Parliament, is conferred on that Parliament; differing in this respect entirely from the constitution of the United States of America, under which the state legislatures retained all the powers of legislation which were not expressly taken away."

[100] 2 S.C.R. 70, at p. 130.

[101] [1902] A.C. 73.

under an Ontario liquor statute against a company licensed under federal excise legislation.[102]

The Supreme Court felt the impact of Privy Council decisions within a decade after the *Severn* case. Thus, Strong J., who had dissented in the *Severn* case, commented in *Pigeon* v. *Recorder's Court* that the *Severn* case had turned on the subordination of the provincial power under section 92(9) to the federal trade and commerce power. And, he asserted further, that "even as regards this construction of the 9th subsection [of s. 92], if the decision in *Severn* v. *The Queen* has not been overruled observations not in accordance with it are certainly to be found in later decisions of the Privy Council."[103] These "later decisions" included, of course, *Bank of Toronto* v. *Lambe* as well as the *Parsons* case and *Hodge* v. *The Queen*.[104] Shortly after the *Lambe* case, the Supreme Court was compelled, as a matter of *stare decisis*, to swallow the views which it had promulgated in *Severn* v. *The Queen*. In *Molson* v. *Lambe*, which raised an issue similar to that in the *Severn* case, the Court was able to base its decision on a procedural point connected with the writ of prohibition, but Ritchie C.J. added a constitutional pronouncement: "In view of the cases determined by the Privy Council since the case of *Severn* v. *The Queen* was decided by this Court, which appear to me to have established conclusively that the right and power to legislate in relation to the issue of licences for the sale of intoxicating liquors by wholesale and retail belong to the local legislature, we are bound to hold that the Quebec License Act of 1878 and its amendments are valid and constitutional."[105] Only Gwynne J. struggled to hold the authority of the *Severn* case by distinguishing the legislation there involved as compared with that in the *Molson* case.

Any discussion of constitutional power in relation to liquor legislation would not be complete without mention of *Fredericton* v. *The Queen* and *In re Liquor License Act, 1883*, the McCarthy Act case. In the *Fredericton* case, the Supreme Court, unlike the Privy Council in the later *Russell* case, sustained the Canada Temperance Act of 1878 under the trade and commerce power. "The right to regulate trade and commerce," said Ritchie

102 [1947] O.R. 1019.

103 (1890), 17 S.C.R. 495, at p. 505.

104 (1883), 9 App. Cas. 117.

105 (1888), 15 S.C.R. 253, at p. 259. Fournier J. came to the same conclusion on the basis of the Supreme Court's views in *In re Dominion Liquor Licence Act, 1883*, Cassel's Dig. S. C. Decisions 279.

C.J., "is not to be overridden by any local legislation in reference to any subject over which power is given to the local legislature."[106] The reasoning of the Supreme Court and its attitude towards the trade and commerce power is in marked contrast to the views expounded by the Privy Council in cases like the *Board of Commerce* and *Snider* decisions. While the Privy Council sought in the *P.A.T.A.* case[107] to redeem section 91(2) from the subordinate (and ancillary) function assigned to it previously, the redemption has had no effect by way of adding anything to the strength of section 91(2) as a source of Dominion legislation.[108] The *Fredericton* case met head on the argument that section 91(2) could not support a prohibitory enactment. "The power to prohibit is within the power to regulate," said Ritchie C.J.[109] "A prohibition is a regulation," said Taschereau J.[110] The Judicial Committee rejected this view of section 91(2) in the *Local Prohibition* case, founding its opinion on a municipal by-law case, *Toronto* v. *Virgo*.[111] Equating a federal constitution with a municipal by-law is one of the Privy Council's more serious lapses. Besides being at odds with common sense, it is in conflict with the Privy Council's own assertion in *Hodge* v. *The Queen* that the provincial legislatures – and, it follows, the Dominion Parliament – are not delegates. A municipal corporation undoubtedly is. Nonetheless, the attenuated meaning so given to section 91(2) by the *Local Prohibition* case has prevailed ever since. There was a suggestion of disapproval by the Supreme Court in *Gold Seal Ltd.* v. *Dominion Express Co,* [112] but it was only recently in the *Margarine* reference that Rinfret C.J.C., in a dissenting judgment, flatly refused to accept the proposition that the power to prohibit is excluded from a power to regulate.[113]

The *McCarthy Act* case represented an overreaching of power by Parliament in the eyes of a court which had sustained federal prohibitory legislation and thrown out provincial regulatory (licensing) legislation. The change of opinion – if there was one – was in line with the Privy Council's judgment in

106 3 S.C.R. 505, at pp. 540-1.
107 [1931] A.C. 310.
108 Cf. the marketing reference, *A.-G. B.C.* v. *A.-G. Can.,* [1937] A.C. 377.
109 3 S.C.R. 505, at p. 537.
110 *Ibid.,* at p. 559.
111 [1896] A.C. 98.
112 (1921), 62 S.C.R. 424.
113 (1949) S.C.R. 1.

Hodge v. *The Queen*. The McCarthy Act – the Dominion Liquor License Act – was enacted in May 1883 and proclaimed to come into force on January 1st, 1884. Its preamble indicated an attempt at conformity to the views of the Judicial Committee in *Russell* v. *The Queen* in 1882. Thus, there was a reference to the desirability of regulating traffic in the sale of intoxicating liquor and an assertion of the expediency of having a uniform law throughout Canada and for the better preservation of peace and order. At the close of 1883, the Judicial Committee gave its judgment in the *Hodge* case sustaining a provincial licensing enactment and enunciating the aspect doctrine. This opinion, added to the earlier Privy Council judgment in the *Parsons* case, established a rather formidable bar to any federal regulatory (as opposed to prohibitory) legislation dealing with local sales of intoxicating liquor. The federal Act of 1883 was an enactment of that character. It provided for the establishment of municipal boards of commissioners to which licensing authority was granted. There was no provision for centralized administration which, had it been provided, might have suggested a national rather than a local aspect to the problem. In the circumstances, the Supreme Court's decision invalidating the Act on a reference in 1885 was hardly a major shift of opinion.[114]

The constitutional story of Dominion-provincial liquor enactments ended, so far as the Supreme Court was concerned, in the *Local Prohibition* case which came before the Court in 1894 as a reference entitled *In re Prohibitory Liquor Laws*.[115] The case is notable for the split of opinion on the Court notwithstanding the compulsion of Privy Council decisions which for a decade up to 1894 had moved decisively towards a greater recognition of provincial legislative authority. The reference concerned *inter alia* the validity of Ontario liquor legislation which was then before the Supreme Court in the case of *Huson* v. *Norwich*.[116] The legislation empowered municipalities, in the circumstances there set out, to pass prohibitory by-laws respecting the retail sale of liquor. Because of the reference, the Court in *Huson* v. *Norwich* reserved judgment until after argument was heard in the reference. A majority of the Court in the *Huson* case (Strong C.J. and Fournier and

---

[114] (1885) Cassel's Dig. S.C. Decisions 279, aff'd by Privy Council without written reasons.
[115] 24 S.C.R. 170.
[116] 24 S.C.R. 145.

Taschereau JJ.) held that the provincial enactment was valid; Gwynne and Sedgewick JJ. dissented. The hearing on the reference was before a court differently constituted: King J. replaced Taschereau J. and he sided with Gwynne and Sedgewick JJ. The result was that a majority on the reference held invalid the same enactment which the Court differently constituted had sustained in *Huson* v. *Norwich*. It is well known that the Judicial Committee on appeal in the reference reversed the Supreme Court.[117] It is instructive, however, to compare the views of the majority and minority of the Supreme Court in the *Huson* case and in the reference. There was no disagreement on the paramount power of the Dominion: the difference in their views was simply on the question whether there was any room for provincial legislation even in the absence of conflicting Dominion legislation. The majority in the *Huson* case was careful to point out that the provincial Act was restricted to retail sales. They were still of opinion that such matters as importation and manufacture belonged exclusively to the Dominion under its trade and commerce power. The reasons given by the Privy Council for its answers in the reference were not only at variance with the majority view of the Supreme Court in that case but were equally at variance with the majority views in the *Huson* case.

The Privy Council in the *Local Prohibition* reference placed the provincial "property and civil rights" power on a solid footing as against the uncertain future presaged for the federal general power and the federal commerce power. The problem was one which the Supreme Court had faced earlier in *Valin* v. *Langlois*, where the potentialities of "property and civil rights in the province" were discussed with the realization that it could not be given full rein in the face of the terms of section 91 of the B.N.A. Act.[118] The collocation argument against the federal

---

[117] [1896] A.C. 348 (the *Local Prohibition* case.)

[118] 3 S.C.R. 1. Thus, for example, Ritchie C.J. said (at p. 15): ". . . The terms 'property and civil rights,' must necessarily be read in a restricted and limited sense, because many matters involving property and civil rights are expressly reserved to the Dominion Parliament, of which the first two items in the enumeration [in section 91] are illustrations, viz., 1. the public debt and property; 2. the regulation of trade and commerce." And Henry J. remarked (at p. 67): "The right of the local legislatures to legislate as to civil rights . . . is subordinated to those civil rights not affected by Dominion powers of legislation and to those *in the province*, and not including matters of a *general* character."

commerce power used by the Privy Council in the *Parsons* case was turned against the property and civil rights power by Sedgewick J. in the *Local Prohibition* reference.[119] He ventured to suggest that material considerations affecting the interpretation of the B.N.A. Act were not presented to the Privy Council in the *Parsons* case. Far from "the property and civil rights" power controlling the federal commerce power, the reverse was true. This was almost the last time that the federal commerce power got such respectful treatment. Less than twenty years later, another Supreme Court judge, in sympathy with the position taken by Sedgewick J., could only remark that "The Judicial Committee has never yet expressly assigned to this power over trade and commerce any Dominion legislation which has come before it."[120] In 1920 a less sympathetic judge of the Supreme Court dismissed the federal commerce power as "the old forlorn hope, so many times tried unsuccessfully upon this court and the court above."[121]

The *Local Prohibition* case, as decided by the Privy Council, was not merely a decisive case on legislative power in respect of liquor control. It also fixed the relation of the component clauses of section 91 to those in section 92 in such a manner as to make the latter the stable point of reference. The result, as has so many times been pointed out, was that only the enumerated powers in section 91 were withdrawn from provincial legislative authority; and the general power of the Dominion became a purely secondary ("supplementary" in the Privy Council's words) source of authority to be invoked in cases falling neither within the enumerations of section 92 nor within those of section 91. It has so remained to this day.[122] A noteworthy feature of the legislative scheme so worked out by the Judicial Committee was that its elaboration occurred in a series of cases concerned with the validity of provincial rather than Dominion legislation.

In the second phase of constitutional interpretation referred to – giving content to the various heads of power – the Supreme

---

[119] 24 S.C.R. 170, at p. 238.

[120] *In re Canadian Insurance Act, 1910* (1913), 48 S.C.R. 260, at p. 270, *per* Davies J.

[121] *In re Board of Commerce Act* (1920), 60 S.C.R. 456, at p. 488, *per* Idington J.

[122] The promise of a revitalization of the general power, held out in *A.-G. Ont.* v. *Canada Temperance Federation*, [1946] A.C. 193, was abruptly dismissed in the margarine reference appeal, [1950] 4 D.L.R. 689.

Court played a less independent role. This was, of course, understandable because the cases up to and including the *Local Prohibition* case had decided particular issues of legislative power besides establishing general principles of interpretation. The particular issues of legislative power were connected with particular legislation. Hence, where the same legislative subject matter came before the Supreme Court it would be difficult to escape a conclusion, on legislative power, similar to that previously reached by the Privy Council. An apt illustration is provided by *In re Sections 4 and 70 of the Canadian Insurance Act, 1910*, better known, after being appealed to the Privy Council, as the *Insurance Reference* case.[123] The Supreme Court was faced with an application of the Judicial Committee's views on insurance legislation in the *Parsons* case. Those views were formulated in a case involving the validity of provincial legislation which merely prescribed standard conditions in fire insurance contracts. The Dominion Act of 1910, now before the Court, was a general licensing statute. Must it fall under the decision in the *Parsons* case or was it legislation in a different aspect? In other words, could the Dominion legislation be supported by the federal trade and commerce power or the federal general power?

The *Parsons* case had gone to the Privy Council from the Supreme Court, where a majority upheld the validity of the Ontario statute which was in question. The grounds for so holding provide an interesting contrast to the fate of the case in the Privy Council and to the subsequent course of Privy Council rulings on insurance legislation.

Nothing in the *Parsons* case called for a pronouncement on the limits of federal authority in relation to insurance. The legislation dealt only with statutory conditions. There was no inconsistent Dominion legislation. In such circumstances, it seemed harsh to deny to a province power to fix the terms of a contract of indemnity respecting property in the province where the contract was made. Yet that is what a minority of the Supreme Court would have done. Thus Taschereau J., dissenting, said:[124]

Insurance business is a trade, and to the federal authority belongs the exclusive power of regulation of that trade in each

[123] 48 S.C.R. 260, aff'd [1916] 1 A.C. 588.
[124] 4 S.C.R. 215, at p. 316.

*and every province in the Dominion. . . . This power to regulate
excludes necessarily the action of all others that would perform
the same operation on the same thing. . . . One of the great
benefits of confederation would be lost if the rules on trade and
commerce were not uniform all through the Dominion.*

And Gwynne J., dissenting, spoke in more portentous terms:[125]

The logical result of a contrary decision [that is, a decision
sustaining the provincial Act] *would afford just grounds to
despair of the stability of the Dominion.*

The majority view was grounded on a strict view of the provincial Act. Said Chief Justice Ritchie:[126]

*I do not understand that by the Act now assailed any supreme
legislative power to regulate and control the business of insurance in Ontario is claimed. . . . In my opinion this Act has no
reference to trade and commerce in the sense in which these
words are used in the B.N.A. Act.*

And almost as if to answer the forebodings of Gwynne J., the
Chief Justice remarked:[127]

*I am happy to say I can foresee and I fear no evil effects what-
ever, as has been suggested, as likely to result to the Dominion
from this view of the case. On the contrary, I believe that while
this decision recognizes and sustains the legislative control of
the Dominion Parliament over all matters confided to its legislative jurisdiction, it at the same time preserves to the local
legislatures those rights and powers conferred on them by the
B.N.A. Act and which a contrary decision would in my opinion
in effect substantially or to a very large extent sweep away.*

In the *Insurance Reference* case there is little resemblance in
the Supreme Court judgments to the views propounded by predecessor members of the Court in the *Parsons* case. A majority
of the Court declared that the Dominion Act of 1910 was
invalid for reasons expressed in Privy Council decisions, and
especially for reasons given by that tribunal in the *Parsons* case.
Only Fitzpatrick C.J., who dissented, placed the *Parsons* case in

125 *Ibid.*, at p. 347.
126 *Ibid.*, at p. 244.
127 *Ibid.*, at p. 248.

the same frame of reference as had the Supreme Court when it decided the case in 1880:[128]

In short it may be safely stated that the whole report of the Parsons *case shews that it was assumed by both sides it was within the power of the Parliament of Canada to grant licences.*

Of the majority judgments in the Supreme Court, that of Mr. Justice Duff requires particular notice for several reasons. In the first place, the learned justice was just nicely settled in his long tenure of office and in a career which was to be the most distinguished of any Supreme Court member. Secondly, the *Insurance Reference* case was the first of several occasions on which he propounded ideas which the Privy Council later took up. Thirdly, the case gave a clue to his constitutional philosophy as expressed through the succeeding thirty years, although it appears that his premises were dictated to him by prior Privy Council judgments. Fourthly, Mr. Justice Duff became the rationalizing agent of Privy Council pronouncements in the two areas which counted most, namely, the scope of the general power and the scope of the trade and commerce power.

Mr. Justice Duff rejected the attempt to support the Insurance Act under the federal general power because, save for its territorial operation, it could be enacted by any province. It is interesting to find that this idea made its appearance about twelve years later in Lord Haldane's judgment in the *Snider* case striking down the federal Industrial Disputes Investigation Act. "I do not think," said Duff J., "that the fact that the business of insurance has grown to great proportions affects the question in the least."[129] Here we have a position to which the learned justice returned when he invalidated the Canada Grain Act, 1912, in *The King* v. *Eastern Terminal Elevator Co.*[130] Equally did he reject the attempt to support the Insurance Act as in relation to the regulation of trade and commerce. According to him, this power "does not embrace the regulation of occupations as such," and "the various kinds of business which are comprehended under the term 'insurance' as used in the Act [of 1910] can [not] be said to be part of the trade and commerce of

128 48 S.C.R. 260, at p. 264.
129 *Ibid.*, at p. 304.
130 [1925] S.C.R. 434.

the country."[131] "Property and civil rights" carried the day here as it did in the notable judgment delivered by Chief Justice Duff, as he then was, almost a quarter century later in *Reference re Natural Products Marketing Act.*[132]

As instructive as the *Insurance Reference* case on the Supreme Court's narrowed role in constitutional interpretation is *In re Board of Commerce Act* in which the Supreme Court split equally on the validity of federal anti-profiteering legislation designed to cope with a post-war economy.[133] The *Board of Commerce* case, dealing as it did with general legislation respecting the price of necessities, as contrasted with the particular legislation involved in the *Insurance Reference* case, provided an excellent opportunity for assessing the attitude of the Supreme Court judges on the content of the federal general power and the commerce power. It was to be expected that Mr. Justice Davies, now Chief Justice, who had dissented in the *Insurance Reference* case, would support the general legislation in the *Board of Commerce* case. Anglin J., who had been with the majority in the earlier case, was won to the support of the federal legislation because of its generality and importance. Not only did he depart in some measure from his views of the "trade and commerce" power in the *Insurance Reference* case but he sought to give some elasticity to the general power by recognizing its appropriateness whenever an economic problem outgrew provincial proportions. He remained faithful to this view, as is evident in his dissent in *The King* v. *Eastern Terminal Elevator Co.*[134] In this he opposed Duff J.

The latter adhered to his "civil rights" view of the "trade and commerce" power as expressed in the *Insurance Reference* case. There was no difference so far as legislative power was concerned between regulating the contracts of a particular occupation, namely, insurance, and regulating the contracts (through price control) of a variety of traders dealing in various commodities. Could the Board of Commerce legislation rest on the federal general power? Said Mr. Justice Duff:[135]

131 48 S.C.R. 260, at p. 302. See, however, another view of the "trade and commerce" power taken by Duff C.J. in *Reference re Alberta Statutes*, [1938] S.C.R. 100.
132 [1936] S.C.R. 398.
133 (1920), 60 S.C.R. 456.
134 [1925] S.C.R. 434, at p. 439.
135 60 S.C.R. 456, at p. 508.

There is no case of which I am aware in which a Dominion statute not referable to one of the classes of legislation included in the enumerated heads of sec. 91 and being of such a character that from a provincial point of view it should be considered legislation dealing with "property and civil rights" has been held competent to the Dominion under the introductory clause.

This view prevailed in the Privy Council and it represents a theme which ran through Lord Haldane's judgments in a number of Privy Council cases. It was a view which rejected social and economic considerations, and which led to the war emergency conception of the general power as finally worked out in the *Fort Frances*[136] and *Snider*[137] cases. In the latter of these cases Lord Haldane purported to destroy once and for all the standing of *Russell* v. *The Queen*. The way for doing this was paved by Duff J. in his strictures on the *Russell* case in *In re Board of Commerce Act*. It was perhaps only proper that Chief Justice Duff's summation of the general power in *Reference re Natural Products Marketing Act* should be accepted as definitive by the Privy Council.[138]

Although by the turn of the century the Supreme Court was clearly a court subordinate to a higher authority, there was still the occasional opportunity for independent evaluation of the limits of various heads of power.[139] The Court as a whole appeared loath to strike out in new directions except where the Judicial Committee itself had given a lead. Differences of opinion among Supreme Court justices rarely reached the delicate stage of dependence on the vote of one justice for a decision, as was and is so often the case in the United States. As Privy Council decisions multiplied, the Supreme Court became engrossed in merely expounding the authoritative pronouncements of its superior. The task of the Supreme Court was not to interpret the constitution but rather to interpret what the Privy Council said the constitution meant. Here and there it might influence the Privy Council, but the direction and initiative in constitutional interpretation belonged to the Privy Council

---

136 *Fort Frances Pulp & Power Co.* v. *Manitoba Free Press*, [1923] A.C. 695.

137 *Toronto Electric Commissioners* v. *Snider*, [1925] A.C. 396.

138 In the *Labour Conventions* case, *A.-G. Can.* v. *A.-G. Ont.*, [1937] A.C. 326.

139 A conspicuous example was *Reference re Privy Council Appeals*, [1940] S.C.R. 49.

alone. With the abolition of Privy Council appeals, the Supreme
Court must now discharge a duty which it assumed, if at all,
only for the first decade or so of its existence.

THE SUPREME COURT AND *STARE DECISIS*

Abolition of Privy Council appeals makes it possible for the
first time to contemplate deviation of Canadian law from English law in all its branches. The Colonial Laws Validity Act,
1865, verified the right to differ in and by legislation even before
Confederation unless English legislation was made applicable
expressly or by necessary intendment;[140] and this qualification
of complete legislative independence has since been removed by
the Statute of Westminster.[141] The authorized abolition of
appeals to the Privy Council, first in criminal cases,[142] and later
in all causes and in all matters,[143] and whether from judgments
of provincial courts or from Supreme Court judgments, will
now force a decision on deviation from English judicial decisions as well.

Three generalized propositions may serve to highlight the
problems which abolition of appeals raises relative to the continuing authority of Privy Council decisions and of English law
generally. First, the Privy Council is not formally bound by its
previous decisions.[144] Secondly, the Supreme Court of Canada
is formally bound by its previous decisions.[145] Thirdly, the
Privy Council is bound on matters of English common law by
the House of Lords which is itself committed to *stare decisis*.[146]
What significance do these propositions have now that the
Supreme Court is an ultimate appellate court?

A distinction must first be made between constitutional and
non-constitutional litigation because only in the former did
Privy Council decisions stand above challenge by any other
judicial authority. In this field, however, the Privy Council
adhered in practice to past decisions notwithstanding its theo-
retical freedom to change its mind. The Judicial Committee has

---

[140] 1865 (Imp.), c. 63.

[141] 1931 (Imp.), c. 4.

[142] Cr. Code, s. 1024(4), as enacted by 1933 (Can.) c. 53, s. 17; and see
British Coal Corp. v. *The King*, [1935] A.C. 500.

[143] *Supra,* footnotes 3 and 5.

[144] See *Tooth* v. *Power*, [1891] A.C. 284, at p. 292.

[145] *Stuart* v. *Bank of Montreal* (1909), 41 S.C.R. 516.

[146] *Robins* v. *National Trust Co.*, [1927] A.C. 515; *London Street Tramways Co.* v. *London County Council*, [1898] A.C. 375.

never overruled any of its constitutional decisions although it has distinguished and explained a number of them, mainly in order to preserve consistency of interpretation.[147] In so doing it has pursued a concept of constitutional certainty from which it was not to be diverted by the profound social and economic changes that have taken place since its assumptions about Canadian federalism first took form in the late 19th century. In one of its last Canadian appeals, the *Margarine* case,[148] it gratuitously shut the door on the possibility of re-examining the federal general power, a possibility held out by the *Canada Temperance Federation* case.[149] It was, however, in the latter case that the Judicial Committee asserted that "on constitutional questions it must be seldom indeed that the Board would depart from a previous decision which it may be assumed will have been acted on both by governments and subjects."[150] The formal reasonableness of such a policy cannot hide the rigidity which it has produced and which has forced the Dominion and provinces into a search for makeshift expedients to escape its consequences.[151] It is, of course, well known that in the case of the Canadian Constitution the Privy Council has never recognized the temporary validity of its interpretations, founded, as they were, on impermanent social and economic considerations which it rarely articulated. Yet in a recent Australian constitutional appeal, the Judicial Committee made this revealing assertion:[152]

The problem to be solved will often be not so much legal as political, social or economic, yet it must be solved by a court of law, for where the dispute is, as here, not only between Commonwealth and citizen but between Commonwealth and intervening States on the one hand and citizens and States on the other, it is only the court that can decide the issue: It is vain to invoke the voice of Parliament.

[147] Cf. *P. A. T. A.* case, [1931] A.C. 310, at p. 326; *A.-G. Ont.* v. *Canada Temperance Federation*, [1946] A.C. 193.

[148] *Canadian Federation of Agriculture* v. *A.-G. Que.*, [1950] 4 D.L.R. 689.

[149] [1946] A.C. 193.

[150] *Ibid.*, at p. 206.

[151] See Gouin and Claxton, Legislative Expedients and Devices Adopted by the Dominion and the Provinces (Appendix 8 to Report of Royal Commission on Dominion-Provincial Relations, 1940).

[152] *Commonwealth of Australia* v. *Bank of N. S. W.*, [1950] A.C. 235, at p. 310.

This is equally true about problems of legislative authority under the B.N.A. Act even though the Privy Council has never expressly said so. Instead, it has sought to apply a legal logic, itself predicated on an accepted social pattern, and has continued to push that logic while seemingly disregarding the fact that its social underpinning has disappeared.

In non-constitutional cases, the Privy Council in *Robins* v. *National Trust Co.* deliberately subordinated itself to the House of Lords.[153] Although there was no necessary relation between the two bodies – one being essentially a court for the Dominions and colonies and the other a court for Great Britain – the British statutes governing the composition of the Privy Council and House of Lords made it practically impossible for a group of men in business suits to ignore their own decisions when dressed in gowns and wigs.[154] Now that appeals to the Privy Council from Canadian courts are abolished, what is the position of House of Lords' decisions? Were they binding on Canadian courts only through the connection of the Privy Council or did they have a force independent of that tribunal? Since the House of Lords, as such, was not part of the Canadian judicial hierarchy, its authority could be binding in Canada only through the link of the Privy Council or the dictate of a competent legislative authority. The link is now gone and the Parliament of Canada, the competent legislative authority, has directed that final appellate authority should reside in the Supreme Court of Canada.

It might be urged that a caveat should be entered because in *Stuart* v. *Bank of Montreal* in 1909, Anglin J., after speaking of the authority of Privy Council decisions, stated that "a decision of the House of Lords should likewise be respected and followed though inconsistent with a previous judgment of this court."[155] We are not told why, but it may be for the reasons just given after the reference to *Robins* v. *National Trust Co.*, or because of the inferior status of Canada in 1909 (an inferiority attaching to its courts as well) or simply because the Supreme Court felt that the House of Lords possessed a superior wisdom as the highest court in the mother-land of the common law. None of these reasons has any present-day validity. The Supreme Court

---

[153] See *supra*, footnote 146.
[154] See Appellate Jurisdiction Act, 1876 (Imp.), c. 59, s. 6; and see amendment of 1887 (Imp.), c. 70, and of 1913 (Imp.), c. 21.
[155] (1909), 41 S.C.R. 516, at p. 548.

is now by statute a final appellate court and this involves a responsibility which it alone must discharge. If it chooses to find help or inspiration in House of Lords decisions, it is open to it to turn to these decisions as it might turn for the same reasons to decisions of final courts in other common law or civil law countries.

Stuart v. *Bank of Montreal* is the case – the only case so far – where the Supreme Court reviewed and announced its attitude to *stare decisis* in respect of its own decisions. There had been dicta in earlier cases where judges of the Court asserted a freedom to reconsider views previously held.[156] But in *Stuart* v. *Bank of Montreal* it was categorically asserted that the Supreme Court is bound by its previous decisions save, as both Duff and Anglin JJ. declared, in very exceptional circumstances. Both judges considered the matter by analogizing the then intermediate position of the Supreme Court to that of the English Court of Appeal; and the latter's current line of decision on the matter was that it was bound by its previous decisions. Duff J. added, however, that "quite apart from this, there are . . . considerations of public convenience too obvious to require statement which make it our duty to apply this principle to the decisions of this court."[157] Several comments are in order. The Supreme Court could not have been expected to list the exceptional circumstances which would justify a departure from previous decisions where such decisions were deliberately made and were not the result of some slip or inadvertence. It was enough to leave open the door to a possible reversal of opinion. One can guess that the considerations of public convenience which Duff J. had in mind were the certainty and predictability of judicial decision and the reliance on them by the citizenry in their transactions and relationships. The "will of the wisp" nature of these considerations, even in the narrow range where *stare decisis* operates, when it operates at all, has been well analysed by others and need not be re-stated here.[158] And, finally, it is only right to point out that the analogy to the English Court of Appeal, even if still apt, would apply only to

[156] See the cases cited by Anglin J. in the *Stuart* case, 41 S.C.R. 516, at pp. 541-2.

[157] (1909), 41 S.C.R. 516, at p. 535.

[158] See Paton and Sawer, Ratio Decidendi and Obiter Dictum in Appellate Courts (1947), 63 L. Q. Rev. 461; Von Moschzisker, Stare Decisis in Courts of Last Resort (1924), 37 Harv. L. Rev. 409.

civil cases, since the English Court of Criminal Appeal has decided that it is not bound by its own decisions.[159]

The cardinal point today is, of course, that the Supreme Court is no longer an intermediate appellate court. Having regard to its present status, there are three ways in which its relation to *stare decisis* can be approached. First, the Supreme Court has succeeded to the position formerly occupied by the Privy Council and, like the latter, is not bound by its previous decisions. This view is quite artificial because it ignores the substantial reason why the Privy Council could not formally admit the application of *stare decisis*.[160] Secondly, the Supreme Court is now an ultimate court for Canada in the same sense as is the House of Lords for Great Britain, and hence like the latter it should continue to be bound by its own decisions. The analogy is imperfect because the House of Lords can afford the luxury of *stare decisis* knowing that Parliament can always supply the correctives for anachronistic rules when moved to do so. In constitutional matters at least, neither the Dominion nor the provinces can overcome ultimate decisions on the distribution of legislative power. Unless the ultimate court is prepared to reconsider outmoded views, we are left only with what has aptly been called "the heroic process of constitutional amendment."[161] The third approach is to adopt a simple rule of adult behaviour and to recognize that law must pay tribute to life; and that in constitutional litigation, especially, *stare decisis* cannot be accepted as an inflexible rule of conduct. It is hardly to the point to say that the House of Lords has proved that strict adherence to *stare decisis* can be a workable rule for an ultimate court.[162] The problems of a unitary state do not bear comparison with those of a federal system. An ultimate court under such a system must take its *stare decisis* diluted so as to be free, as the

---

[159] *Rex* v. *Taylor*, [1950] 2 All E. R. 170.

[160] The theory of the Privy Council as a body, not strictly a court, to advise His Majesty who must not be subjected to conflicting advice is today (and has been for long) just too romantic. The Privy Council itself no longer believes in this myth: see *A.-G. Ont.* v. *A.-G. Can.*, [1896] A.C. 348, at p. 370; *British Coal Corp.* v. *The King*, [1935] A.C. 500, at p. 511.

[161] Freund, On Understanding the Supreme Court, at p. 72.

[162] The House of Lords has been very circumspect in its obedience to its previous decisions. Even such notable decisions as *Donoghue* v. *Stevenson*, [1932] A.C. 562, do not, strictly speaking, represent a departure from previous views. Of course, comparatively few cases go to the House of Lords.

occasion warrants, to modify particular views. This has been the case in Australia where the High Court holds to the formal rule that it will follow its own decisions except where manifestly wrong.[163] The Supreme Court of the United States, on the other hand, has refused to accord to *stare decisis* anything more than a limited application in constitutional cases, taking the position that here (notwithstanding that there is a procedure for constitutional amendment) legislative correction is practically impossible. "The Court," said the late Mr. Justice Brandeis, "bows to the lessons of experience and the force of better reasoning, recognizing that the process of trial and error, so fruitful in the physical sciences, is appropriate also in the judicial function."[164] In non-constitutional cases, too, changes of opinion may well be warranted by the lessons of experience and the force of better reasoning. Despite the possibility of legislative correction, it may be difficult to achieve in a day and age when the trend is to legislate a general policy and not to bother with the minutiae of private relationships. Not only the pressure of time and events but good sense dictates that in the area of so-called private law the legislature should expect the Supreme Court to discharge a creative role of law-making through constant re-examination of previously accepted doctrine. It will suffice to refer to a recent judgment of Mr. Justice Jackson retreating from a position which he took when he was Attorney-General; he said, in *McGrath* v. *Kristensen*:[165]

Precedent, however, is not lacking for ways by which a Judge may recede from a prior opinion that has proven untenable and perhaps misled others. See Chief Justice Taney, License Cases, 5 How. 504, recanting views he had pressed upon the Court as Attorney-General of Maryland in Brown v. State of Maryland, 12 Wheat. 419. Baron Bramwell extricated himself from a somewhat similar embarrassment by saying, "The matter does not appear to me now as it appears to have appeared to me then." Andrew v. Styrap, 26 L.T.R. (N.S.) 704, 706. And Mr.

---

[163] See *Rex* v. *Commonwealth Court of Conciliation & Arbitration and Australian Tramways Employees' Association* (1914), 18 C.L.R. 54; and cf. Stone, A Government of Laws and Yet of Men, Being a Survey of Half a Century of the Australian Commerce Power (1950), 25 N.Y.U.L.Q. Rev. 451, at pp. 455 ff.

[164] *Burnet* v. *Coronado Oil & Gas Co.* (1932), 285 U.S. 393, at pp. 405 ff. See also *St. Joseph Stock Yards Co.* v. *U.S.* (1936), 298 U.S. 38, at p. 94.

[165] (1950), 71 Sup. Ct. 224, at p. 233.

Justice Story, accounting for his contradiction of his own former opinion, quite properly put the matter: "My own error, however, can furnish no ground for its being adopted by this Court. . . ." U.S. v. Gooding, 12 Wheat. 460, 478. If there are other ways of gracefully and good naturedly surrendering former views to a better considered position, I invoke them all.

Since, in my submission, the Supreme Court is now free to adopt its own canons of judicial behaviour, the question arises as to how it will deal with the accumulated body of Privy Council and House of Lords doctrine. Even if it should choose to pay homage to *Stuart* v. *Bank of Montreal*, what are Supreme Court decisions within the meaning of the rule in that case? Sensibly, it could hardly be said that decisions of the Supreme Court which were reversed are now automatically restored because of *stare decisis*. Further, since neither the Privy Council nor the House of Lords can dictate to the Supreme Court for the future, is the Court none the less going to hold itself bound by the decisions of those tribunals given in the past? At the best or worst, it can treat these decisions as its own, and we are thus back to our starting point, namely, whether the Supreme Court will continue to subscribe to *stare decisis* in respect of its own decisions.[166] There is also the subsidiary question of how ready

[166] The recent judgment of the Supreme Court in *Woods Manufacturing Co. Ltd.* v. *The King*, [1951] 2 D.L.R. 465, supports the suggestion that the Supreme Court will regard Privy Council decisions as governing decisions although subject to such interpretation or exposition as the Supreme Court may choose to give them. The case involved issues of valuation in expropriation proceedings and the seven-judge Supreme Court, speaking through Rinfret C.J.C., declared that the Exchequer Court had failed to apply the relevant law as declared by Privy Council decisions and followed by the Supreme Court. Rinfret C.J.C. concluded his judgment as follows: "It is fundamental to the due administration of justice that the authority of decisions be scrupulously respected by all courts upon which they are binding. Without this uniform and consistent adherence the administration of justice becomes disordered, the law becomes uncertain, and the confidence of the public in it is undermined. Nothing is more important than that the law as pronounced, including the interpretation by this Court of the decisions of the Judicial Committee, should be accepted and applied as our tradition requires; and even at the risk of that fallibility to which all judges are liable, we must maintain the complete integrity of relationship between the courts. If the rules in question are to be accorded any further examination or review, it must come either from this Court or from the Judicial Committee." It may be noted that since this case was commenced before the abolition of appeals, the Privy Council was still competent to entertain a further appeal.

it will be to break a three-fourths century habit of obedience and uncritical deference to English decisions, regardless of the removal of compulsion to that end.

It is worth remembering that for a final court consistency in decisions is merely a convenience and not a necessity. No one expects the Supreme Court to break out in a rash of reversals of previous holdings, even if it should formally dissociate itself from *stare decisis*. In my view, such a dissociation, whether formally expressed or not, is imperative if the Court is to develop a personality of its own. It has for too long been a captive court so that it is difficult, indeed, to ascribe any body of doctrine to it which is distinctively its own, save, perhaps, in the field of criminal law. What is required is the same free range of inquiry which animated the Court in the early days of its existence, especially in constitutional cases where it took its inspiration from Canadian sources. Empiricism not dogmatism, imagination rather than literalness, are the qualities through which the judges can give their Court the stamp of personality. In *Boucher* v. *The King*,[167] a recent case on sedition, the Supreme Court conceded the inconclusiveness of its reasoning after a first hearing by granting a re-hearing; and Mr. Justice Kerwin gave a welcome illustration of open-mindedness by modifying his conclusion about the case. In the result, an acquittal was directed rather than a new trial. Only the Court can tell us, by its conduct in the cases that lie ahead, whether this signalizes the spirit of its new status.

[167] (1950), 96 Can. C.C. 48; on rehearing, (1951), 99 Can. C.C. 1.

Legislative Power and The Supreme Court in the Fifties

THE HONOURABLE VINCENT C. MAC DONALD

[Editor's Note. Pages 5 to 9 of the original published lecture are omitted, along with the relevant footnotes. The omitted portion is purely preliminary to the main theme, consideration of which starts with the second part of the lecture, where the question of validity of statutes is examined.]

II

THE PROBLEM OF PREDICTION

It seems safe for me to assume that you students are fully aware of the provisions in Sections 91 and 92 of the Act of 1867 involved in the determination of the validity of a statute in a typical case and how, in general, those provisions allocate jurisdiction to make laws in relation to matters coming within this or that class of subject.

I shall not discuss the technique followed, or the tests applied, in the total process which leads to the conclusion of validity or otherwise – a difficult subject well explored by competent Canadian scholars, e.g., Laskin, Lederman and your own Professor Mundell.[1]

I do wish to remind you that this conclusion comes after a Court has first, scrutinized the statute in its entirety to discover its true nature and aspect and second, has ascertained (with or without the aid of authority) within which head of jurisdiction a statute of that type must fall.

Lectures delivered at the Osgoode Hall Law School, March, 1960. Published by Butterworth and Company (Canada) Ltd., 1961. By permission of the author and publisher.

[1] As to the illusion involved in such phrases as "pith and substance," see *Commonwealth of Australia* v. *Bank of New South Wales*, [1950] A.C. 235, at p. 311.

Every statute enacted in Canada runs the risk of subjection to this process. Some live a long time in honour, as the famous Lemieux Act, or in infamy, as the notorious Padlock Act, before being questioned and slain; others die early in life at the first challenge; others die aborning whilst still in the Bill stage, as did the Nova Scotia Bill respecting Delegation of Legislative Powers; and still others have been held *ultra vires*, on a Reference, whilst still in draft form. The unpredictability of such results confronts every lawyer called upon to draft Bills for enactment, or to give his opinion as to the validity of existing or proposed legislation.

Roscoe Pound said that the element of stability in any system stems from the practice of a known and uniform technique, and, as you know, the ordinary technique is one wherein courts apply the principles of past decisions as binding precedents for the determination of present cases – in accordance with the grade of authority of the courts concerned.

Varcoe tells us that up to 1954 the Privy Council had dealt with 120 cases relating to questions of validity and since then, the Supreme Court of Canada has dealt with about twenty-five cases of this kind.[2]

The art of the lawyer has been said to be that of predicting the decisions of the future from the principles of past decisions in reliance on the doctrine of *stare decisis*. But, as Justice Douglas has warned us in terms very applicable in constitutional cases: "The difficulty is to estimate what effect a slightly different shade of facts will have, and to predict the speed of the current in a changing stream of the law; [for] the predictions are, indeed, appraisals of a host of imponderables."[3]

Predictability of statutory validity in Canada is extremely difficult for three reasons:

1. The relatively small number of such decisions is a handicap. For though they have defined the area of certain heads of jurisdiction, and have enunciated various doctrines applicable to the process, there are many unexplored gaps. Moreover there have been many inconsistent statements of principle and definition and above all, the diverse trends of approach and decisions, manifested in various periods as to important issues, must be taken into account.

2. The truth is that *stare decisis* has little effect in such cases,

[2] Varcoe, Legislative Power in Canada, at p. 1 (Carswell Co., 1954).
[3] *Stare Decisis* (1949), 49 Columbia Law Review, at p. 737.

notwithstanding the usual parade of authorities, for illustrations abound of decisions being explained away or gradually eroded as authorities. Indeed, such is the nature of the process of validity that the ultimate Court is invested with great discretion in classifying the matter of statutes, and jurisdiction is so often conferred in vague and general terms, that the ultimate decision often presents a choice between alternatives of equal force.

3. These wide areas of discretion and choice are largely free from binding authority (except, perhaps, where the statute in question has been held valid before) and the ultimate decision depends, to an unusual extent, upon qualities personal to the judges of last resort. No judge is free from the influence of his own conception of the basis of our Federal system, of what has been called his "Ideal Constitution." Every judge has his own theory of his function, as requiring him to call the shots, in terms of whatever scrap of authority he can find, on the one hand, or permitting him to consider that freedom from exact authority entitles him to write into the law his own views of public policy, on the other hand. There are, of course, limits to the free exercise of such a discretion but they are imposed by way of professional self-restraint rather than by law. It was in the light of such considerations that Freund said: "The first requisite for one who sits in judgment on legislative acts is that he be a philosopher (able to see social and economic measures under the aspect of a wide perspective); but the second requisite is that he be not too philosophical, i.e., that he should absorb himself in the facts rather than in deductions from large and rigidly held abstractions."[4]

However put, the point is that predictability in respect of statutory validity is affected by the nature of the adjudicative process; by the extent to which judicial discretion enters into that process; and by the potential influence of the human equation. I venture to think that success in this field of law will come most surely to the lawyer who realizes how largely considerations of policy influence the exercise of a judicial discretion more independent than in other fields of law and who, in his opinions or in his arguments, attempts to gauge the extent to which the changing context of affairs will infiltrate into the minds of the judges, as material for future decision.

[4] Freund, Umpiring the Federal System (1954), 54 Columbia Law Review, at p. 561.

THE CASES ON VALIDITY

I propose now to run through the decisions of the Court in the fifties which involved determinations as to the validity of various types of statute, actual or proposed. For the sake of brevity, I shall refer to them, where possible, by a short title.

The list is long and may prove tedious; particularly as it covers cases which you have studied under various topics of your course. It is because they form, in their sum, but a small proportion of the aggregate number of precedents on the subject, that there is the danger that their significance may escape you. Unlike those which preceded them, these are the decisions of the ultimate Court of today; it is in these accumulating decisions of the Supreme Court, and in the judicial attitudes and techniques exhibited in them, that the seeds of future decisions by the Court are most immediately revealed. Moreover, it is in them that a special element of predictability resides; as indicating to what extent the Court is likely to look at the B.N.A. Act anew, or to look at it through spectacles tinted by eighty years of Privy Council decisions.

The decisions of the last decade are varied and complex, and present new aspects of old subjects as well as entirely new subjects created by new types of legislation. I can do no more than outline the nature and result of the cases, with occasional comment as to the things of significance in them, regarding them telescopically rather than microscopically.

In the third part of these lectures I shall discuss matters related to the functions of the Court as a constitutional expositor, and to its methods of adjudication. Before I embark on these topics, however, there is a point I wish to stress. It is that I was invited to give these lectures because for many years I taught Constitutional Law, and wrote upon it with great frequency. It so happens that I am now a Judge and, alas, a Judge of a Court which, officially, is inferior to the Court whose decisions and methods I wish to review. I must ask you to relieve me from the danger that an abiding sense of my judicial lowliness might so paralyse my critical faculties as to make me unworthy of this great occasion by regarding me rather as a teacher, speaking in a class-room to students, and to accord me that freedom of expression proper to one speaking in that great capacity.

a *Emergency and Transitional Powers*

In the *Wartime Leasehold Reference*, [1950] S.C.R. 124, the Court held that the Regulations, though dealing with matters normally within Provincial jurisdiction, had been validly made in time of war, and had remained validly in force thereafter, by virtue of statutes providing for an orderly transition to peacetime conditions.

This was a straight application of the doctrine of implied emergency powers as extending to the aftermath of war.[5]

In the *Canadian Wheat Board Case* (*Canadian Wheat Board v. Nolan et al.*, [1951] S.C.R. 81), the Court held invalid an Order-in-Council made under the National Emergency Transitional Powers Act of 1945 providing for the compulsory appropriation of title to certain barley, and its vesting in the Board at fixed prices. I refrain from discussion of this case as the Privy Council reversed the Court ([1952] 3 D.L.R. 433), in upholding the Order.[6]

b *Regulation of Motor Transport*

Similarly I merely note that the judgment of the Court in the *Winner Case* in 1951 (*Winner* v. *S.M.T. (Eastern) Ltd. and the Attorney-General of Canada*, [1951] S.C.R. 887), as to the validity of Provincial legislation regulating the interprovincial activities of an American bus company, was varied by the Privy Council ([1954] 3 All E.R. 177), which held that the company's undertaking could not be divided into phases, as the Supreme Court had held, but was one indivisible undertaking extending beyond the Province, and therefore solely within Dominion jurisdiction to regulate. It was conceded, however, that Provin-

---

[5] Some interesting things were said (1) as to the duty of the Court on such a Reference to rely on declarations in such statutes as to the continuing need for such controls; (2) as to its right to take judicial notice as to the continuance of economic disturbances; and (3) as to the Court's being confined on such a Reference to the material in the Order of Reference except, perhaps, where challenge is made on the ground of colourability, in which case resort to litigation rather than to References should be had. See also Murphy, The War Power of the Dominion (1952). 30 Canadian Bar Review 791.

[6] The Supreme Court decision did, however, evoke a good deal of discussion in the Canadian Bar Review, notably as to the use of legislative history in aid of interpretation; see Willis (1951), 29 Canadian Bar Review, 296; Kilgour, 30 *ibid*. 769; Davis, 31 *ibid*. 1; Milner, *ibid*. 228; Corry, 32 *ibid*. 624.

cial legislation for the regulation of highway traffic would apply to such an undertaking.

The case in the Supreme Court was notable for the enunciation by Rand, J., of a doctrine as to the inherent rights of citizenship as limiting Provincial jurisdiction, which he has subsequently elaborated in some of the civil liberties cases, viz., *Saumur* and *Birks Cases* (see p. 163, *post*).[7]

A remarkable result of the Privy Council judgment was the consequent enactment by Parliament of The Motor Vehicle Transport Act of 1954, designed to give Provincial licensing boards power to license extra-Provincial motor carriers operating in the Provinces, and to regulate their tolls and charges, etc., (subject to certain reserved powers) upon Provincial proclamations bringing the Act into force, as has been done by all Provinces save Quebec and Newfoundland. The Act thus represents an attempt to free Parliament from the necessity of exercising the very jurisdiction it had been found to possess in relation to extra-Provincial highway traffic. This expedient was one of delegation by Parliament to Provincially-appointed boards; and seemingly was based on the similar power of delegation upheld by the Court in 1952 in the *Potato Marketing Reference* (see p. 00, *post*) in relation to the regulation of marketing.

This reference to Delegation leads to the two cases on that subject decided by the Court in this period.

c *Delegation of Jurisdiction between Parliament and Legislatures*

The *Nova Scotia Delegation Reference*, [1951] S.C.R. 31, was a Reference of Questions as to the competence of the Province to enact measures referred to in a Bill, introduced into the Legislature of Nova Scotia in 1948. By this Bill the Legislature purported to authorize the delegation to Parliament of its authority to make laws in relation to stated matters within Provincial jurisdiction and to apply to the Province the provisions of any Dominion Act delegating to that Legislature certain powers possessed by Parliament, etc. The Supreme Court held that the Bill, if enacted, would not be valid since it contemplated delegation by Parliament of powers, exclusively vested

---

[7] See comments, McWhinney (1952), 30 Canadian Bar Review 832; Ballem, 32 *ibid*. 788; and Price, 16 University of Toronto Faculty of Law Review 16.

in it to the Legislature, and delegation to Parliament of powers, exclusively vested in Provincial Legislatures. The Court said that Parliament and each Provincial Legislature is a sovereign body possessed of exclusive jurisdiction to legislate with regard to the subject matters assigned to it and therefore, neither is capable of delegating to the other the powers with which it has been vested, nor is it capable of receiving from the other, the powers with which the other has been vested.[8]

As this is a recent and unanimous decision of the Court there is little value in comment upon it, except to note that it relates to an expedient which, carefully used, might have enabled escape from the concept of "water-tight compartments" as descriptive of legislative jurisdiction.

I may note that the idea of a constitutional amendment to enable such delegation to, and from, Parliament and the Legislatures found much favour with the Dominion-Provincial Conference of 1950, and it is not inconceivable that the future may produce such an amendment some day.

d *Delegation from Parliament to Provincial Boards in the Regulation of Marketing*

The *Potato Marketing Board Reference*, [1952] 2 S.C.R. 392, is remarkable in that it validates the technique of delegation of Dominion powers to a Provincially-created and controlled Board. The Privy Council, in drawing sharp lines between the exclusive powers of Parliament and Legislature, has frequently suggested each might legislate in such a way, as together to cover a topic of divided jurisdiction in the manner desired; but always with the reminder that in the "complementary" attempt neither must invade the field of the other.

The conventional position has been that the Dominion has jurisdiction to regulate interprovincial and external trade as and from the point of its external movement and the Provinces to regulate trade beginning and ending in the Province. In the thirties a great co-operative attempt was made when the Natural Products Marketing Act of Canada was designed to dovetail with Provincial Acts in respect of marketing. The scheme, however, failed because the Dominion Act, in addition to dealing

[8] See comments by F. R. Scott (1948), 26 Canadian Bar Review 984; Ballem (1951), 29 *ibid*. 79.

with foreign and interprovincial trade, also covered transactions completed entirely within a Province.[9]

In the *Potato Marketing Reference* another such co-operative attempt succeeded: for the Court upheld the device of a Provincial Act for the regulation of marketing in the Province setting up Marketing Boards to administer same and of a Dominion Act authorizing delegation to such a Provincial Board of the Dominion's power to regulate marketing outside the Province. In short, the Court held that the Dominion could delegate, and had validly delegated, its power in respect of the non-local aspects of marketing.

However tenuous may be the distinction between delegation by Parliament to Legislature or vice versa (held to be forbidden by the very nature of their powers), and delegation by Parliament to a Provincial Board of the right to exercise the jurisdiction of Parliament in respect of marketing, it must be admitted that the result is to get a degree of practical efficacy into the conjoint regulation of trade, heretofore regarded as impossible.[10]

e *The Regulation of Trade*

In two other cases the Court dealt with other aspects of trade regulation:

 i. In the *Farm Products Marketing Reference*, [1957] S.C.R. 198, the Court was faced with eight very detailed Questions as to the validity of parts of the Ontario Act in question, and of Orders and Regulations made under it, in relation to certain marketing schemes, declared to have been passed to provide for the regulation of the marketing of farm products within the Province, including the prohibition of such marketing, in whole or in part. The case relates chiefly to the limitations upon provincial marketing power as regards dealing with articles marketed in interprovincial or export trade, or in matters of interprovincial concern.

[9] Responding to the plea of counsel that there was great practical need for supporting such dovetailing legislation in relation to marketing, the Privy Council expressed its appreciation of this aim, but warned that though "satisfactory results for both can only be obtained by co-operation . . . it will not be achieved by either party leaving its own sphere and encroaching upon that of the other" (*Natural Products Marketing Case* (*A.G. for British Columbia* v. *A.G. for Canada*, [1937] A.C. 377)).

[10] Comment, Ballem (1952), 30 Canadian Bar Review 1050; and see Cowen, 31 *ibid*. 814, as to legislative co-operation in Australia.

It is impossible to summarize the six opinions expressed in sixty pages, with sundry qualifications on various points; but there is much exploration of the nature of the processes of trade itself, and how it may be regulated by unitary or co-operative action.[11]

ii. *Murphy* v. *C.P.R. and A.G. of Canada*, [1958] S.C.R. 626, involved the Canadian Wheat Board Act which purports to regulate the activities of producers of grain, railroads and elevators, in respect of the export of grain from a Province, by providing that all grain entering interprovincial or foreign trade must be purchased and marketed by the Board exclusively. The Act was held valid as a comprehensive scheme for the regulation of extra-Provincial trade and as prohibiting persons from buying grain grown by others in one Province for export to another.[12]

The decision was unanimous; it evoked a discussion by Rand, J., as to the contrast between the Federal systems of Australia and Canada.

These two recent cases, together with the *Potato Marketing Reference* of 1952, represent a maturing of opinion in the Supreme Court as to the processes of trade and the problems inherent in its regulation, marking a great advance from the negative approach of the Privy Council cases, and, it seems to me, constitute good ground for hope that precise limits will be found for dividing Provincial and Dominion powers, upon such a functional basis as will enable their practical exercise by each, or by both in co-operation.[13]

But it is to be noted that the delegation technique depends upon consent and is difficult to accomplish. In many matters regulation of trade by Canada or by a Province must be attempted by a solo effort; and until the limits of jurisdiction are more clearly plotted, the attempt to combine legal with practical considerations will remain difficult.

[11] There was also adjudication as to the invalidity of licence fees and their use to meet losses and equalize returns, as constituting indirect taxation, as to which see Laskin's article, Provincial Marketing Levies (1959), 13 University of Toronto Law Journal, 1.

[12] Held, further, the administrative expenses of the Board deductible from the return on sales by it, being mere service charges, are not custom duties which offend against the "free trade" principle of s. 121. (As to the validity of such deductions in terms of taxation powers, see Laskin, *op. cit.*).

[13] Cf. Laskin's note on the revival of the Trade and Commerce power (1959), 37 Canadian Bar Review 630.

f . *Miscellaneous*

i. The Mineral Taxation Act of Saskatchewan, imposing three varieties of taxation on the ownership of "minerals," was held *intra vires*, each tax being a direct tax on land, in *C.P.R.* v. *A.G. for Saskatchewan*, [1952] 2 S.C.R. 231.

ii. A provision of the Ontario Assessment Act imposing a tax on a person using Crown land in connection with his residence was held *intra vires* as a direct tax on that person, as distinct from a tax on the Crown lands, in *Phillips and Taylor* v. *Sault Ste. Marie*, [1954] S.C.R. 404.

iii. S. 198 of the Railway Act of Canada was held valid, as merely limiting the general power of a railway respecting the expropriation of land, by stipulating that minerals can only be acquired by express agreement of purchase in *A.G. of Canada* v. *C.P.R. and C.N.R.*, [1958] S.C.R. 285.

iv. An interprovincial oil pipeline, operated by a company subject to Federal control under s. 92 (10) (a), was held not subject to Provincial mechanics' lien legislation, involving the possibility of sale of that portion of the Federal undertaking within the county where the lien is declared to exist, in *Campbell-Bennett Ltd.* v. *Comstock Midwestern Ltd., et al.*, [1954] S.C.R. 207. *Semble*, the situation may be different where the work is one locally situate in a Province and passes into Dominion jurisdiction by declaration under s. 92 (10) (c); for it has been held, that in such case mechanics' lien legislation is applicable in *Re Perini* (1959), 15 D.L.R. 375.

v. The Moratorium Act of Saskatchewan was held *ultra vires* as invading the field of insolvency in *Can. Bankers Assn.* v. *A.G. for Saskatchewan*, [1956] S.C.R. 31.

vi. The Reciprocal Enforcement of Maintenance Orders Act of Ontario was upheld in *Attorney-General for Ontario* v. *Scott*, [1956] S.C.R. 137.[14]

g *Provincial Courts and Tribunals*

The Court made three incursions into the jungle-land of case-law which has arisen out of the interpretation of s. 96 as restricting Provincial power to create, or vest jurisdiction in, Provincial or municipal bodies, broadly conforming to the type of jurisdiction exercised by the Superior, District or County Courts before Union. This is a complex subject.

[14] See comment, Laskin (1956), 34 Canadian Bar Review 215.

In *Dupont* v. *Inglis*, [1958] S.C.R. 535, an amendment to the Ontario Mining Act creating a Mining Commissioner, and defining his jurisdiction so as to include a right of appeal from the Recorder, was held valid as being primarily legislation for the administration of Provincially-owned mining resources, from which the Superior Courts had been excluded before 1867 in preference to persons of practical competence.

In *Toronto* v. *Olympic Edward Recreation Club*, [1955] S.C.R. 454, the Court held that a Province cannot give a municipal assessment tribunal exclusive authority to determine the assessability of property to municipal taxation, or exclude the right of taxpayers to resort to the ordinary Courts.[15]

And in a very recent case, *A.G. for Ontario et al.* v. *Victoria Medical Bldg. Ltd.* (1960), 21 D.L.R. 97, the Court held invalid a section of the Ontario Mechanics' Lien Act purporting to transfer to the Master jurisdiction to try, and (subject to appeal) finally to dispose of mechanics' lien actions.

Perhaps this is a good place to remind you of the great burden which falls on the Provincial Courts of interpreting the decisions of the Supreme Court, and of applying them to diverse circumstances which have yet to reach the ultimate Court, and of the fact that both types of decision must be considered by the lawyer in his daily tasks.

h *Criminal Law*

The criminal law power was held to extend to a provision for the forfeiture of vehicles used in connection with a narcotic drug offence, whether or not owned by the offender, in *Industrial Acceptance Corp.* v. *The Queen*, [1953] 2 S.C.R. 273. Provincial slot machine legislation, also providing for confiscation, was held invalid as conflicting with the Criminal Code as to gaming in *Johnson* v. *A.G. of Alberta*, [1954] S.C.R. 127.[16]

A section of the Combines Act providing for the issuance of an Order prohibiting acts relating to conspiracy to lessen competition was held valid in *Goodyear Tire & Rubber Co.* v. *R.*, [1956] 2 S.C.R. 303. Provincial legislation for suspension of the licence of the driver of a motor vehicle refusing to give a breath sample in certain circumstances was held to be valid and not

---

[15] See Laskin, Municipal Tax Assessment and S. 96 (1955), 33 Canadian Bar Review 993.
[16] Cf. *De Ware* v. *Queen*, [1954] S.C.R. 182, where the Court divided on the issue of validity.

to be in conflict with provisions of the Criminal Code as to drunken and impaired driving, in the *Breathalizer Reference*, [1958] S.C.R. 608.[17]

A Quebec Act requiring the compulsory closing of stores on six Catholic Holy Days was held invalid as prohibitory legislation analogous to Sunday or religious observance laws in *Birks* v. *City of Montreal*, [1955] S.C.R. 799.[18] On the other hand, in the *Sunday Sport Reference* (1959), 19 D.L.R. 97, Provincial legislation authorizing Sunday sports was upheld as coming within an exception in the Lord's Day Act of Canada.

In *Switzman* v. *Elbing and A.G. of Quebec*, [1957] S.C.R. 285, the Court held invalid the so-called Padlock Act of Quebec which prohibited the use of any house to propagate Communism and enabled the Attorney-General to order the closing of any house used for such purposes. The chief ground was that the Act was in relation to criminal law. Certain of the Judges, however, found in it an attempt to control freedom of speech which, so far as it was essential to the democratic operation of parliamentary institutions in Canada, transcended Provincial power and fell within the sole control of Parliament; one, Abbott, J., was of opinion that curtailment of this right was beyond the power of Parliament as well.

Saumur v. *City of Quebec*, [1953] 2 S.C.R. 299, concerned the validity of a city by-law forbidding the distribution in the streets of the city of any book, pamphlet, etc., without having obtained the written permission of the Chief of Police. One of the members of Jehovah's Witnesses, having been convicted for distributing religious tracts, challenged the validity of the by-law. It was held, by a majority, that the prohibition in the by-law did not apply to members of Jehovah's Witnesses; but more important in terms of principle, four of the Judges, at least, were of the opinion that such a by-law could be valid if made under provincial authority. There is a wide diversity of opinion among writers as to the grounds upon which the individual Judges reached their conclusions, and as to the effect of the case as a whole upon the issues of freedom of speech and religion, and as to legislative competence to deal with them in those aspects. This case also illustrates the frequent difficulty of determining the *ratio* of a judgment as a whole and what great divergencies

---

[17] Cf. Article (1959), 2 Canadian Bar Journal 103.
[18] Comment by Brewin (1956), 34 Canadian Bar Review 81.

can exist in the matter of classifying a statute in terms of its true nature and aspect.

These two cases, together with certain others, have been hailed as going a long way towards the establishment of freedom of speech, of the press and of religion and as constituting, in a sense, a Bill of Rights, written into the Constitution by judicial decision, removing such subjects from legislative invasion.[19]

I do not feel I am free to discuss them in this aspect, except to note: (1) that they stem largely from dicta of Duff, J., in the *Alberta Press Reference*, [1938] S.C.R. 100, at pp. 132-5, as to the nature of Canadian federalism as inferred from the Preamble to the B.N.A. Act and the general structure of Canadian Government: (2) that because of recent changes in the Court, it is uncertain to what extent such far-ranging opinions, based upon the "fundamental postulates" of an "open society," or on some sort of natural law, will influence the Court in future.

I think it permissible to observe, however, that these two cases together illustrate to what lengths an unrestricted method of seriatim opinion-writing may lead, for they evoked fifteen opinions totalling 125 pages of text.

i *Collective Bargaining and Dominion Works etc.*

In *Reference re the Industrial Relations and Disputes Investigation Act of Canada*,[1955] S.C.R. 529, the Court upheld the validity of sections 1-53 of the Act dealing with labour relations, including collective bargaining, the prevention and conciliation of strikes, etc., as made applicable therein to employees "employed upon or in connection with the operation of any works, undertakings, or business that is within the legislative authority of the Parliament of Canada," including those connected with navigation and shipping, railways, ferries, aerodromes, works declared to be for the general advantage of Canada, etc. The Court also held that the application of such provisions will depend on the circumstances of particular cases.

The particular case presented in the other Question was of

[19] See Laskin, Our Civil Liberties (1955), 41 Queen's Quarterly 455; Scott, Civil Liberties and Canadian Federalism (Toronto 1959); The Symposium on the Bill of Rights contained in (1959), 37 Canadian Bar Review for March; Brewin, note (1957), 35 Canadian Bar Review 554; MacKay in Canadian Jurisprudence at pp. 293-300. (Carswell Co. 1958).

this character. It related to a stevedoring company engaged in Toronto in supplying stevedoring services for lines of ships plying regularly between Canadian and non-Canadian ports. In holding that its employee-employer relations were subject to Dominion rather than to the Provincial law, some important reservations were made, confining the application of the Dominion Act to stevedoring companies not engaged in local shipping, etc. Such is the generality of this decision that many specific cases and much wisdom will be required to pin-point the exact extent of its application. It has already led to a notable decision by McLennan, J., of the High Court in the *Pronto Case* (see p. 169, *post*) that the labour relations of mine owners and their employees engaged in any stage of the production and use of atomic energy in mines under federal control, are subject to exclusive regulation by Dominion legislation under the residuary clause, even where such mines are situate entirely within a Province.[20]

It will be appreciated that this decision involves a bifurcation of the general topic of labour relations. Moreover, it negates Provincial jurisdiction to deal with employees engaged upon Dominion "works and undertakings" extending beyond a province or which are the subject of a declaration, or engaged in shipping, aerodromes, radio activities, etc. This is a large subtraction from the area of Provincial control and it may grow wider as particular industries and firms are brought within the scope of the Act. Accordingly it appears that the Court has taken a truly gigantic step from the conclusions of the Privy Council in *Snider's Case* in 1925 (*Toronto Electric Comrs.* v. *Snider*, [1925] A.C. 396). It will be interesting to see what will result from this bifurcation of such a generic topic, and the duplication of legislation and functionaries which it entails; and whether the difficulties of divided control will prompt the use of expedients by way of delegation, such as have occurred recently in the realms of marketing and motor-carriers.[21]

Meanwhile it may not be amiss to recall what was said with reference to the C.P.R. by Lord Watson in the *Bonsecours Case* (*C.P.R.* v. *Notre Dame de Bonsecours Corpn.*, [1899] A.C. at p.

[20] Comment, Laskin, 35 Canadian Bar Review 101; see also *Underwater Gas Developers Ltd.* v. *Ontario Labour Relations Board* (1960), 21 D.L.R. 345, Smily, J.

[21] For an interesting review of the present situation see F. R. Scott, Federal Jurisdiction over Labour Relations, (1960), 6 McGill Law Journal 153.

372), that the B.N.A. Act "whilst it gives the legislative control of the appellant's railway, qua railway, to the Parliament of Canada, does not declare that the railway shall cease to be part of the provinces in which it is situate, or that it shall, in other respects, be exempted from the jurisdiction of the provincial legislatures." Since then the subjection of railways and other extra-provincial works and undertakings to various types of provincial law has been recognized in other cases, such as *Workmen's Compensation Board* v. *C.P.R.*, [1920] A.C. 184, the *Winner* (see p. 156, *ante*) and the *Industrial Relations Cases* (see p. 164, *ante*). Accordingly you must not conclude that such extra-provincial works or undertakings are within Dominion jurisdiction in all respects as if they constitute enclaves or foreign territories within the Provinces, such as Embassies, whereas they should be regarded rather as similar to that small plot of soil within Edinburgh Castle which ranks as part of Nova Scotia for very special purposes.

j Aeronautics

In *Johannesson* v. *West St. Paul*, [1952] 1 S.C.R. 292, it was held that a provincial statute (and a by-law thereunder), authorizing a municipality to pass by-laws for the licensing and prohibition of the erection of aerodromes, were *ultra vires*.

It had been held by the Privy Council in the *Aeronautics Reference,* [1932] A.C. 54, that a Convention relating to aerial navigation made by "the British Empire" empowered Canada under s. 132 of the B.N.A. Act to enact legislation for performance of its obligations thereunder. Lord Sankey, having relied on s. 132, referred to "a small portion of the field" of aeronautics not covered by the specific heads of s. 91 or s. 92, and went on to say that "their Lordships are influenced by the facts that the subject of aerial navigation and the fulfilment of Canadian obligations under s. 132, are matters of national importance; and that aerial navigation is a class of subject which has attained such dimensions as to affect the body politic of the Dominion."[22]

In the *Labour Conventions Reference,* [1937] A.C. 326, the

---

[22] This was an obvious reference to a doctrine enunciated by Lord Watson in the *Local Prohibition Case* of 1896 (*A.G. for Ontario* v. *A.G. for the Dominion*, [1896] A.C. 348) which formed one of the "four propositions" stated in the *B.C. Canneries Case* of 1930 (*A.G. for Canada* v. *A.G. for British Columbia*, [1930] A.C. 111), and which Lord Sankey had quoted a few pages before.

Privy Council invalidated several Dominion Acts passed for the performance of certain Labour Conventions, the subject matter of which lay in the Provincial field. In doing so it emphatically rejected (as it also did in the *Employment and Social Insurance Reference*, [1937] A.C. 405) the proposition that legislation might come under the Residuary Clause if concerned with matters of such general importance as to have "ceased to be merely local or provincial" and have "become matter of national concern."[23]

In the *Johannesson Case* the Court was faced with municipal-provincial legislation zoning and restricting aerodromes – a matter also covered by the Aeronautics Act (and by an Aviation Convention outside the scope of s. 132). The Judges anxiously dwelt on Lord Sankey's words (in the *Aeronautics Case*) as implying a judgment, or at least an opinion, that aeronautics fell under the Residuary Clause as a matter of national importance. They stressed also a dictum of Lord Simon in the *Canada Temperance Case* of 1946 (*A.-G. for Ontario* v. *Canada Temperance Federation*, [1946] A.C. 193), that if a matter of legislation "must from its inherent nature be the concern of the Dominion as a whole, then it will fall within the competence of the Dominion Parliament as a matter affecting the peace, order and good government of Canada."[24]

Paying scant attention to the fact that "national importance" had been rejected twice in 1937, the Judges carefully pieced together the dicta in the *Aeronautics* and *Canada Temperance References*, and concluded that the municipal-provincial zoning of aerodromes could not stand against the Aeronautics Act of Canada which dealt with a matter – aeronautics – which as such lies outside s. 92 and falls within the Residuary Clause as a matter of national importance.

No one can doubt that as a matter of notorious fact aeronautics is a matter of national concern. The difficulty lies in the

---

23 Holding that Lord Watson's words had "laid down no principle of Constitutional Law," an opinion endorsed in *The Empress Hotel Case* (*C.P.R.* v. *A.G. for British Columbia and A.G. for Canada*, [1950] A.C. 122, at pp. 138-40).
24 The force of this dictum was badly impaired in the *Dairy Industry Act Case*, [1951] A.C. 179, wherein the Privy Council expressly limited Lord Simon's words by reference to those of Lord Atkin in the *Labour Conventions Case* in the passage in which he rejected Lord Watson's proposition as to "national importance." However, the former case, decided on Oct. 16, 1951, was not available when the *Johannesson Case* was decided on Oct. 12, 1951.

doubt which the chain of reasoning raises as to how far we may consider that the Residuary Clause now applies to similar topics of demonstrable national importance, and which, unlike those covered by the Aeronautics Act, may normally lie within Provincial jurisdiction.[25]

Moreover in estimating its future influence, regard must be had to the fact that the Dominion legislation involved had been held valid previously by the Privy Council. This was a fact of which the Court must have been very conscious at that early stage of its new-found freedom; that is probably why it felt constrained to dress up its conclusion in an attire of precedent, however tenuous, rather than to decide the issue starkly in terms of principle.

Meanwhile this sphinx-like case holds out some hope for the future application of the doctrine of "aspects" of the Residuary Clause so that Parliament may have overriding power to legislate in relation to the national aspects of matters otherwise within Provincial classes of subjects, and which though not affected with the urgency of emergency have nevertheless become "matters of national concern."[26]

III

It seems fitting to conclude with some examination of the methods whereby our final court reached and set forth its conclusions, together with some reflections upon the functions of such a court in this area of its jurisdiction, and its future.

METHODS OF ADJUDICATION

In proceeding to a closer look at the content and form of the opinions which make up the judgments under consideration, I remind you of the old axiom that "a Court must decide and, having decided, is then given over to criticism."

The Court disposed of the 24 cases under review in 108 written opinions aggregating 675 pages of text, or an average of 4½ opinions and 28 pages per case. In the 13 cases of unanimity

---

[25] Cf. Szablowski, Creation and Implementation of Treaties in Canada (1956), 34 Canadian Bar Review, at pp. 52-55.

[26] Such considerations have already produced an interesting decision whereby the control of atomic energy has been assigned to the Residuary Clause by an Ontario Judge; *Pronto Uranium Mines Ltd.* v. *Ontario Labour Relations Board*, [1956] O.R. 862.

the Justices wrote an average of 3 opinions, averaging 17 pages of text; in only 2 of these cases – both of minor importance – was there a single Court-opinion. In terms of numbers of Judges the full Court sat in 8 cases, 8 Judges sat in 4 cases, 7 in 8 cases, and 6 sat in 4 cases. It is only fair to note that the later cases show a reduction in the number of opinions and of pages.

As other commentators have noted, the opinions as a whole present the picture of having been written in complete or partial isolation. It appears desirable in this class of case that the Court should establish, or more closely adhere to, an official procedure providing for conferences of all the Justices, at intervals during the writing stage, designed to secure whatever measure of uniformity is possible among the Judges as a whole, or within the several groups into which the Court seems likely to divide; and, still later, to see to what extent individual views may find expression in one Opinion satisfactory to the Court, or to the majority, or to the dissenting group, as the case may be.

These are not mere counsels of perfection as to form. The present practice makes it very difficult for even an acute lawyer to estimate the net effect of the several Opinions which reach the same result (particularly where a Justice concurs in two Opinions which are far from identical in their reasoning), for often there is no clearly articulated common ground to which the majority or dissenting Opinions, as such, can be related.[27]

Accordingly it seems to me that the Court as a whole should accept as one of its greater functions the duty to make explicit the *ratio* of every decision, whether it be a majority or an unanimous decision. Whatever leeway should be extended to Justices to dissent, in solitude or in groups, on varying grounds, there is a special responsibility on those writing the several Opinions which in sum constitute the judgment of the Court, to proceed, if possible, to the common conclusion by reasoning which has a common basis in principle, and which is more patent than tacit.

I do not for a moment contend for an integrated unitary Opinion such as characterizes Privy Council decisions for, as

[27] This is indicated by the number of decisions in which the headnote having stated that the Court "held" a statute valid or invalid (or answered a Question in a Reference in the affirmative or negative), proceeds to summarize the Opinions of particular Justices or groups of Justices, thus contenting itself with providing materials from which the *ratio* of the decision is left to be pieced together by the reader.

we have learned, under a guise of unanimity these may mask an actuality of hidden dissent among its members.[28]

I do suggest that the operative Opinions should manifest explicitly the ground upon which the Court decided, no matter how restricted that common ground may be. This is of crucial importance; for in every such case the Court (in addition to disposing of it as regards the litigants, or answering Questions on a Reference) is making a precedent – upon the true principle of which citizens, governments and lawyers will predicate their future conduct in matters of moment. Moreover, since dissents often contain the seeds of future trends in the law, there is a similar duty resting on Judges writing a plurality of dissenting Opinions to explore the possibility of putting their dissents explicitly upon a common ground, if possible, so that together they may represent some degree of unified opposition to the majority view, rather than individual sniping at that view for a diversity of reasons.[29]

In any event the Court might well exemplify the policy of the Privy Council, early avowed and often restated, that in passing on questions of validity involving the B.N.A. Act "it will be a wise course . . . to decide each case which arises . . . without entering more largely upon an interpretation of the statute than is necessary for the decision of the particular question in hand" (*Citizens Insurance Co. of Canada* v. *Parsons, Queen Insurance Co.* v. *Parsons* (1881), 7 A.C. 96, at p. 109) "the object as far as possible [being] to prevent too rigid declarations of the Courts from interfering with such elasticity as is given in the written constitution" (*The Combines Investigation Act Case* (*Proprietary Articles Trade Assocn.* v. *A.-G. for Canada*, [1931] A.C. 310, at p. 317)). The Privy Council often disregarded these cautionary precepts to the detriment of that orderly elucidation of the law which results from gradual clarification of terms, as new cases present new aspects of meaning, rather than from great advances marked by subsequent retreats or enervating "explanations."

Of course there are occasions when a Court must forsake Judicial Caution and exemplify Judicial Valour as these antitheses were explained by Sir Frederick Pollock in a memorable essay.

[28] Cf. Lord Wright's disclosures in (1935), 33 Canadian Bar Review 123, and comments thereon 34 *ibid*. at pp. 114-17, 243.

[29] See generally McWhinney, Judicial Concurrences and Dissents (1953), 31 Canadian Bar Review 595; and Friedmann, 31 *ibid*. at p. 749.

Indeed, when to adopt one attitude rather than the other is a perennial problem of the judicial art, beautifully described in these words:

> The most delicate of the problems of judicial craftsmanship is no doubt that of determining when it is wise to decide a matter on the narrowest possible basis and when it is both legitimate and salutary to grasp the opportunity to formulate general principles in the hope that they may have an influence extending far beyond the immediate case. Every great judge from Coke and Marshall to our own day has been confronted with the dilemma and dilemma it will necessarily remain in every successive case in which the problem arises. The skill with which the dilemma is resolved is perhaps the ultimate test of both judicial craftsmanship and judicial statesmanship.[30]

References

One-third of the cases of the decade (including some of the most important) came to the court as References of Questions submitted by the Executive. These have ranged from questions as to the validity of legislation already in force or in progress through a Legislature, to abstract questions relating to legislative power as such, without reference to any text. Some were very detailed as to specific provisions or situations and often the Terms of Reference stated the factual background from which they arose or recited matters of government opinion.

In many of the cases the Judges obviously felt embarrassed by the Terms of Reference or the matters recited therein and above all, by the absence of such concrete evidence as would be before them in ordinary litigation. It is clear that constitutional validity depends largely upon the actual or contemplated effect of legislation upon the relevant context of affairs; and yet the required Answers must be made in large ignorance of the facts on which the legislation operates, or legislation consequent on those Answers will operate.

It is not surprising that Answers based so largely on speculation, rather than experience, have often been conceptual in nature, or couched in such terms of assumption or qualification

---

[30] C. Wilfred Jenks, Craftsmanship in International Law (1956), 50 American Journal of International Law 32, at pp. 59-60.

as to destroy much of their value as authorities.[31] Yet authorities they remain in fact however limited in theory; for it is difficult for a Court to recede from solemn pronouncements so made.[32] All these considerations have their echoes in the References of this decade, and they recall various expressions of judicial aversion to this type of case, particularly where abstract Questions are concerned.[33]

This type of adjudication has also the disadvantage of requiring immediate declarations as to conclusions normally reached by gradual stages of evolution in relation to specific fact-situations. It may well be that in the matter of statutory validity "deliberate speed" is preferable to "majestic instancy." It would conduce to the orderly development of the law if this procedure should be restricted, in practice, to Questions arising from the text of an Act or draft Bill.

THE EDUCATIONAL ROLE OF THE COURT

It is well recognized that the ultimate court in a Federal system plays two roles in relation to public opinion. It is first the institutional symbol of balance in the national life, the instrument which seeks to preserve unity in the system of diversity of interest and legal power involved in Federalism. Secondly, its deliverances help to educate the public mind as to the historic purposes of the Constitution, and the principles applied in the determination of great internal issues. Our Court will discharge these functions best when it speaks unanimously as a Court, or substantially so, and when its decision is so expressed as to make explicit, in terms easily understood, the principle leading to its result, and the relation of that principle to the Constitution itself. Its corporate influence is diminished by the degree of minority dissent and whenever the principles are not integrated into a governing court or majority opinion and thus, have to be gathered from a plexus of individual opinions. Moreover, this educational and symbolic effect is dissipated also, to the extent that the governing opinion, or opinions, do not embody careful

[31] Compare, e.g. the Questions submitted in the *Farm Products Marketing Reference*, [1957] S.C.R. 198, at p. 221, with the Answers made thereto.

[32] Rubin, The Nature, Use and Effect of Reference Cases (1960), 6 McGill Law Journal at pp. 175-80.

[33] See Rinfret, J., in the *Wartime Leasehold Reference*, [1950] S.C.R. 124, at p. 126ff.; Davidson (1938), 3 University of Toronto Law Journal, at p. 275; LaBrie (1950), 8 *ibid*, at pp. 347-51.

craftsmanship in the statement of issues and principles. Accordingly, there are compelling reasons why the Court should strive for whatever unity of view is possible, and against obscurity of statement.[34]

It is of some importance, in my view, that constitutional decisions should not emanate from a faceless court but from one whose members are known to the public. In an article written in 1952 the Associate Editor of The Ottawa Journal remarked that "now that the Supreme Court is all powerful . . . it is advisable that Canadians learn something about it; [for] up to now it has been an unknown, and the Chief Justice himself could probably not be named by one-twentieth of the people of Canada." It seems a good bet to say that relatively few lawyers could recite the names of the majority of its present members. In the United States the Justices do not enjoy or suffer from a similar anonymity in public discussion but even there a book, *Mr. Justice*, has recently been written concerning a group of its Justices, for the avowed purpose of "rescuing the Court from the limbo of impersonality."[35]

In my view it would be a gain if members of the Court should write in terms more commonly intelligible and thus more likely to evoke a degree of public recognition, commensurate with their importance in our national affairs.

THE COURT AS UMPIRE OF THE FEDERAL SYSTEM

It is the prime function of the final Court to keep the exercise of legislative powers by Parliament or Legislatures within the limits marked out for them. For that purpose it must interpret the heads of jurisdiction relevant to each exercise of asserted legislative power in reaching its conclusion of validity or invalidity. A Constitution consists of two things: the words in which legislative powers were distributed, and the purpose and philosophy of the document as a whole, as enshrining the original concept of the kind of government envisaged for the future.

[34] See Zo Bell, Division of Opinion in the Supreme Court (1959), 44 Cornell Law Quarterly, 186; Blaustein & Field, Overruling Opinions in the Supreme Court (1958), 57 Michigan Law Review, 151.

[35] Freund attributes the lack of identification of our own Supreme Court Justices in the public mind as deriving from our method of "treating constitutional issues as mere matters of statutory construction not lending themselves to the exposition of a philosophy" or from "the unfocussed nature of seriatim opinions" (A Supreme Court in a Federation (1953), 53 Columbia Law Review 597).

Implicit in any Constitution, in my opinion, is the idea of continuous review by the court of the terms of the Constitution, and their adaptation to developing needs and curcumstances as they present themselves in the cases which arise for decisions; an attitude made imperative by the difficulty of the amending process in Canada.

A perennial difficulty is that the Constitution was penned in terms expressive of the ideas and desiderata of an age long gone and the Courts often must face the task of reading the words so as to encompass developments unforeseen by their authors. This is never too hard when these are in the nature of new physical phenomena, or come slowly. When, however, as in Canada, there arise new and rapid developments in matters social and economic, and in the formation of new concepts of government as to finance and social welfare (to say nothing of the new state of affairs incident to impending nuclear horrors), the Courts are faced by a revolutionary change in the environment to which the old words must be applied. Experience has proved to us that such a pattern of fact and opinion cannot be ignored in favour of a literalistic interpretation of a sacred text; but, on the contrary, must be admitted as data of decision in keeping the Constitution adapted to the conditions and needs of the day, and to allow the several Legislatures room to experiment in their regulation.

This does not imply that the Courts must become dedicated to the promotion of their own views of what is proper or expedient, for that area of policy belongs to the Legislators. Nor does it mean that they should remould the Constitution into something alien from its basic purpose and underlying philosophy. On the contrary, it is their function to maintain that purpose and philosophy in stability, to maintain the dichotomy of powers in the same relative position in a world of movement, as existed in the world of its original conception.[36] This does involve some element of judicial policy but if marked by due restraint is merely the exercise of that degree of discretion proper to all constitutional interpretation. In a word, the Courts must allow the facts of modern life to enter into their formulations as materials of decision, in order that the Constitution of 1867 shall aid rather than shackle the legislative solution of the

[36] Cf. generally, ten Brock (1939), 27 California Law Review 399.

problems of today.[37] For, as Frankfurter has wisely said, "The Constitution cannot be applied in disregard to the external circumstances in which men live, and move, and have their being" (*Martin* v. *Struthers* (1943), 319 U.S. 141).

The Supreme Court is no longer bound to adopt Privy Council pronouncements as the premises of its own reasoning, and we must recognize that future results of its deliberations will depend, alike, upon its attitude of approach to the B.N.A. Act, and to those pronouncements. The score or so of decisions in the last decade provide reasonable evidence of an intention to adopt a policy of gradual adaptation of Privy Council decisions and doctrines. I venture to think that the Court, in time, will prove itself to be as free of that ghostly influence in fact as it is in law and that it will re-work its way through the precedents of its predecessor in such a way as gradually to make the Constitution as well adapted to the twentieth century as it was to the conditions which gave it birth.

That is the view of Rand, J. (who has recently bereaved us all by departing from the Court he has served so well), as expressed in the *Farm Marketing Products Reference*, [1957] S.C.R. 198, at p. 212:

The powers of this Court in the exercise of its jurisdiction are no less in scope than those formerly exercised in relation to Canada by the Judicial Committee. From time to time the Committee has modified the language used by it in the attribution of legislation to the various heads of ss. 91 and 92, and in its general interpretative formulations; and that incident of judicial power must, now, in the same manner and with the same authority, wherever deemed necessary, be exercised in revising or restating those formulations that have come down to us. This is a function inseparable from constitutional decision. It involves no departure from the basic principles of jurisdictional distribution; it is rather a refinement of interpretation in application to the particularized and evolving features and aspects of matters, which the expansion of the life of the country inevitably presents.[38]

---

[37] Cf. MacDonald, Constitution in a Changing World (1948), 26 Canadian Bar Review 21; and The Privy Council and the Canadian Constitution (1948), 29 *ibid*, 1021.

[38] See Joanes, *Stare Decisis* in the Supreme Court of Canada (1958), 36 Canadian Bar Review 215.

If this passage were to be adopted by the Court as an official axiom of approach to Privy Council decisions and if it were extended to comprehend a willingness to correct error in its own formulations and decisions as such error becomes manifest, we should be able to face the future with even greater confidence in our final court, as one which "bows to the lessons of experience and the force of better reasoning" (*Burnet* v. *Coranado Oil & Gas Co.* (1932), 285 U.S. 393 per Brandeis, J.).

Meanwhile I venture to assert that the record of the Court, in its first decade of freedom, goes far to vindicate Edward Blake's high estimate of the value of a Canadian Court of last resort, as one possessing "the daily learning and experience which Canadians, living under the Canadian Constitution, acquire . . . and which can be given only by residence upon the spot." At all events I trust you will agree that the record has been one of very high achievement indeed.

PART THREE

THE PROCESS

OF INTERPRETATION

Classification of Laws and the British North America Act

W. R. LEDERMAN

The heart of Canada's federal constitution is the distribution of legislative powers that is made by the British North America Act[1] between the central Parliament on the one hand and the provincial legislatures on the other. Laws, both actual and potential, have been separated into certain classes and those classes respectively assigned either to the central or to the provincial authority. Thus the law-making powers of Parliament are confined to the classes of laws allotted to it, and likewise with the various provincial legislatures. Accordingly, when a provision of the pre-Confederation law is to be altered or when a new law of some kind is proposed, the law or proposed law in question must be classified to determine which authority has power to alter it, in the former instance, or to enact it, in the latter. If our federal constitution is to endure and to work tolerably, this task of interpretation is plainly an exclusive judicial function and requires the services of independent tribunals of the first rank. "It is of the essence of the Canadian constitution that the determination of the legislative powers of the Dominion and of provinces respectively shall not be withdrawn from the judiciary."[2]

From: *Legal Essays in Honour of Arthur Moxon*, University of Toronto Press, 1953. By permission of the author and publisher.

[1] The British North America Act, 1867, 30 Vict., c. 3.
[2] *Ottawa Valley Power Co.* v. *A.G. for Ontario*, [1936] 4 D.L.R. 594 at p. 603.

It is clear then that this task rests upon our courts, in particular now upon the Supreme Court of Canada, but it is not quite so clear that the task is as difficult as it is important. Indeed, the thesis of this essay is that the processes of classification concerned involve inevitable complexities which too often are only vaguely appreciated even in professional circles. First then, the nature of the process of classification in general will be examined. It will be found, for instance, that a basic distinction must be made between the classification of facts on the one hand, and the classification of laws on the other. Then the attempt will be made in the light of this general analysis to criticize and restate the accepted doctrine for interpretation of the B.N.A. Act.

GENERAL CONSIDERATIONS ON CLASSIFICATION

Since we are to be concerned with divisions of the power to make or alter rules of law in the country, our first step must be to analyse carefully the nature of an ordinary rule of law. We have to examine the relation of a given particular rule to concrete facts on the one hand, and the grouping of such rules by systems for classification of them on the other. Certain basic considerations of analytical jurisprudence must be our first concern, and their nature is well described by Sir Frederick Pollock in a passage in which he clearly differentiates classification of laws from classification of facts:

It is not possible to make any clear-cut division of the subject-matter of legal rules. The same facts are often the subject of two or more distinct rules, and give rise at the same time to distinct and different sets of duties and rights. The divisions of law, as we are in the habit of elliptically naming them, are in truth divisions not of facts but of rules; or, if we like to say so, of the legal aspect of facts. Legal rules are the lawyer's measures for reducing the world of human action to manageable items, and singling out what has to be dealt with for the time being, in the same way as number and numerical standards enable us to reduce the continuous and ever-changing world of matter and motion to portions which can be considered apart.[3]

By enlarging upon the last sentence of this quotation for the

[3] Sir F. Pollock, *A First Book of Jurisprudence* (2nd ed., London, 1904).

moment, more light can be shed on the nature of the legal classifications of facts. Rules of law as we know them are precepts of human conduct employed as a means of social control in a politically mature community. They must deal with such non-legal realities or facts as persons, things, conduct, and states of mind. They operate by discriminating between different kinds of persons and things, different kinds of conduct and states of mind, for purposes of defining the entitlement of the persons concerned to certain legal rights, privileges, powers, or immunities. Laws then must contain notional categories of facts, and must prescribe the criteria to be used in differentiating facts in order to define or establish these classes of them for legal purposes. For example, it is a natural fact that John Smith has passed his twenty-first birthday anniversary, but it is our law of contract which prescribes that before he does so he has no capacity to bind himself by a contract of loan and that after-wards this power does attach to him. It is the law which invests the attaining of age twenty-one with this significance; the fact of reaching that age is in itself legally quite neutral. . . .

[Editor's Note: Pages 185 to 189 of the original essay are omitted here, along with the relevant footnotes, numbered 4 to 8 inclusive. The omitted portion is concerned in detail with the process of classifying facts involved in applying ordinary laws to real-life situations. For example, the law prescribes that a person is forbidden to drive a car with wanton or reckless disregard for the lives or safety of other persons, with severe penalties for breach. To determine that John Smith in particular circumstances was driving in this way is to classify those particular facts as relevant to the rule – that is, as a valid particular instance of the general category "driving with wanton or reckless disregard." But this process of classifying facts is not to be confused with the process of classifying laws themselves as of one kind or another. You are calling for a different process of classification if you ask whether the above rule against dangerous driving is criminal law or property law or motor vehicle law.]

Let us turn now by way of contrast to a general consideration of the classification of rules of law. Of course, classification itself as a basic procedure does not alter. It is simply the arrangement into distinct classes of an undifferentiated mass of data by criteria which take account of various attributes inherent in the things concerned. However, as rules of law and concrete facts

are different orders of things, obviously the criteria of classification are different depending on whether facts or laws are the
subject-matter being classified. Rules of law attach prescribed
rights and duties to some hypothetical condition or state of facts
(here called a fact-category) and are thus norms, principles, or
standards. They are concerned with the "ought" of human
conduct, with what *should be* and not merely what *is*. The fact-
categories they contain, while no doubt suggested by certain
real-life situations, past, present, or anticipated, are nevertheless
independent of actual facts. The legal fact-category is thus
notional, and can exist even though concrete facts relevant to
it have never occurred but are merely anticipated. There must
be many examples of this in the statutes, in the dicta of judges,
and in the speculations of jurists. This being so, it is proper and
essential to distinguish the classification of laws as a different
process from that of the classification of facts.[9]

Legal rules, then, considered in isolation from concrete
facts, may be grouped in various classes by criteria which
select uniform features of the concepts they contain, including
the rights and duties they prescribe. As Dr. Martin Wolff
puts it, "Classification may be compared with the mathematical
process of placing a factor common to several numbers outside
the bracket."[10] Thus rules of law may be classified (1) on the
basis of some uniform feature of their fact-categories (that
is the classes of persons, things, conduct, or intentions they
contain); or (2) on the basis of some uniform features of the
legal results they prescribe (that is the rights and duties they
specify). For example, for purposes of the Canadian constitution we find that the class "criminal law" is defined as including
all rules which in pith and substance *forbid* any conduct in the
public interest.[11] Hence the criterion of this class is the pro-
hibitive features common to the legal prescriptions of the rules
so grouped. The type of conduct thus prohibited might be any
sin of omission or commission. However, more often than not
the groupings of rules in classes depends cumulatively on

---

[9] "In value judgments there are always some individual words that are
referential, but the statement as a whole does not purport to state
past, present, or future reality." Dr. Glanville Williams, "Language
and the Law: IV" in (1945) 61 *Law Quarterly Review* 384 at p. 395.
By "referential" is meant "descriptive of fact."

[10] M. Wolff, *Private International Law* (Oxford, 1945), p. 148.

[11] *A.G. for British Columbia* v. *A.G. for Canada*, [1937] A.C. 368 at
p. 375.

several criteria. For instance, certain rules are grouped as rules for the sale of goods because (i) their fact-categories are limited to tangible movable things, and (ii) their legal prescriptions concern only the transfer for money of the bundle of legal rights and privileges which make up "ownership" of such things.

Clearly, then, legal rules can be classified by a great number of criteria for any number of purposes. There is no one universal system of classification of laws valid for all purposes, though there have been several attempts by jurists to outline systems for which this claim is made. (The schemes of Professor Holland and Albert Kocourek might be cited as examples.) However, the true view is that systems of classification will be as various as the purposes which classification may be used to serve. In the words of Dean Roscoe Pound: "Classification is not an end. Legal precepts are classified in order to make the materials of the legal system effective for the ends of law."[12] The history of the categories "realty" and "personalty" in English law provides an interesting illustration of classification as a tool of policy. "Realty" is a class comprising those legal rules which confer proprietary rights over land to endure for an uncertain period. Thus, there are three criteria which form the basis of this particular class of rules of law: (i) they must be rules concerning rights over land; (ii) these rights must be rights in rem, i.e. they must avail against all comers, or nearly all; and (iii) these rights must be uncertain in the length of time for which they are to endure. (This third requirement refers to the well-known common law doctrine of estates.) It will be noted that rules concerning leasehold rights over land are excluded from the above class because the duration of the rights concerned is certain, being fixed between definite dates. Hence, they are characterized as rules of personalty; a class which came to include all rules conferring proprietary rights over things (including land) not classifiable as rules of realty. As Pollock and Maitland point out, the classing of rules conferring leasehold rights as rules of personalty served a very definite economic purpose in the thirteenth and fourteenth centuries. In medieval England land was the principal form of wealth and "real" rights over land were not freely transferable, being fettered by all the rigidities of the feudal system. For instance, prior to 1540, they were not freely alienable by will. On the other hand, proprietary rights over chattels could be freely disposed of by will, and thus by classifying leasehold rights over land as personalty, a valuable and freely bequeathable form of investment in land was made available. This peculiar legal dichotomy of "realty" and "personalty," then, enabled the law to satisfy a genuine economic need in medieval England.[13]

Perhaps it will have been noticed that we have just been speaking of the classification of legal rights as well as of rules of law. This should not be confusing if it is remembered that only laws can confer legal rights and hence a classification of rights is *ipso facto* a classification of laws, whether the laws concerned are being considered in relation to concrete or hypothetical facts. Again Sir Frederick Pollock's words are apt: "The divisions of law . . . are in truth divisions not of facts but of rules; or, if we like to say so, of the legal aspect of facts."

Usually systems for the classification of laws result from the meditations of jurists and derive what authority they have from the prestige of their respective authors. But it is otherwise with a federal constitution which of necessity contains a complete and authoritative system for the classification of laws as the basis of its allocation of law-making powers between the different legislatures concerned. In the B.N.A. Act such rules are found primarily in the well-known sections 91 and 92. These contain respectively enumerations of federal and provincial law-making powers. It is important to realize that these enumerated "subjects" or "matters" are classes of laws, not classes of facts. It is impossible for instance to look at a set of economic facts and say that the activity is trade and commerce within section 91(2) and therefore any law concerning it must be federal law. Rather, one must take a specific law (either actual or proposed) which is relevant to those facts and then ask if that rule is classifiable as a trade or commercial law. The Act very wisely recognizes this necessity in the wording of section 91(2). It does not say just "trade and commerce," it says rather "the regulation of trade and commerce," meaning of course "laws regulating trade and commerce."

The same can be said of all the enumerated classes in both sections 91 and 92. Some of them are obviously classes of laws on their face for they speak of rights, institutions, relations, or

[13] Sir F. Pollock and F. W. Maitland, *History of English Law* (2nd ed., Cambridge, 1898), II, 116, 117.

operations which have necessarily to be created or provided for by appropriate laws, e.g. taxation, legal tender, patents of invention and discovery, copyrights, marriage and divorce, criminal law, incorporation, municipal institutions, solemnization of marriage, and property and civil rights. The wording used for certain other classes makes them seem classes of fact, but these they cannot be. They must be read as the "trade and commerce" clause is worded: thus "seacoast and inland fisheries" truly means "laws regulating seacoast and inland fisheries." Similarly with such classes or categories as postal service, defence, banking, insolvency, and local works and undertakings. The late Chief Justice Harvey of Alberta seems to have put his finger on the point here being made when he said, in a recent case concerned with "banking" in section 91(15). "The word is used as the Statute [The B.N.A. Act] says as describing a subject for legislation, not a definite object."[14] We do not look just for banking as a matter of economic fact, we must look for regulation of banking as a matter of law.

It is important to insist that these enumerated classes are categories of legal rules and not of facts for the implications of this are too frequently forgotten. Thus concrete facts alone cannot provide the mass of data appropriate for grouping under these categories, since facts as such are legally neutral. Or, to put it the other way around, facts alone cannot be characterized by subsumption within these classes as they are not classes of fact. They are classes of laws depending on normative or prescriptive criteria, and hence concrete facts alone are simply not relevant data, because they have no such attributes. For instance, facts alone cannot be characterized as criminal or proprietary or procedural, though particular legal rules appropriate to concrete facts may be one or the other. It is the country's ordinary rules of law, disposing of the rights, duties, liberties, capacities, and immunities of its citizens, that are the raw materials – the undifferentiated mass of data – relevant to the scheme of distribution of powers in the B.N.A. Act. You must talk in terms of such specific laws, actual or proposed, if you would determine whether the relevant legislative power is federal or provincial under the B.N.A. Act.

It follows that it is quite feasible to refer a challenged law (whether a bill or a statute) to our highest courts for a decision

---

[14] *Reference Re Alberta Bill of Rights Act*, [1946] 3 W.W.R. 772 at p. 778.

on where the power to enact it lies in the absence of any concrete litigious fact-situation involving adverse parties. Indeed, this is frequently done. Nevertheless the separate problems of the classification of facts cannot be entirely dismissed even from this picture. In order to classify the challenged rule, the court must first reach a conclusion regarding its true meaning – the full significance of the words in which it is expressed. Only thus are the various features by which it may be classified revealed. This decision will include the meaning of the words expressing that part of the rule which is its fact-category, which can best be assessed by testing its applicability to particular situations of fact, hypothetical or real. It is a recognized part of the reasoning process to gain additional insight concerning the meaning of a principle of conduct by making test applications of it to particular fact-situations to which it is deemed relevant, in order to determine what the effects of its observance would be. In this way all the problems of the classification of facts certainly enter the picture. No doubt this is why judges seem happier when a challenged law comes before them as a result of specific litigation, rather than by government reference. It is then easier to construe what the law means. Nevertheless, the classification of facts is still not our crucial problem in interpreting sections 91 and 92. We can admit that that process bears on the true meaning of the challenged law, but classification of that law cannot begin anyway until its true meaning is established, whether the issue of validity arises out of specific litigation or by government reference. The classification of facts is important, but anterior to the problem of whether a law is intra or ultra vires.

THE APPLICATION OF SECTIONS 91 AND 92 OF THE B.N.A. ACT

Certain of the essential principles for the interpretation of the B.N.A. Act now require consideration in detail in light of the foregoing analysis. In the first place the categories of laws enumerated in sections 91 and 92 are not in the logical sense mutually exclusive; they overlap or encroach upon one another in many more respects than is usually realized. To put it another way, many rules of law have one feature that renders them relevant to a provincial class of laws and another feature which renders them equally relevant logically to a federal class of laws. It is inherent in the nature of classification as a process that this should be so, and hence the concluding words of section 91 represent aspiration for the unattainable. It will be recalled that they read as follows: "And any Matter coming within any of the classes of subjects enumerated in this Section shall not be deemed to come within the Class of Matters of a local or private Nature comprised in the Enumeration of the Classes of Subjects by this Act assigned exclusively to the Legislatures of the Provinces." Over eighty years of judicial interpretation have demonstrated conclusively the impossibility of such mutual exclusion. "The language of [sections 91 and 92] and of the various heads which they contain obviously cannot be construed as having been intended to embody the exact disjunctions of a perfect locical scheme."[15]

For a simple illustration, take the well-known rule that a will made by an unmarried person becomes void if and when he marries. Is this a rule of "marriage" (s. 91(26)) or of "property and civil rights" (s. 92(13))? In England and the common law provinces of Canada it occurs in the respective "Wills Acts," and its validity in Canada as provincial law has not been challenged. This would suggest it is deemed a rule of "property and civil rights" for constitutional purposes. Yet if we turn to Private International Law (which has similar problems of classification) we find English and Canadian courts in agreement that this provision about marriage voiding a pre-nuptial will is to be deemed a matrimonial law for purposes of Private International Law.[16] Obviously, this rule could in addition be classed as testamentary or successive. In truth it is logically quite correct to classify it as matrimonial or successive or testamentary or as concerning property and civil rights. It is any or all of these things. The decision as to which classification is to be used for a given purpose has to be made on non-logical grounds of policy and justice by the legal authority with the duty and power of decision in that respect. The criteria of relative importance involved in such a decision cannot be logical ones, for logic merely displays to us as of equivalent logical value all the possible classifications. There are as many possible classifications of a rule of law as that rule has distinct characteristics or attributes which may be isolated as criteria of classification. Dr.

---

[15] *John Deere Plow Co., Ltd.* v. *Wharton*, [1915] A.C. 330 at p. 338.
[16] *Re Martin*, (1900) P. 211; *Seifert* v. *Seifert*, [1915] 23 D.L.R. 440. See also W. R. Lederman, "Classification in Private International Law" in (1951) 29 *Canadian Bar Review* 3 and 168.

Glanville Williams expresses this point very well in the following passage: "The above view as to definition . . . involves a rejection of Aristotle's doctrine of essences. Aristotle taught that essences are fixed in nature and that a definition is a phrase signifying this essence. On this view it is possible to dispute about 'true' definitions as though they are matters of fact. We now know that 'essence' simply means 'important feature,' and that what is important is a subjective or emotional matter. No definition ever states the sum total of the qualities that seem to go to the being of a thing; it always involves a selection from those qualities, and the exact selection made depends very much on the purpose of the definition."[17] By "definition" Dr. Williams means the same thing as "classification." Definition is a process of classification. Thus there is not just one universally valid classification of a given rule of law good for all purposes. As has been said, several classifications are always possible, and which is best for a given purpose is a matter of judgment on higher grounds than logical ones.

How then do we determine the several features of a law by any one of which or by any combination of which it may be classified? This question takes us back to the question of the true meaning of the challenged law. In many of the cases we are told that it all depends on what is determined to be the "subject-matter" of the rule. Presumably this phraseology coupling "subject and "matter" comes from the wording of the opening parts of sections 91 and 92, which speak of "exclusive Legislative Authority" extending "to all Matters coming within the Classes of Subjects next hereinafter enumerated" (s. 91), and "Laws in relation to Matters coming within the Classes of Subjects next hereinafter enumerated" (s. 92). As has been pointed out, what is really being dealt with is power to enact *laws coming within the classes of laws next hereinafter enumerated*, and the B.N.A. Act could well be more concisely and clearly phrased in that way. "Subjects" and "matters" simply refer to meaning. Everything in a rule of law is "subject-matter" of it. "Subject-matter" can only refer to all features of its fact-category and the rights and duties prescribed. You must construe meaning before you can talk of subject-matter, and you only know what is subject-matter when you have settled meaning.

Further, in other cases a false antithesis is set up between the subject-matter of a rule on the one hand and its object or purpose

[17] 61 *Law Quarterly Review* at pp. 388-9.

on the other. For instance, Dr. MacRae states: "The Court, having regard to the language used in Sections 91 and 92, has to find what the 'matter' is which is being legislated in relation to; and in doing this it must look, not merely at the subject-matter of the legislation (in the sense of the thing legislated about), but also at the object or purpose of the legislation. In other words, it has to look not merely at the thing legislated *about*, but the object or purpose legislated *for*."[18] This sounds plausible, but is not as helpful as it seems. In addition to speaking of the object or purpose of a rule, we may also speak of its intention and of its effects or consequences. But all these words lead us back to the one primary problem, the full or total meaning of the rule. There is an essential unity here that defies these grammatical attempts at separation. A rule of law expresses what should be human action or conduct in a given factual situation. We assume enforcement and observance of the rule and hence judge its meaning in terms of the consequences of the action called for. It is the effects of observance of the rule that constitute at least in part its intent, object, or purpose. Certainly the total meaning of the rule cannot be assessed apart from these effects. We must seek the full meaning of the challenged law because the classes of laws in sections 91 and 92 depend on criteria which touch on all possible phases of the meaning of a law.

It should be noted that the problem of the colourable statement cannot be dealt with except in accordance with the foregoing analysis of total meaning. A colourable law is one which really means something more than or different from what its words seem at first glance to say. A law may have been so worded as to make it seem that it has only provincially classifiable features of meaning, and only when the effects of it (if enforced) are assessed can one ascertain a fuller or different meaning which supplies federally classifiable features. The Alberta Bill of Rights Act of 1946 is a classic example; it did not say "banks" or "banking" once, but it was classified as banking legislation none the less.[19]

The matter of intention also causes some confusion at this point. It is virtually impossible to find determinate human intenders behind most statutes. The examination of Hansard would not be nearly as helpful as many jurists suggest, though

18 D. A. MacRae, *Constitutional Law* (mimeo.), p. 118.
19 *Reference Re Alberta Bill of Rights Act,* [1947] 4 D.L.R. 1 (P.C.).

it might have some value. On the whole, the position is as the Privy Council itself has stated it; "The question is, not what may be supposed to have been intended, *but what has been said*."[20] Here, as in other departments of the law, it has to be taken that ordinary consequences are intended consequences. Ordinary consequences are those reasonably informed men would expect as effects of the course of conduct the rule prescribes. The word intention, with or without adjectives such as "real," "true," or "essential," could well be completely dispensed with. It is superfluous, and at best represents a pseudo-subjective approach to meaning. Rules of law are for all manner of people, and hence the meaning ascribed to the words expressing them should be objectively and not subjectively determined.

Nevertheless, while all the effects of a particular rule are features of its meaning, it by no means follows that all are equally important. Let us suppose that the federal Government proposes to enact a heavy tax on the consumers of liquor. It can be seen that enforcement of the law will (*a*) bring in some revenue and (*b*) reduce consumption of liquor, which in turn will gladden the hearts of members of the W.C.T.U., facilitate the diversion of more alcohol to the manufacture of explosives, and put some marginal distillers out of business. These are all effects of the law and features of its meaning by which, severally or in combination, it may be classified in different ways. Which of the logically possible classifications is to prevail? As this law would put certain distillers in the province out of business it is a law concerning "Property and Civil Rights in the Provinces." But in a time of national peril there would be little difficulty in deciding that country-wide diversion of alcohol to the manufacture of explosives was its most important object, purpose, effect, or feature of meaning. Thus this circumstance would be the crucial feature of meaning for purposes of the division of legislative powers, and the law would be deemed a law of the national emergency class allotted to the central Parliament.

This suggests the main thesis of this essay: *That a rule of law for purposes of the distribution of legislative powers is to be classified by that feature of its meaning which is judged the most important one in that respect*. The thesis so stated points to the heart of the problem of interpretation, i.e. whence come the criteria of relative importance necessary for such a decision? In this inquiry, the judges are beyond the aid of logic, because

[20] *Brophy* v. *A.G. for Manitoba*, [1895] A.C. 202 at p. 216.

logic merely displays the many possible classifications, it does not assist in a choice between them. If we assume that the purpose of the constitution is to promote the well-being of the people, then some of the necessary criteria will start to emerge. When a particular rule has features of meaning relevant to both federal and provincial classes of laws, then the question must be asked, Is it better for the people that this thing be done on a national level, or on a provincial level? In other words, is the feature of the challenged law which falls within the federal class more important to the well-being of the country than that which falls within the provincial class of laws? Such considerations as the relative value of uniformity and regional diversity, the relative merits of local *versus* central administration, and the justice of minority claims, would have to be weighed. Inevitably, widely prevailing beliefs in the country about these issues will be influential and presumably the judges should strive to implement such beliefs. Inevitably there will be some tendency for them to identify their own convictions as those which generally prevail or which at least are the right ones. On some matters there will not be an ascertainable general belief anyway. In the making of these very difficult relative-value decisions, all that can rightly be required of judges is straight thinking, industry, good faith, and a capacity to discount their own prejudices. No doubt it is also fair to ask that they be men of high attainment, and that they be representative in their thinking of the better standards of their times and their countrymen.

Furthermore, our judges need all the assistance they can be afforded by the provision of data relevant for their constitutional decisions. What is wanted is emphasis on the approach pioneered in the United States by Mr. Justice Brandeis when at the Bar. In the so-called "Brandeis Brief," he would gather and place before the Supreme Court of that country an account of the *contemporary* economic and social factors which underlay the challenged law, to assist the judges there with the value-decisions confronting them. It might be said that the problem of ultra vires in the United States often differs too much from that in Canada for a parallel to be drawn, since the Americans have "Bill of Rights" clauses written into their Constitution defining things none of their legislatures can do by ordinary statute. Consider, for instance, a minimum wage law. The American courts have had to ask themselves whether such a law is urgent enough in the public interest to justify the limitation on freedom of contract that is involved, such freedom being deemed guaranteed in the Constitution except to the extent that it conflicts with some vital public interest. True enough, Canadian judges do not have to consider the substantive merit of a challenged law in this sense; indeed they are accustomed to labour the point that they are not concerned with whether such a law is good or bad, necessary or unnecessary. They say in effect that the malady and its proper cure are not their concern, rather that they have to ask only, Who is to be the physician? Yet does not the choice of physician depend to an important degree on the nature of the malady and of the proposed remedy? Admittedly if the challenged law is logically classifiable in only one way there is no problem, but the main thesis here is that such a situation will be rare, and that often so far as logic is concerned the challenged law will have features of meaning relevant to both federal and provincial classes of laws. Then our judges cannot be content simply to ask, Who is to be the physician? They must rather ask, Who is the better physician to prescribe in this way for this malady? To give a meritorious answer to this second question they need to consider as many factors as their American brothers. As was indicated earlier, widely accepted standards and beliefs are vital considerations in choosing the better alternative in this type of decision, but at least the principles of relative value should be ascertained and applied in the light of everything important that can be known about the need for the challenged law and what it would involve if observed and enforced.

Lest a false impression of complete uncertainty and fluidity be conveyed by the foregoing, the importance of the rules of precedent that obtain in our courts should be remembered. However open logically the classification of a given type of law may have been when first it was considered by the highest court, that decision will in all probability foreclose the question of the correct classification should the same type of law come up again. For instance it was argued that the federal Industrial Disputes Investigation Act of 1907 was within the power of the Canadian Parliament because its provisions regulating the settlement of industrial disputes were classifiable as "regulation of trade and commerce," "criminal law," and rules for "peace, order, and good government." Nevertheless the Judicial Committee pointed out that these provisions were also classifiable as laws concerning "property and civil rights in the province" and in effect ruled that such was *the* important or significant classification for constitutional purposes.[21] Hence the Act was declared ultra vires of the Canadian Parliament. Incidentally, in his argument for the validity of the Act, Sir John Simon had pointed to the absence of economic division in Canada on provincial lines; in other words many industries and labour organizations were national or at least interprovincial in scope and hence national regulation of industrial relations was desirable. But the Judicial Committee was not impressed. Tacitly but effectively they decided that provincial autonomy and diversity in the regulation of employer-employee relations were more important when they ruled that the challenged statute "in its pith and substance" interfered with civil rights. Thus the classification of this type of industrial regulation critical for constitutional purposes has been settled by precedent, and in like manner many other classifications are authoritatively settled. It is not clear yet whether the Supreme Court of Canada, supreme now in law as well as name, will assert a right to depart in exceptional circumstances from particular decisions in the accumulation of Privy Council precedents. Certainly it would seem that explicit departures, if any, will be rare. Nevertheless, some new and different scheme of industrial regulation, for example, might well be deemed outside the scope of the precedent just discussed, and then its classification in turn would have to be considered as a matter of first impression with all the problems here explained once more in full bloom.

Moreover, frequently there will be new laws, both federal and provincial, which the precedents on classification will not touch decisively or concerning which indeed there may be conflicting analogies. Thus in spite of the principles of precedent the full-blown problem of classification described earlier is often with us. Therefore, it is not merely those who would make or amend the federal constitution who must ask themselves and each other, What is truly of national concern and what is truly of provincial concern for purposes of law? Within the limits set by the terms of particular laws being challenged before them from time to time, the judges frequently confront this question *just as starkly as did the original constitution-makers themselves.* Further, as conditions change with the years, the relative importance of various classifiable features of particular laws may change as well. For instance the motor vehicle has brought

[21] *Toronto Electric Commissioners* v. *Snider*, [1925] A.C. 396.

to highway traffic today an interprovincial and international character undreamed of forty years ago; hence regulation of highway-using enterprises is now to be regarded to some extent in a new light.[22] Another way to put this point is to say that changed economic and social conditions and a different moral climate will give to present or proposed laws new features of meaning by which they may be classified and may also alter judgments on the relative importance of their several classifiable features. As their Lordships of the Privy Council have said: "It is . . . irrelevant that the question is one that might have seemed unreal at the date of the B.N.A. Act. To such an organic statute the flexible interpretation must be given that changing circumstances require."[23] The authority of appropriate precedents then will remove much of the uncertainty just described as implicit in the process of classification but inevitably much unpredictability will remain. The principles of stare decisis are important in our courts, but the degree of certainty and predictability their operation can provide is often much overestimated or misconceived.

Having explored the main problem of interpretation regarding our constitutional division of legislative powers, we may now attend in detail to the particular doctrines developed by the judges to facilitate the making of the necessary decisions. In the cases of many, if not most, particular laws, the overlapping of federal and provincial categories of laws logically relevant is inevitable, no matter how often the B.N.A. Act cries "exclusive." The courts have dealt with this overlapping in a number of ways. For one thing, they have limited the generality of the classes of laws in sections 91 and 92 by the so-called principle of "mutual modification," and have thus eliminated some of the encroachment of one upon the other. For example, consider the relation of the federal class, "regulation of trade and commerce," with the provincial class, "property and civil rights." Trade and commerce is carried on in articles in which persons have property and in respect of which they have civil rights. Obviously, in the logical sense there is here a wide overlapping. However, speaking generally, the courts have said that "regulation of trade and commerce" is to be reduced in generality and read as "regulation of interprovincial and international trade and commerce." Likewise, "property and civil rights" is to be

[22] *Winner* v. *S.M.T.* (*Eastern*), *Ltd.*, [1951] S.C.R. 887.
[23] *Privy Council Appeals Case*, [1947] 1 D.L.R. 801 at p. 814.

rendered "property and civil rights except those involved in interprovincial and international trade and commerce." By these operations the overlapping of the literal words of the statute is reduced and some additional degree of exclusiveness is imparted to federal and provincial classes of laws. The reading of sections 91 and 92 as a whole certainly makes it clear that some of this rewording is necessary.

Nevertheless, in spite of all that can or should be done by mutual modification, some overlapping inevitably remains. Where this occurs, either one of two things has then been done. First, the feature of the challenged law relevant to a provincial class of powers has been completely ignored as only an "incidental affectation" of the provincial sphere, and the law concerned has been classed only by that feature of it relevant to a federal class of laws. Thus, in spite of the logical overlap the decision is made that only the federal Parliament has power to enact the challenged law. Obviously this decision involves a judgment that the provincial feature of the law is quite unimportant relative to its federal feature. On the other hand if the federal feature be deemed quite unimportant relative to the provincial feature, then the converse decision would be made.

But if the contrast between the relative importance of the two features is not so sharp, what then? Here we come upon the double-aspect theory of interpretation, which constitutes the second way in which the courts have dealt with inevitably overlapping categories. When the court considers that the federal and provincial features of the challenged rule are of roughly equivalent importance so that neither should be ignored respecting the division of legislative powers, the decision is made that the challenged rule could be enacted by either the federal Parliament or a provincial legislature. In the language of the Privy Council, "subjects which in one aspect and for one purpose fall within sect. 92, may in another aspect and for another purpose fall within sect. 91."[24] Clearly this decision raises some further problems. Under such principles of interpretation there may well be both a valid federal law and a valid provincial law directed to the same persons concerning the same things, but requiring from them different courses of conduct and thus having certain differing effects. Now if these different courses of conduct and effects are merely cumulative and not conflicting,

[24] *Hodge* v. *The Queen*, (1883) 9 App. Cas. 117.

then both rules may operate. But, if the two rules call for inconsistent behaviour from the same people, they are in conflict or collision and both cannot be obeyed. In these circumstances the courts have laid it down that the federal rule is to prevail and the provincial one is inoperative and need not be observed. The suspension of the provincial law continues so long as there is a federal law inconsistent in the sense explained. This is known as the doctrine of "Dominion paramountcy." Thus, it is a principle of our constitution that in the event of collision between a federal law and a provincial law each valid under the double-aspect theory, the federal features of the former law are considered in the last analysis more important than the provincial features of the latter. At this ultimate point of conflict, presumably the federal classes and features relevant to them are deemed the more important simply because they have a national as opposed to a sectional reference. At any rate, "Dominion paramountcy" is said to be called for by the concluding words of section 91, quoted earlier.

It is clear then that in dealing with the overlapping of federal and provincial classes of laws, the courts must make the types of value-decisions described about the relative importance of the federal and provincial features of the challenged law. Some examples may now be examined. The Vacant Property Act of Quebec (1939) provided, to put it briefly, that all financial deposits in credit institutions unclaimed for thirty years became the property of the Crown in right of the Province of Quebec. The validity of this law was challenged. It was a question of the federal "banking" clause *versus* the provincial "property and civil rights" clause. The law was declared beyond the powers of a province, and in the course of judgment in the Privy Council the following passages occur:

If that be the main object and effect *of the provincial Act it does in their Lordships' view invade the field of banking. It comes in* pith and substance *within that class and the fact that it may* incidentally affect *certain other institutions cannot take away its* primary object and effect.

In their [Lordships'] *view a provincial legislature enters upon the field of banking when it interferes with the right of depositors to receive payment of their deposits, as in their view it would if it confiscated loans made by a bank to its customers. Both are* in a sense *matters of property and civil rights, but in* essence *they are included within the category "banking."*[25]

Further, in the *Alberta Bill of Rights Case* (1947) where there was the same type of problem concerning banking and property and civil rights, the Judicial Committee said:

> *It is true of course, that in one aspect provincial legislation on this subject* affects *property and civil rights, but if, as their Lordships hold to be the case, the* pith and substance *of the legislation is "Banking" . . . this is* the aspect that matters *and Part II is beyond the powers of the Alberta Legislature to enact.*[26]

In these two cases the property and civil rights features of the challenged laws were deemed relatively so unimportant in contrast to their banking features that classification for the purpose of determining legislative power was by the latter features only. The former were ignored. This may look like just another way of describing the result arrived at by the principle of mutual modification. For instance the decision in these banking cases could perhaps be put as a decision that "property and civil rights" should be read "property and civil rights except those of banking." Even so, one still has to decide whether the *non-banking* property and civil rights features or the banking features of a challenged statute are the more important, where such a statute logically has both aspects, as it did in the Quebec and Alberta cases.

The quoted passages display the language which has become standard for expressing this judgment on value. The feature of the meaning of the rule deemed of outstanding importance is said to be "the pith and substance," "the essence," or "the aspect that matters." The feature deemed relatively unimportant is dismissed as merely "incidental." Other adjectives might be used to express the same contrast – the feature deemed of outstanding importance could be designated as "vital," "principal," or "capital," whereas the feature deemed unimportant could be called "secondary," "subordinate," "inferior," and so on. Also, some courts have put it this way, that what a rule is "in relation to" is primary, whereas that which it merely "affects" is secondary. In ordinary usage, there is no such contrast between "in relation to" and "affects." There is in fact no special magic in

---

[25] *A.G. for Canada* v. *A.G. for Quebec,* [1947] 1 D.L.R. 81 at pp. 87-8 (author's emphasis).

[26] [1947] 4 D.L.R. 1 at p. 10 (author's emphasis).

any of these incantations. Plainly, *whatever the form of expression adopted there is only one thing to be expressed: judgment on the relative importance of the federal and provincial features respectively of the meaning of the challenged law, for purposes of the distribution of legislative powers.* All the foregoing verbiage could be dispensed with and the words "important" and "unimportant" (or "more important" and "less important") substituted. Indeed, words like "pith and substance" or "essence" should be dropped entirely because they suggest that as a matter of final truth in philosophy or logic there is only one correct classification of a challenged rule. As we have already seen, this is a fallacy. Nevertheless, at times judges do so concentrate their gaze upon the feature of the challenged law they deem most important that they are found asserting that such law does not have other features relevant to the classes of the B.N.A. Act at all. In effect, the inevitable value-judgment is made, but its nature as a necessary choice between logically equal alternatives is unfortunately obscured for all concerned.

Finally we may examine an example of the application of the double-aspect theory. A good one is explained in the case of *Provincial Secretary of P.E.I.* v. *Egan* (1941) in the Supreme Court of Canada.[27] The Criminal Code of Canada provided that it was an offence to drive a motor vehicle while intoxicated and that in addition to any other punishment the court might on conviction make an order prohibiting the convict from driving a motor vehicle anywhere in Canada for a period not exceeding three years. On the other hand the Highway Traffic Act of Prince Edward Island provided for the licensing of drivers on the Island and that on a first conviction for driving while intoxicated the licence of such driver would be automatically and irrevocably suspended for twelve months. Suspension was to be for twenty-four months on a second conviction and for life on a third one. The Court found that the federal rule was valid as criminal law, and that the provincial rule was valid, inter alia, as licensing law and as a law defining provincial civil rights. It was further found that these laws were not inconsistent and that both were operative, presumably because the respective suspensions of the right to drive could be regarded as concurrent and cumulative rather than as conflicting. Thus, at the back of this decision must be at least the tacit judgment that the provincial features of the challenged part of the Highway Act were of

[27] [1941] 3 D.L.R. 305.

equivalent importance with the federal features of the very similar provisions of the federal Criminal Code. In the words of Sir Lyman Duff: "It is important to remember that matters which, from one point of view and for one purpose, fall exclusively within the Dominion authority, may, nevertheless, be proper subjects for legislation by the Province from a different point of view, although this is a principle that must be 'applied only with great caution.' "[28]

One other allegedly separate principle of interpretation remains to be noticed, that known as the "ancillary doctrine." According to an eminent authority, the purport of this doctrine is as follows: "Provisions of a Dominion Statute which directly intrude upon provincial classes of jurisdiction and which, standing alone, would be incompetent to the Dominion, may nevertheless be valid as being necessarily incidental to full-rounded legislation upon a Dominion subject-matter, or to the effective exercise of an enumerated Dominion power, or to prevent the scheme of an otherwise valid Act from being defeated."[29] It is sometimes put alternatively that, in these circumstances, the Dominion can *trench upon* provincial jurisdiction. An example of this approach is found in the judgment of the Privy Council in the *Voluntary Assignments Case*: "Their Lordships would observe that a system of bankruptcy legislation may frequently require various ancillary provisions for the purpose of preventing the scheme of the Act from being defeated. It may be necessary for this purpose to deal with the effect of executions and others matters which would otherwise be within the legislative competence of the provincial legislature."[30] It should be apparent that this talk of the "necessarily incidental," or the "ancillary" is just another way of describing a dual-aspect situation and thus does not represent a separate problem in or approach to interpretation at all. We are not interested in what some part of a Dominion statute would have meant standing alone, because it does not stand alone. It takes some features of meaning from its context which it would not have if isolated. In its context it has both federal and provincial features deemed of equivalent importance and hence we have nothing more nor less than the double-aspect situation already considered.

[28] *Ibid.* at p. 309.
[29] Vincent C. MacDonald, "Judicial Interpretation of the Canadian Constitution" in (1935) 1 *University of Toronto Law Journal* 260 at pp. 273-4.
[30] [1894] A.C. 189 at p. 200.

Nevertheless, such talk does suggest one angle of the interpretation or classification problem not yet explored. So far the argument in this paper has proceeded largely on the footing of assessing certain simple and concise rules of law. This was necessary for clarity of exposition, but of course constitutional issues do not always arise in such simple forms. A given statute is frequently a complex of particular rules, all facets of a single plan or scheme. Such a statute will stand or fall as a whole when its validity is questioned. On the other hand, the single plan or scheme or pattern concerned may be expressed in two or three statutes all of which have to be read together. By contrast, it may be that a single statute will fall into parts which can be taken as separate units for purposes of determining which authority has power to enact them. This would be a case where "severance" is said to be appropriate. Clearly, because of the influence of context on meaning, it is going to be important what group of particular legal provisions the court selects as the unit for classification within federal or provincial classes of laws. It seems impossible to lay down any standard tests for grouping rules into a single pattern for this purpose, though presumably well-drafted statutes have only one principal theme. It seems a matter for the reasoning power and common sense of judges in each particular case. Judicial pronouncements, it is submitted, do make it plain that this question of the unit to be classified is a real one. For instance, in one of the cases concerning interest on Alberta bonds, Mr. Justice Ewing said, "A composite Act may be declared ultra vires in its entirety but it does not follow that each of its component parts if enacted separately would necessarily be declared to be ultra vires."[31] Likewise, in the *Alberta Bill of Rights Case* already referred to, Viscount Simon said:

This sort of question arises not infrequently and is often raised (as in the present instance) by asking whether the legislation is ultra vires "either in whole or in part," but this does not mean that when Part II is declared invalid what remains of the Act is to be examined bit by bit in order to determine whether the Legislature would be acting within its powers if it passed what remains. The real question is whether what remains is so inextricably bound up with the part declared invalid that what remains cannot independently survive or, as it has sometimes been put, whether on a fair review of the whole matter it can be

[31] *I.O.O.F.* v. *Trustees of Lethbridge Northern Irrigation District,* [1937] 4 D.L.R. 398 at p. 400.

assumed that the Legislature would have enacted what survives without enacting the part that is ultra vires at all.[32]

The Supreme Court of Alberta had held that Part I of the Act was intra vires and Part II ultra vires. The Privy Council held that the two parts were not severable and that the whole was ultra vires.

By way of conclusion, the main points of the foregoing analysis may be summarized:

1. Basically, in applying sections 91 and 92 of the B.N.A. Act, we are concerned with a classification problem, which is really the problem of language itself. There are certain difficulties inherent in all processes of classification.

2. In legal analysis, classification of facts must be distinguished from classification of laws, since facts and laws are different orders of things.

3. When the constitutional validity of a law is challenged, we must seek to ascertain its full or total meaning. In part, this involves the process of classifying facts, and in part it calls for determining the effects of doing what the law requires.

4. Logically, a given law may be classified by any one or by any combination of the distinct features of meaning which it has. Thus, a given law can be classified in many different ways. The idea that there is only one true classification is a fallacy.

5. The application of sections 91 and 92 of the B.N.A. Act is a process of classification of laws, but inevitably the categories there specified are largely overlapping. Therefore a challenged law with features of meaning relevant to both federal and provincial categories of laws has to be classified by that feature of it deemed most important for purposes of the division of legislative powers in the country. The heart of the interpretative process thus often lies in the criteria of relative importance employed by the judges in making this type of choice.

6. Precedents on classification are important, but the degree of certainty they can afford is usually much overestimated.[33]

7. The task of the judges in this regard is as difficult as it is important. Criticism of what the courts have done, if it is to be constructive, should acknowledge with some humility that this is a field in which honest and able men may differ.

[32] [1947] 4 D.L.R. 1 at p. 11.
[33] For an exhaustive analysis relevant to this point, see F. E. LaBrie, "Constitutional Interpretation and Legislative Review" in (1950) 8 *University of Toronto Law Journal* 298.

The Concurrent Operation of Federal and Provincial Laws in Canada

W. R. LEDERMAN

DEFINITION OF CONCURRENT FIELDS

The federal distribution of legislative powers and responsibilities in Canada is one of the facts of life when we concern ourselves with the many important social, political, economic, or cultural problems of our country. Over the whole range of actual and potential law-making, our constitution distributes powers and responsibilities by two lists of categories or classes – one list for the federal parliament (primarily section 91 of the B.N.A. Act),[1] the other for each of the provincial legislatures (primarily section 92 of the B.N.A. Act). For instance, the federal list includes regulation of trade and commerce, criminal law, and a general power to make laws in all matters not assigned to the provinces. Examples from the provincial list are property and civil rights in the province, local works and undertakings, and all matters of a merely local or private nature in the province.

These federal and provincial categories of power are expressed, and indeed have to be expressed, in quite general terms. This permits considerable flexibility in constitutional interpretation, but also it brings much overlapping and potential conflict between the various definitions of powers and responsibilities. To put the same point in another way, our community life – social, economic, political, and cultural – is very complex and will not fit neatly into any scheme of categories or classes with-

From: *The McGill Law Journal*, Volume 9 (1962-63), pages 185-99.
By permission of the author and publisher.

[1] 30 & 31 Victoria (U.K.), c. 3.

out considerable overlap and ambiguity occurring.[2] There are inevitable difficulties arising from this that we must live with so long as we have a federal constitution.

Accordingly the courts must continually assess the competing federal and provincial lists of powers against one another in the judicial task of interpreting the constitution. In the course of judicial decisions on the B.N.A. Act, the judges have basically done one of two things. First, they have attempted to define mutually exclusive spheres for federal and provincial powers, with partial success. But, where mutual exclusion did not seem feasible or proper, the courts have implied the existence of concurrent federal and provincial powers in the overlapping area, with the result that either or both authorities have been permitted to legislate provided their statutes did not in some way conflict one with the other in the common area. It is the problems arising from such concurrency that are the primary concern of this article.

But, before proceeding specifically to the problems that arise after concurrency has been found, it is necessary to examine carefully the interpretative process whereby the courts strive first to establish mutually exclusive spheres of federal and provincial law-making powers. The words "exclusive" or "exclusively" occur in section 91 of the B.N.A. Act respecting federal powers and in section 92 respecting provincial powers, hence the priority for the attempt at mutual exclusion. Only if this attempt fails do the judges then proceed to define by necessary implication certain spheres of common powers to regulate the same matter.

Here we encounter important considerations that go under the name of "the aspect theory." As Lord Fitzgerald said long ago in *Hodge* v. *The Queen*, "subjects which in one aspect and for one purpose fall within Sect. 92, may in another aspect and for another purpose fall within Sect. 91."[3] For instance, a law providing for suspension or revocation of the right to drive a car upon a highway because the driver was drunk has the provincial

---

[2] ". . . It is necessary to realize the relation to each other of ss. 91 and 92 and the character of the expressions used in them. The language of these sections and of the various heads which they contain obviously cannot be construed as having been intended to embody the exact disjunctions of a perfect logical scheme." – Viscount Haldane in *John Deere Plow Company Ltd.* v. *Wharton* [1915] A.C. 330, at 338.

[3] (1883-84) 9 A.C. 117, at 130.

aspects of control of highways as local works and of the right to drive as a civil right in the province, these things reflecting the provincial responsibility for safe and efficient circulation of traffic. The law mentioned has also the federal aspect of criminal law, reflecting the federal responsibility to forbid and punish such dangerous anti-social conduct.[4] Where does the power to suspend and revoke drivers' licences reside, or do both parties have it? Such laws with double aspects in the logical sense are the usual and not the exceptional case.

In other words, simply as a rational or logical matter, the challenged law displays several features of meaning some one of which at least falls within a federal class of laws, and another one of which falls within a provincial class of laws. Rationally the challenged law is classified both ways – how then do we determine whether power to pass such a law is exclusively federal or exclusively provincial or is something both legislative authorities have? The basic solution here comes by decisions on the relative importance of the federal features and the provincial features respectively of the challenged law in contrast to one another. Respecting the detailed aspects raised by the challenged law, one must ask – when does the need for a national standard by federal law outweigh the need for provincial autonomy and possible variety as developed by the laws of the several provinces, or vice versa? The criteria of relative importance here arise from the social, economic, political, and cultural conditions of the country and its various regions and parts, and of course involve the systems of value that obtain in our society. The answers must be guided by and related to the categories and concepts of the British North America Act, and so at this point we find that the two interpretative situations mentioned earlier emerge.

a *Mutual Modifications and Exclusive Powers*

If the federal features of the challenged law are deemed clearly to be more important than the provincial features of it, then the power to pass that law is exclusively federal. In other words, for this purpose the challenged law is classified by its leading feature, by its more important characteristic, by its pith and substance. And if, on the other hand, the provincial features are deemed clearly more important than the federal ones, then

[4] See: *Provincial Secretary of P.E.I.* v. *Egan and A.G. of P.E.I.* [1941] S.C.R. 396; [1941] 3 D.L.R. 305.

power to pass the law in question is exclusively provincial.[5]

In some instances, the solution to this dilemma of competing classifications may be grammatically obvious if one simply reads sections 91 and 92 together. For example, the provincial power "Solemnization of Marriage" (92(12)) is obviously to be read as an exception to the federal power "Marriage and Divorce" (91(26)). As a matter of construction the former is a particular sub-class completely comprehended by and carved out of the latter as a more general class or category. Only the provincial legislatures then can make law for marriage ceremonies, but only the federal parliament can make divorce law. Another example is afforded by "Patents" and "Copyrights" (91(22) and (23)) as small subdivisions of the general category of "Property" (92(13)). In these cases the B.N.A. Act seems explicit enough on the priorities between competing classifications, and to the extent that the words of the Act are clear on such issues they are conclusive.

Nevertheless, most of the problems of competing classifications that arise are not so easily soluble. Take for instance the competition between "Trade and Commerce" (91(2)) and "Property and Civil Rights" (92(13)) considered in the *Parsons* case.[6] Neither of these classes of laws is grammatically or logically an all-inclusive general category of which the other is obviously a sub-division. As a matter of construction it can properly be said that each is to be read subject to the other, that neither should be permitted to push the other out of the picture completely, but the question remains: where is the line to be drawn? There is no answer to this to be found by a simple reading of the statutory words. The answer is not grammatically internal to the Act. These are simply two wide or general categories that overlap a large common area – all property or civil rights laws that are also trading or commercial laws fall both ways as a matter of simple logic. From the legal point of view, most trade and commerce is the transfer of property rights by contract, or the provision of services by contract. In the *Parsons* case, the judgment of relative importance called for at this point was a compromise. The general line of distinction between section 91(2) and section 92(13) was drawn as follows: given that the challenged law is both property or contract law and

---

[5] See: *Union Colliery Company of B.C.* v. *Bryden* [1899] A.C. 580, at 587.

[6] *Citizens Insurance Company* v. *Parsons* (1881-82) 7 A.C. 96.

trading or commercial law, if the trade or commerce is internal to a single province, then the property and civil rights aspect is the more important and provincial power is exclusive. But, if the challenged law is property or contract law about interprovincial or international trade or commerce, then its trading or commercial aspect is the more important and the federal power is exclusive. In this way an issue of relative importance originally open so far as the words of the Act are concerned becomes settled as a matter of judicial precedent.

Accordingly, if there is sufficient contrast in relative importance between the competing federal and provincial features of the challenged law, then in spite of extensive overlap the interpretative tribunal can still allot exclusive legislative power one way or the other. Once exclusive power has been determined to exist for either legislature, then the so-called doctrine of abstinence simply expresses the implication of this negatively. If the federal parliament does not choose to use its power of regulation in a particular *exclusive* federal field, nevertheless a province cannot enter the field with provincial legislation. The activity concerned simply remains unregulated.

But what if the federal and provincial aspects of the challenged law seem to be of equivalent importance? What if there is no real contrast in this respect? This leads to the second main interpretative situation.

b *The Double-Aspect Doctrine and Concurrent Powers*

If reasoning (a) has been attempted, but it develops that the federal and provincial aspects of the challenged law are of equivalent importance – that they are on the same level of significance – then the allocation of *exclusive* power one way or the other is not possible. For example, in the *Voluntary Assignments* case,[7] the Court pointed out that the federal parliament must be able to deal with priority among the execution creditors of an insolvent debtor from the point of view of effective bankruptcy legislation, but that, equally, provincial legislatures had to deal with priorities among such execution creditors from the point of view of the provincial responsibility for civil procedure and civil rights. Hence the provincial legislation was valid, there being no federal bankruptcy statute at the time.

Accordingy the idea of mutual exclusion if practical, but

---

[7] *A.G. of Ontario* v. *A.G. of Canada* [1894] A.C. 189.

concurrency if necessary, explains much of Canadian constitutional law. For instance, one may ask, if Quebec was to be denied power to pass the Padlock Law because this invaded the exclusive federal criminal law sphere,[8] how is it that other provinces were permitted their provincial offences of simple careless driving, these not being considered to be such an invasion?[9] The judicial answers take the lines already suggested. True, the Padlock Law was in a sense property legislation as well as treason legislation, but its treason aspect was much more important than its property aspect, the latter being really a subterfuge. Hence, treason was the "pith and substance" and federal power was found to be exclusive. But, where the offence of simple careless driving was concerned, the provincial aspect of responsibility for safe and efficient circulation of traffic on highways was real and was deemed equivalent in importance to the federal aspect of responsibility to forbid and punish grave and dangerous anti-social conduct of all kinds. Hence the finding was made that dangerous driving offences are a concurrent matter or field.

There seems a definite increase in the number and importance of concurrent fields being presently established by the courts. Of course, agriculture and immigration are expressly concurrent fields by section 95 of the B.N.A. Act, while temperance and insolvency have been with us by judicial implication since the nineteenth century.[10] Recent cases have added concurrency concerning conduct on highways, sale of securities, validity of trading stamps in retail stores, and aspects of Sunday observance.[11] This list is by no means exhaustive. So, precisely

---

[8] *Act Respecting Communistic Propaganda* (Province of Quebec) R.S.Q. 1941, c. 52. Generally speaking, the Act provided that any house or building used by the tenant or owner as a place from which communistic propaganda was distributed could be padlocked on order of the Attorney-General for a year and thus withdrawn from any use whatsoever for that period. It was held to be *ultra vires* of the Province. See: *Switzman* v. *Elbling and A.G. of Quebec* [1957] S.C.R. 285.

[9] See: *The Queen* v. *Yolles* (1959) 19 D.L.R. (2d) 19; *O'Grady* v. *Sparling* [1960] S.C.R. 804.

[10] See: *A.G. of Ontario* v. *A.G. of Canada* [1896] A.C. 348, and footnote 7.

[11] Highways – *P.E.I.* v. *Egan, supra*, footnote 4; *The Queen* v. *Yolles, supra*, footnote 9; *O'Grady* v. *Sparling, supra*, footnote 9. Securities – *Smith* v. *The Queen* [1960] S.C.R. 776. Trading stamps – *The Queen* v. *Fleming* (1962) 35 D.L.R. (2d) 483. Sunday observance – *Lord's Day Alliance of Canada* v. *A.G. of B.C.* [1959] S.C.R. 497.

what concurrency means requires and deserves careful analysis. In 1907 in the Judicial Committee of the Privy Council, Lord Dunedin said that two propositions were established:[12]

First, that there can be a domain in which provincial and Dominion legislation may overlap, in which case neither legislation will be ultra vires, if the field is clear; and secondly, that if the field is not clear, and in such a domain the two legislations meet, then the Dominion legislation must prevail.

The word "meet" is used here in the sense of collision, but there may be joint occupation of a concurrent field without collision necessarily occurring. The different conditions of joint legislative tenancy will be discussed below under the headings *"Conflict," "Supplement"* and *"Duplication."*

CONFLICT, SUPPLEMENT AND DUPLICATION RESPECTING FEDERAL AND PROVINCIAL LAWS IN CONCURRENT FIELDS

Given that a concurrent sphere or field has been established, what if both the federal parliament and a provincial legislature have entered the field with statutes? What if "the two legislations meet"?

If the meeting is a collision, *i.e.* if conflict or inconsistency or repugnancy is the result, the federal statute prevails and the provincial one is displaced and inoperative. But it is far from obvious what amounts to sufficient conflict or inconsistency or repugnance to effect this result.

We start with two statutes that are somehow concerned with the same matter, that matter being the respect in which a concurrent field has been found to exist. The two statutes may differ in what they prescribe about the concurrent matter, or they may be the same in what they prescribe about it. This can soon be discovered by construing and comparing their respective terms, remembering that the search is for substantial differences or substantial identities. As in other constitutional matters, one must not be put off by merely verbal differences or identities. Does the provincial statute differ from the federal one or does it duplicate the federal one? That is the first question, because the reasoning appropriate to difference is not the same as that appropriate to duplication.

[12] *G.T. Rlwy Company of Canada* v. *A.G. of Canada* [1907] A.C. 65, at 68.

And even difference has its variations. The provincial statute may differ from the federal one in either one of two ways – it may be inconsistent with the federal one or it may be merely supplemental to the federal one, adding something to what the federal statute does but not contradicting it. So, in considering the relation of a provincial statute to a federal one in a concurrent field, there are three basic states: (a) conflict, (b) supplement, and (c) duplication. For the sake of developing the analysis clearly, it is assumed to start with that we have provincial statutes that are pure examples of each of these states, *i.e.* first a provincial statute that is purely conflicting, second a provincial statute that is purely supplemental, and finally a provincial statute that is purely duplicative. The problems presented by a mixed provincial statute – one that combines any two or all three of these types of provisions – can be disposed of if we know what is appropriate for the pure cases.

a Conflict

The situation envisaged here is actual conflict between the comparable terms of the provincial statute and the federal one. One finds that the same citizens are being told to do inconsistent things. One statute blows hot and the other cold. For example, a provincial statute says that a certain creditor is a secured creditor, but the federal Bankruptcy Act says he is an unsecured creditor. There can only be one scheme for priority among creditors in the event of bankruptcy of the debtor, hence the federal statute prevails and the provincial one is inoperative for repugnancy.[13] Another example is found in the *Local Prohibition* case of 1896.[14] There, Lord Watson compared the details of the Ontario statutory liquor prohibition scheme with the details of the federal liquor prohibition scheme of the Canada Temperance Act and found that the two differed sufficiently and that it would be impossible for both to be in force in the same county or town at the same time. Had it not been for its local option voting provisions, the Canada Temperance Act would automatically have displaced the provincial statutory scheme.

It thus appears that, in their local application within the province of Ontario, there would be considerable difference between

[13] *Royal Bank of Canada* v. *La Rue* [1926] S.C.R. 218; [1928] A.C. 187.
[14] *A.G. of Ontario* v. *A.G. of Canada* [1896] A.C. 343.

the two laws; but it is obvious that their provisions could not be in force within the same district or province at one and the same time.[15]

Thus, Lord Watson made it clear that if any district voted the Canada Temperance Act into force, the provincial statutory scheme would be precluded or superseded in that district.

Thus the pure case of express conflict is clear on the authorities – the federal statute prevails. At least the doctrine of Dominion paramountcy must go this far, but there has been some suggestion recently that it goes no further – that this is *all* it means. In the recent case of *Smith* v. *The Queen* (1960),[16] which concerned federal and provincial offences of knowingly issuing a false prospectus to induce the sale of company shares, Mr. Justice Martland of the Supreme Court of Canada said that, unless the federal and provincial provisions in question conflict *"in the sense that compliance with one law involves breach of the other,"* they can operate concurrently.[17] If only such patent and positive conflict of comparable terms can invoke the doctrine of Dominion paramountcy, then that doctrine is indeed confined to the narrowest significance it could possibly be given. On this view, any supplemental or duplicative provincial legislation could operate concurrently with the federal legislation it supplemented or duplicated, and our enquiry into the scope of the doctrine of Dominion paramountcy could end right here. But, as we shall see, this does not seem to be the state of the authorities.

In addition to the patent and positive conflict of terms just considered, there is another type of conflict or inconsistency to be examined. The federal legislation in a concurrent field may carry the express or tacit implication that there shall not be any other legislation on the concurrent subject by a province. If this negative implication is present, any supplemental provincial statute would be in conflict with it, though there is no conflict between comparable terms of the two statutes. It would be normal to find this implication in a federal statute that could properly be construed as a complete code for the concurrent

[15] [1896] A.C. 343; see also 369-70.

[16] *Supra,* footnote 11.

[17] [1960] S.C.R. 776, at 800; (italics added). In the context of the *Smith* case it may not be right to fix Mr. Justice Martland with the full implications of these words. Nevertheless, their full implications do mark out the narrowest possible meaning of Dominion paramountcy, and perhaps this *is* what Mr. Justice Martland intended.

subject. To revert to the matter of priority among various kinds of creditors in a bankruptcy, the federal code of priorities would clearly have this negative implication, even if there were gaps in it here or there where something might be added or even if there were room for further refinements. It should be noted at this point that Mr. Justice Cartwright of the Supreme Court of Canada has carried this idea of conflict by negative implication to its ultimate limit. In *O'Grady* v. *Sparling* (1960),[18] the Supreme Court was considering the relation of two different dangerous driving offences. The Criminal Code of Canada at this time made it an offence to drive a car with "wanton or reckless disregard for the lives or safety of other persons."[19] The Highway Traffic Act of Manitoba made it an offence to drive a car on a highway "without due care and attention or without reasonable consideration for other persons using the highway."[20] The provincial offence is much wider than the federal one, but overlaps and includes it. Mr. Justice Cartwright (dissenting) said:[21]

In my opinion when Parliament has expressed in an Act its decision that a certain kind or degree of negligence in the operation of a motor vehicle shall be punishable as a crime against the state it follows that it has decided that no less culpable kind or degree of negligence in such operation shall be so punishable. By necessary implication the Act says not only what kinds or degrees of negligence shall be punishable but also what kinds or degrees shall not.

In other words, he is saying that if there is a federal statute of any kind in a concurrent field, this alone necessarily and invariably implies that there shall be no other legal regulation by a province of the concurrent subject. To carry negative implication this far would ban all supplemental or duplicative provincial legislation. To use the metaphor of the "field," the effect of this view is that any federal statute touching a concurrent field constitutes total excluding occupation of that field by the federal parliament. This is the opposite extreme from the view of Mr. Justice Martland and thus represents the broadest sweep that could possibly be given the doctrine of Dominion paramountcy.

[18] *Supra*, footnote 11.
[19] *Criminal Code*, 2-3 Eliz. II, S.C. 1953-54 c. 51, ss. 191(1), 221(1).
[20] R.S.M. 1954, c. 112, s. 55(1).
[21] [1960] S.C.R. 804, at 820-1.

Mr. Justice Cartwright's view is not the law, but, as stated, it does mark out one of the two extreme positions possible and so aids this attempt at analysis.

As suggested earlier, the negative implication discussed here is legitimate and realistic in some circumstances, and when it is present, the rule of Dominion paramountcy operates to cause the exclusion or suspension of any provincial legislation on the subject in hand. But this is by no means automatically the case for every federal statute in a concurrent field.

Finally, if one has a provincial statute that mixes repugnant provisions with supplemental or duplicative ones, it may be that the repugnant provisions can be severed. This depends on the normal tests for severance in a constitutional case – does the provincial statute still constitute a viable and sensible legislative scheme without the obnoxious section or sections?[22] If severance is not proper, then the whole provincial statute becomes inoperative. If severance is possible, then one goes on to the question whether the supplemental or duplicative provisions are respectively valid in their own right. The case of pure supplement is then next.

b *Supplement*

The sitution envisaged here is that of a provincial statute which simply adds something to regulation of the concurrent matter without contradicting the federal statute in the field in either the positive or the negative sense explained in **(a)**. A. H. F. Lefroy gives a good example of this.[23]

Thus, where the Dominion Companies Act provided a method for serving summonses, notices, and other documents on a company incorporated under that Act, this was held not to prevent provincial, or rather North-West Territorial, legislation, providing that such companies must file a power of attorney to some person in the Territories upon whom process might be served, before they could be registered and enabled to carry on their business in the Territories, thus providing another and more convenient method for the service of process upon such company.

Accordingly, provincial supplemental legislation in these

[22] See: *Toronto Corporation* v. *York Corporation* [1938] A.C. 415, at 427; *A.G. for B.C.* v. *A.G. for Canada* [1937] A.C. 377, at 388-9.
[23] A. H. F. Lefroy, *Canada's Federal System* (Toronto, 1913), p. 126.

circumstances is valid and operates concurrently with the relevant federal legislation. A refinement of this position was approved by the Supreme Court of Canada in the case of *Lord's Day Alliance of Canada* v. *Attorney-General of British Columbia*.[24] The federal statute in question was the Lord's Day Act,[25] section 6(1) of which is as follows:

6(1) It is not lawful for any person, on the Lord's Day, except as provided in any provincial Act or law now or hereafter in force, to engage in any public game or contest for gain, or for any prize or reward, or to be present thereat, or to provide, engage in, or be present at any performance or public meeting, elsewhere than in a church, at which any fee is charged, directly or indirectly, either for admission to such performance or meeting, or to any place within which the same is provided, or for any service or privilege thereat.

If it were not for the words *except as provided in any provincial law now or hereafter in force*, the field of regulation of Sunday commercial sports and movies would be completely occupied by the federal prohibition by virtue of the federal criminal law power. The Supreme Court considered that permissive Sunday observance legislation would also be proper for a province as a matter of civil rights in the province or as a matter of merely a local nature in the province, and that the federal parliament had deliberately and effectively made room for such permissive provincial legislation by the statutory words just quoted. Here then we have the federal parliament explicitly drawing back from full occupation of the concurrent field to allow a different provincial provision on the subject to operate without conflict. It is the strongest possible case for the validity of non-repugnant and supplemental provincial legislation because, on the facts, a prohibition was withdrawn to make room for a permission to operate. The extreme view of the scope of negative implication explained earlier under (**a**) is inconsistent with the *Lord's Day Alliance* case of 1959.

The Saskatchewan *Breathalyser* case of 1957[26] is also a decision of the Supreme Court of Canada upholding the validity of a non-repugnant supplemental provincial statute. The matter

[24] *Supra*, footnote 11.
[25] R.S.C. 1952, c. 171.
[26] *Reference Re Section* 92(4) *of The Vehicles Act*, 1957 (Sask.), *c.* 93 [1958] S.C.R. 608.

involved was the legal status and effect of the result of tests by the breathalyser machine to determine whether a driver on the highway was drunk. The federal Criminal Code, addressing itself to the evidentiary problem only, stated that

No person is required to give a sample of blood, urine, breath or other bodily substance or chemical analysis for the purpose of this section.[27]

but also provided in effect that, if such sample was in fact given, the result of the chemical analysis was admissible evidence in the trial of a relevant charge under the Criminal Code.

The Saskatchewan statute provided that a driver suspected of being drunk who refused to take the breathalyser test at the request of a policeman was liable to have his licence to drive suspended or revoked. The Supreme Court of Canada held that the provincial legislation was not inconsistent with the federal legislation and was therefore fully operative, and moreover that breathalyser evidence obtained in Saskatchewan was admissible in the trial of the relevant federal offence.

The writer agrees with Mr. Justice Cartwright in this case that the finding of "no conflict" here is wrong. As the learned judge put it:[28]

. . . I am of opinion that a statute declaring that a person who refuses to do an act shall be liable to suffer a serious and permanent economic disadvantage does "require" the doing of the act. With deference to those who hold a contrary view, it appears to me to be playing with words to say that a person who is made liable to a penalty (whether economic, pecuniary, corporal or, I suppose, capital) if he fails to do an act is not required to do the act because he is free to choose to suffer the penalty instead.

There is at least partial repugnance here, and the better decision would have been that the Saskatchewan requirement could not operate to create evidence admissible in the trial of the relevant federal offences but could operate as the evidentiary basis for a decision by the Saskatchewan Motor Vehicle Board to suspend or revoke a driver's licence. Nevertheless, given the majority finding that there was no conflict between the provincial and federal statutory provisions concerned, the case is authority, as stated earlier, for the proposition that supplemental provincial legislation remains operative. Now, only the final case of pure duplication remains to be examined.

c Duplication

The situation envisaged here is that of a provincial statute that literally or in substance duplicates the provisions of the federal statute in the field. (It does not matter which statute was passed first once both are in the field.) The authorities establish one of the implications of Dominion paramountcy to be that provincial duplicative legislation is suspended and inoperative. Simple duplication by a province is not permitted.[29] But, given that this *is* the state of the precedents, why *should* it be so? My submission is that there are proper reasons for this result, but they are not explained in the opinions of the judges in Canadian constitutional cases.

Where the provincial statute differs from the federal one, we have seen that the provincial provisions are suspended if they are directly or indirectly repugnant to the federal ones (**a**), but the provincial provisions are operative if they merely supplement the federal ones (**b**). Necessity born of repugnance accounts for the former result (**a**) and the logic of being different for the latter (**b**). But in the case of simple duplication we have neither repugnance nor difference. *In fact what one now finds by comparing the provincial and federal statutes in question is the ultimate in harmony*. Obviously this is what substantial duplication means. Yet at times the judges persist in saying that there is "conflict" here, and that such "conflict" somehow calls for the suspension of the provincial duplicative legislation. For instance, in *Smith* v. *The Queen*, Mr. Justice Ritchie (dissenting), after concluding that the provincial and federal offences there in question were the same, said: "I am of opinion . . . that there

[29] See: *Home Insurance Co.* v. *Lindal & Beattie* [1934] S.C.R. 33, *per* Lamont, J. at p. 40; *Lymburn* v. *Mayland* [1932] A.C. 318, *per* Lord Atkin, at p. 326-7. Also, in the *Yolles*, *O'Grady* and *Smith* cases most of the judges (whether of the majority or dissenting) assumed that if the federal and provincial offences being compared were substantially the same, the provincial offence was suspended and inoperative.

In an excellent note on this subject, Professor Bora Laskin points out that simple duplication of federal legislation by a state is forbidden in both the United States and Australia. See Bora Laskin, *Canadian Constitutional Law* (Toronto, 1960), p. 98.

is a direct conflict between the impugned provisions of the provincial statute and those of the Criminal Code and that it is not within the competence of the Legislature of Ontario to create the offences here in question."[30] Likewise, Chief Justice Kerwin, giving one of the majority judgments in the same case, said there was *"no repugnancy"* between the provincial and federal offences because it was *not* the same conduct that was being dealt with by the two legislative bodies.[31] Obviously he implies that there would be repugnancy if the offences had been exactly the same.

Nevertheless, though it is not proper at all to speak of conflict or repugnance of terms when a provincial statute simply duplicates a federal one, is there a conflict in some other sense when this happens? Is it somehow an affront to the federal parliament that a provincial legislature should repeat the terms of a federal statute? No doubt the doctrine of Dominion paramountcy means that in a concurrent field the federal parliament is the senior partner, but what is repugnant about the junior partner merely repeating the senior one? In truth there is no conflict or repugnance of any kind in this situation. As seen in Part I, the provincial legislature and the federal parliament are properly making laws in the concurrent field in pursuance of legislative responsibilities and powers conferred by their respective aspects of interest. These aspects are equivalent as a matter of authority stemming from the constitution, so there is no clash of authority in the absence of actual inconsistency of statutory terms as explained earlier. Why then is duplicative provincial legislation suspended? The reason seems a very simple one – economy. It is wasteful of legislative and administrative resources to allow simple duplication, besides being confusing for all concerned. Since the province in effect admits that the federal legislation is in exactly the terms it wants, the federal legislation is serving the provincial interest just as the provincial legislature wishes it to be served. But still the provincial spokesman may ask, why not suspend the federal legislation then and avoid duplication that way? The answer in favour of the federal legislation would seem to be twofold: (i) the federal parliament is in the better position to effect economy and avoid confusion because of its wider territorial jurisdiction, hence the provincial duplicative legislation should be suspended, and, anyway, (ii)

30 [1960] S.C.R. 776, at 804.
31 [1960] S.C.R. 776, at 780-1. Italics added.

the nation is greater than its parts, hence when the scales are evenly balanced, as here, the national parliament should be preferred over the provincial legislature. So, the normal rule is that a provincial statutory provision is suspended and inoperative if it simply duplicates a federal one.

But what if the provincial provision in question is a mixed one in the sense that it both duplicates and supplements the corresponding federal one? This was the position in both *Yolles* v. *The Queen* and *O'Grady* v. *Sparling*.[32] In both these cases, the provincial offence was to drive a car on a highway "without due care and attention or without reasonable consideration for other persons using the highway," while the corresponding federal law made it an offence to drive a car with "wanton or reckless disregard for the lives or safety of other persons." Mr. Justice Roach pointed out in the *Yolles* case that the provincial offence as expressed cannot really be severed into its duplicative and its supplemental parts so as to suspend the former and save the latter. "Section 29(1) does not confine the lack of 'due care and attention' or the absence of 'reasonable consideration for others' to an attitude that is less than wanton or reckless. The Court cannot unscramble s. 29(1) or rewrite it. The Legislature alone can do that."[33] Mr. Justice Roach was right to consider this not a proper case for severence, but was he right to conclude that therefore the whole provincial section was suspended? In the latter conclusion he was dissenting, the majority decisions in both the *Yolles* and *O'Grady* cases being to the contrary.

The majority decisions seem correct and justifiable. A provincial section that combines inseverably duplicative and supplemental elements does not necessarily require the same treatment as one that combines inseverably repugnant and supplemental elements. Logically, economy permits exceptions that inconsistency must deny, and in the cases mentioned the majority judges took advantage of this. Here is the importance of elucidating the different reasons for superseding duplicative provisions on the one hand and repugnant ones on the other. The normal rule is that duplicative provincial provisions are inoperative, but, by way of exception, when a provincial provision is an inseverable combination of duplicative and supplemental elements, the whole provincial provision stands and operates concurrently with the federal provision it both dupli-

[32] *Supra*, footnote 11.
[33] (1959) 19 D.L.R. (2d) 19, at 44.

cates and supplements. This is the proper rationale of the
Yolles, O'Grady, Stephens, and *Smith* cases.[34] This exception to
the general rule is important but quite limited, and it contrasts
of course sharply with the position that obtains when a provincial provision inseverably combines *repugnant* and supplemental elements – the whole of such a provision is necessarily
superseded by the federal one. In other words, when the duplicative is in combination with the supplemental, the former is
operative because of its combination with the latter, but when
the repugnant is combined with the supplemental, the latter
goes into suspension with the former.[35]

Unfortunately the reasons for the exception just explained
and the limited nature of the exception do not come out too
clearly in the majority opinions of the four leading cases just
mentioned. There is a tendency among some of the learned
judges to deny the existence of the duplicative or overlapping
element, and to say that because there is *some* difference between the provincial and federal offences as to the mental state
required, this makes them *totally* different, so that the provincial
offence is merely supplemental after all. But it does not really
make sense to deny the genuine though partial duplicative element in these cases. Also, in the same cases, there is a tendency
among some of the learned judges to argue that, because the
concurrent matter in issue has a provincial aspect and a different
federal aspect, partially overlapping provincial and federal
laws enacted respectively under these aspects of authority are
themselves entirely different laws because the two aspects of
authority involved are different. This does not stand up either.
As we have already seen, it is the existence of two equivalent but
different aspects of authority that establishes a concurrent field
in the first place. The double-aspect theory opens two gates to
the same field, but there it leaves us. It does not resolve any of
the *subsequent* difficulties of conflict, duplication, or supplement being analysed here.

There has been a new development since the decision of

[34] *Supra*, footnote 11. *Stephens* v. *The Queen* [1960] S.C.R. 823.
[35] Of course, a provincial statute may combine provisions exclusively
within provincial powers with others in a concurrent field of one or
more of the three types discussed here – conflicting, supplemental or
duplicative. This was true of both the Ontario and Manitoba Highway Traffic Acts. The argument made here is not affected by this
circumstance, though the application of the rules for severance might
become rather complex in some situations.

O'Grady v. *Sparling*, the implications of which serve to illustrate the effect of this group of cases. In the session of 1960-61, the Parliament of Canada added to the Criminal Code a new provision making it an offence to drive a motor vehicle "in a manner that is dangerous to the public, having regard to all the circumstances."[36] This is in addition to the federal offence of driving with "wanton or reckless disregard" that was the sole federal provision at the time of the *Yolles* and *O'Grady* decisions. There is really no difference between driving in a manner dangerous to the public, and driving with lack of due care and attention (simple negligence). Negligence is defined by whether a reasonable man would foresee the likelihood of causing harm to others by his conduct, *i.e.* by whether his conduct was *dangerous* to the public. In *O'Grady* v. *Sparling* the Supreme Court of Canada expressly adopted the twofold distinction of these offences into advertent negligence and inadvertent negligence, pointing out that inadvertent negligence was the respect in which the provincial offence was wider than the federal one of showing wanton and reckless disregard. It follows that the provincial "lack of due care" offence now merely duplicates the new federal offence of simple dangerous driving. Hence provincial careless driving offences like those of Ontario and Manitoba are now suspended and inoperative, and any charge laid under such a provincial section should be quashed.[37] This is the effect of the general rule that a provincial provision that is severable and merely duplicative is to be severed and superseded by the federal provisions duplicated. Authority for this proposition has already been quoted.

[36] 9-10 Eliz. II, S.C. 1960-61, c. 43, s. 3.

[37] It is true that some authorities consider there are three grades of negligence for these purposes. See the judgment of LeBel, J. A. in the *Yolles* case, (1959) 19 D.L.R. (2d), 19, at 49-50. Mr. Justice LeBel referred to *McLean* v. *Pettigrew* [1945] S.C.R. 62, as supporting this view. *McLean* v. *Pettigrew* is a conflict of laws case in tort and such a threefold distinction was unnecessary to the decision. In any event, the Supreme Court of Canada in the *O'Grady* case has adopted two grades of negligence as the governing distinction for purposes of the issues touching Dominion paramountcy – the distinction being that between advertent negligence and inadvertent negligence.

There has also been some suggestion that Lord Atkin sanctioned a threefold distinction in the case of *Andrews* v. *Director of Public Prosecutions* [1937] A.C. 576, when discussing parallel sections in the English Road Traffic Act of 1930. I cannot find any such threefold distinction in Lord Atkin's judgment. See [1937] A.C. at 576, at 584.

Subject then to the limited exception explained, the general rule requiring the suspension of provincial duplicative legislation is a salutary one. If the possibility of effective provincial duplicative legislation was wide open, then, for example, a provincial legislature could duplicate the whole of the federal law of theft as legislation to protect property rights in the province. Crown attorneys could take their choice of whether to prosecute under the federal theft sections or the provincial ones, and the provincial Attorneys-General could control this choice. Awkward questions about double jeopardy or the right to trial by jury could arise. Fortunately, under the present rules, there are two reasons why a province could not duplicate the federal law of theft in the Criminal Code. In the first place the federal theft sections are by their nature comprehensive, constituting what purports to be a complete code on the subject of theft. Hence the negative implication discussed under (a) earlier is genuinely present and precludes any provincial theft legislation operating. Even if this were not so, simple duplication is not allowed anyway, as we have seen in the analysis just concluded under (c).

The position of provincial legislation in a concurrent field then may be summarized as follows. Provincial legislation may operate if there is no federal legislation in the field or if the provincial legislation is merely supplemental to federal legislation that is in the field. Duplicative provincial legislation may operate concurrently only when inseverably connected with supplemental provincial legislation, otherwise duplicative provincial legislation is suspended and inoperative. Repugnant provincial legislation is always suspended and inoperative. These are the implications of the doctrine of Dominion paramountcy developed by the courts.[38]

In conclusion, it should be noted that the existence of a concurrent field means that there is room for political agreement between provincial and federal governments about whether the federal parliament or a provincial legislature undertakes the

---

[38] It should be noted that in one respect, old age pensions, we have a doctrine of provincial paramountcy, by virtue of section 94A of the B.N.A. Act, added in 1951 by 14-15 Geo. VI(U.K.), c. 32:

94A. It is hereby declared that the Parliament of Canada may from time to time make laws in relation to old age pensions in Canada, but no law made by the Parliament of Canada in relation to old age pensions shall affect the operation of any law present or future of a Provincial Legislature in relation to old age pensions.

regulation of this or that phase of a concurrent matter. The precise equilibrium point in practice then would become a matter for political and administrative decision. As governmental activities continue to expand in our modern urban and industrial society, we can expect much more concurrent operation of federal and provincial laws in the old areas of joint occupation and in new areas as well. The adjustments involved will continue to call for both judicial and political decisions of a high order.[39]

[39] As Dr. J. A. Corry has pointed out, our country is increasingly moving away from the older classical federalism of "watertight compartments" with provincial legislatures and federal parliament carefully keeping clear of one another. We seem to be moving towards a co-operative federalism. "The co-ordinate governments no longer work in splendid isolation from one another but are increasingly engaged in co-operative ventures in which each relies heavily on the other." See J. A. Corry. "Constitutional Trends and Federalism," in the volume of essays *Evolving Canadian Federalism* (Durham, N.C., U.S.A., 1958), p. 96. The multiplication of concurrent fields is one of the facets of this trend. Even if the precise equilibrium point in a concurrent field is reached by political decision or agreement, nevertheless the bargaining position of federal and provincial governments is defined by the judicial decisions about concurrency and the doctrine of Dominion paramountcy.

The Nature, Use and Effect of Reference Cases in Canadian Constitutional Law

GERALD RUBIN

THE NATURE OF REFERENCE CASES

An analysis of the nature of "reference cases" requires a working definition of that term and a term which is synonymous with it: "advisory opinions." An "advisory opinion" has been defined as follows:[1]

A formal opinion by judge or judges or a court of law or a law officer upon a question of law submitted by a legislative body or a governmental official, but not actually presented in a concrete case at law.

It is the concluding words of this definition which point most clearly to the outstanding characteristics of a reference case. A "concrete case at law" is characterized by at least two features: rival litigants, and a specific actual fact situation out of which their dispute arose. It is the peculiar mark of the reference case that it has neither of these features.

The absence of the first feature is one of the key factors distinguishing the reference or advisory opinion from the declaratory judgment, while the absence of the second feature is the basic distinction between the reference and the stated case.

It has been stressed that the advisory opinion differs "funda-

From: *The McGill Law Journal*, Volume 6 (1959-60), pages 168-90. By permission of the author and publisher. This article is a condensation of a thesis that tied for the Public Law Prize in third year at McGill University.

[1] *Black's Law Dictionary*, 4th ed. (1951), p. 75. The definition continues: "Merely opinion of judges or court which adjudicates nothing and is binding on no one, in exercise of wholly non- or extra-judicial function. The expression ordinarily connotes the practice which existed in England from very early times of extra-judicial consultation of the judges by the Crown and the House of Lords."

mentally" from the declaratory judgment and that the function of rendering advisory opinions belongs properly to the law officers or the attorney-general. The power has been exercised by the courts simply because there has been no constitutional bar and the courts have been unable to decline.

The advisory opinion binds no one, not even the judges, is not rendered between parties, is given to the asking official or department and is often rendered without hearing argument. In all these respects it differs from the declaratory judgment. Even if argument is heard by parties with opposing interests . . . it lacks one of the essential elements of a judgment in that it is rendered not on demand of and to an aggrieved or complaining party, but on demand of and to an administrative body.[2]

The distinction between the stated case and the reference must also be borne in mind. "It is absolutely settled law," writes an Australian judge,[3] "in both England and Australia that the expression 'state a case' involves stating facts, that is, the ultimate facts, requiring only the certainty of some point of law applied to those facts to determine either the whole case or some particular stage of it." It is just this factual basis which is lacking in the reference case.[4]

[2] Borchard, E. M., *Declaratory Judgments*, 1st ed., (1934), pp. 51-2, cited by J. F. Davison in "The Constitutionality and Utility of Advisory Opinions," (1937-8), 2 University of Toronto L.J. 2593, n. 24. See also the second edition of Borchard's work, 1941, at pp. 71-3. *Osborn's Concise Law Dictionary*, 4th ed. (1954), defines a declaratory judgment as follows: "A judgment which conclusively declares the pre-existing rights of the litigants without the appendage of any coercive decree. See also *Wharton's Law Lexicon*, 14th ed., (1938), p. 307; *Black's Law Dictionary*, 4th ed., p. 497. The Judicature Act, R.S.O., 1950, c. 190, s. 20. For cases under declaratory judgment legislation in Canada see *Attorney-General for Canada* v. *Attorney-General for Ontario*, (1891-92), 19 O.A.R. 31, *Attorney-General for Ontario* v. *Attorney-General for Canada*, [1931] 2 D.L.R. 297; *Motor Car Supply Co.* v. *Attorney-General for Alberta*, [1939] 3 D.L.R. 660.

[3] *Australian Commonwealth Shipping Board* v. *Federated Seamen's Union of Australasia*, (1925), 36 C.L.R. 442, *per* Isaacs J., at p. 450, cited in *Words and Phrases Judicially Defined*, (1945), Vol. V, p. 152.

[4] See Borchard, *op. cit.*, 2nd ed. pp. 221-3 for a discussion of the special case – "an agreed statement of facts for the determination of a disputed issue of law" – and its variation in the special case stated – "used by certain special courts and administrative tribunals to test the validity of their orders." At p. 223, n. 65, Borchard cautions against confusing the special case stated with the advisory opinion.

The distinctions we have attempted to make are not matters of purely academic interest. In *Re Board of Commerce*[5] the Supreme Court of Canada rebuffed an attempt to submit to it what was in reality a reference under the guise of a stated case. Section 32 of The Board of Commerce Act of 1919 empowered the Board of Commerce to state a case in writing for the opinion of the Supreme Court upon any question which, in the opinion of the Board, was a question of law or jurisdiction. Acting, or claiming to act, under this section, the Board of Commerce drew up a list of six questions.

Three of the questions were concerned with the constitutional validity of certain provisions of the Combines and Fair Prices Act of 1919, the others with the construction of certain sections of the same statute. When the matter came to be considered by the Court, it found that the questions presented did not constitute a "stated case" within the meaning of the Board of Commerce Act. The Board then inserted a typewritten memorandum into the record stating that the question had arisen as a result of certain matters actually pending before the Board, but this too was rejected because, in the words of Anglin J., "it did not contain any statement out of which the questions formulated arose." The Court based itself upon an English decision, *Re Cardigan County Council*,[6] where it was held that in stating a case for the High Court under s. 29 of The Local Government Act of 1888, "the facts which have actually arisen" and the decision thereon, must be set forth, and that the High Court would not answer questions as to the construction of the statute "unless arising out of acts which have actually occurred." The justices of the Supreme Court looked upon the questions submitted by the Board, again in the words of Anglin J., as an unintentional assumption, under the guise of a stated case, of the power conferred on the Governor-General in Council by the Supreme Court Act for hearing and considering the constitutionality of any federal or provincial legislation.[7]

For purposes of this paper, reference cases may be defined as matters referred to the courts under the provisions of the

[5] (1920), 60 S.C.R. 456.

[6] (1890), 54 J.P. 792.

[7] The difficulty was finally overcome when the Board made a third submission to the Court containing the required statement of facts. For the account of the Board's difficulties in obtaining a hearing, see the remarks of Anglin J., (1920), 60 S.C.R. 456 at pp. 457-9 and those of Idington J. at pp. 475-80.

Supreme Court Act, R.S.C., 1952, c. 259, ss. 55,56,37 and corresponding provincial legislation.[8]

Thus, the term "reference case," as we intend to use it, is at once wider and narrower than the definition we cited at the beginning of this paper. It is wider in the sense that matters of law *and* fact can be submitted under the federal or provincial reference legislation, narrower in that references to the law officers of the Crown are not included in it.

THE USE OF REFERENCE CASES

a Constitutional references – general

Generally speaking, the strongest moving force for use of the reference power is a desire by both the federal and provincial executives for a speedy judicial determination of legal problems arising out of the interpretation of the provisions of the British North America Act and especially the provisions allotting legislative jurisdiction. The question as to which legislative authority has the power to implement treaty obligations, one involving ss. 91, 92, and 132, is an excellent example. The answer to this question has been, almost in its entirety, furnished by the Supreme Court and the Judicial Committee in answer to references submitted to them.[9]

In terms of the actual content of the British North America Act references, there is no very significant difference between the use of the federal reference power and the use of the provincial reference power. But in terms of motivation, beyond the common federal and provincial interest in obtaining information as to the working of that Act, there are special factors peculiar to the use of the federal power which will now be considered.

b Constitutional reference – disallowance

Reference has long been considered as a useful aid to the

---

[8] R.S.N.S., 1954, c. 50; R.S.P.E.I., 1951, c. 79; R.S.N.B., c. 120, s. 24A; Statutes of Newfoundland, 1953, No. 3; R.S.Q., 1941, c. 8; R.S. Man., 1954, c. 44; R.S. Sask., 1953, c. 18; R.S. Alta., 1955, c. 55; R.S.B.C., 1948, c. 66.

[9] *Reference re Employment of Aliens*, (1922), 63 S.C.R. 293; *Reference re Waters and Water Powers*, [1929] S.C.R. 200; *Reference re Hours of Labour*, [1925] S.C.R. 505; *Reference re Regulation and Control of Aeronautics*, [1930] S.C.R. 663; *Reference re Regulation of Radio Communication*, [1931] S.C.R. 541. *The Labour Conventions Reference*, [1936] S.C.R. 461.

federal executive in the exercise of its disallowance power. This was one of the principal reasons behind the introduction in the House of Commons, of the Hon. Edward Blake's resolution of 1890 on references which in turn led to the amendment in 1891 of the reference provisions of the Supreme Court Act. In supporting his resolution in the Commons, Blake outlined his view of the relationship between the reference power he desired and disallowance.[10]

Now, Sir, in the exercise of this power of disallowance by the Government, political questions may ... arise. Questions of policy may present themselves, that is, questions of expediency, of convenience, of the public interest, of the spirit of the constitution or of the form of legislation. All these are clearly, exclusively for the executive and legislative, that is, for the political departments of the Government. But it is equally clear that when, in order to determine your course you must find whether a particular act is ultra *or* intra vires, *you are discharging a legal and judicial function. . . . Now, I aver that in the decision of all legal questions, it is important that the political executive should not, more than can be avoided, arrogate to itself judicial powers; and that when in the discharge of its political duties, it is called upon to deal with legal questions, it ought to have the power, in cases of solemnity and importance where it may be thought expedient so to do, to call in aid the judicial department in order to arrive at a correct solution.*

The decision that an act was *ultra vires*, he continued, and its consequent disallowance by the federal executive were incidents peculiar to Canada. It was a most delicate function and its exercise involved grave ulterior consequences. The question whether the act disallowed was or was not valid was removed from judicial cognizance forever. Thus, by repeated exercises of the power of disallowance, in respect to repeated provincial legislation, a province might practically be deprived of that which might be a right justly claimed. One of two limited governments might practically decide the extent of the limits of what was, in a sense, its rival government. A decision under such circumstances would necessarily be suspect. It would, in a sense, be the decision of a party in its own cause. The concur-

---

[10] For the speeches on the resolution by Blake and Sir John Macdonald see Debates, House of Commons, Canada, 1890, Vol. II, 4084-94.

rence of a neutral and respected court was necessary to strengthen the decision of the executive.

My own opinion is that whenever, in opposition to the continued view of a Provincial Executive and Legislature, it is contemplated by the Dominion Executive to disallow a provincial Act because it is ultra vires, *there ought to be a reference; and also that there ought to be a reference in certain cases where the condition of public opinion renders expedient a solution of legal problems, dissociated from those elements of passion and expediency which are rightly or wrongly too often attributed to the action of political bodies.*[11]

The relationship between references and disallowance was also discussed by the Federal Minister of Justice, Sir John Thompson, during the debate on the amendment of 1891. The disallowance power, explained Sir John, was exercised in two classes of cases: first, where an act of a provincial legislature was in conflict with Dominion policy, Dominion rights, or Dominion property; and secondly, where it was felt by the Dominion executive that the legislature, in passing the act in question, had exceeded its powers. It was with regard to the second class of cases that Sir John felt the reference power, as provided for in the amendment, would be of assistance. As matters presently stood, he said, when it was felt that the operation of an unconstitutional act would create public inconvenience, its disallowance was recommended, but the basis for this was merely the opinion of the Minister of Justice. Henceforth, he declared, he took it for granted that in nearly every case of that kind, reference would be had with a view to understanding what were the constitutional rights of the legislature. If the Court held the act to be *intra vires*, since the opinions would be only advisory, the bare power of disallowance for constitutional reasons would remain. However, he acknowledged[12]

. . . it would be more absurd and practically impossible for the Minister of Justice to advise that it should be disallowed, after the highest tribunal had decided that the Act was within the powers of the Provincial Legislature.

It will be at once perceived that Blake and Thompson had advanced definite criteria which were to guide the federal

[11] *Ibid.*
[12] Debates, House of Commons, Canada, 1891, Vol. II, 3586-7.

executive in using the reference in disallowance cases. "Constitutional" cases involving questions of *ultra vires* were to be referred to the Court, while cases involving "policy" were, as Blake said, "clearly, exclusively for the executive and legislative, that is for the political departments of the Government." However, there is often no clear cut line between "constitutional" cases and "policy" cases. "Constitutional" cases often involve strong elements of "policy" and vice versa. There is thus a danger that the federal executive, where a case involves *both* the constitutional issue and highly controversial questions of policy will shirk its disallowance responsibility and pass political "hot potatoes" to the Supreme Court under the guise of following the rule that cases involving the constitutionality of a statute should not be decided by the executive but by the courts. It has been suggested that this was indeed the policy of the Federal Cabinet during the great storm that arose in the thirties over Alberta legislation. When the first group of Alberta statutes was enacted, the first move of Prime Minister King was to suggest a reference. It was only when this tactic, and others, had failed that the Federal Cabinet, "smoked out," as it were, resorted to disallowance.[13]

Sir John Macdonald was aware that a danger existed but felt that the terms of Blake's resolution, the substantial basis for s. 55 of the Supreme Court Act as it is enacted today, would enable it to be avoided. He told the Commons, in accepting Blake's resolution, that it had at first seemed to him to be a step toward the American system which transferred the responsibility of the Ministry of the day to a judicial tribunal, but he saw now that Blake had been careful not to propose in his resolution that the opinions would bind the executive. It was, he noted, explicitly declared that the decision was only for the information of the government. The executive was not released from all

[13] Mallory, J. R., Disallowance and the National Interest, 1948, Canadian Journal of Economics and Political Science, p. 357. Eugene Forsey writes: "Authentic copies [of the Alberta Acts] reached the Governor General August 10th [1937]. On the same day the Minister of Justice wrote a long and elaborate report recommending disallowance. On August 11th the Prime Minister telegraphed Mr. Aberhart, Premier of Alberta, that the Minister of Justice 'is considering' disallowance and offered to refer the Acts to the Supreme Court if Mr. Aberhart would suspend their operation. Mr. Aberhart refused. Six days later, August 17th, the Acts were formally disallowed." "Canada and Alberta: The Revival of Dominion Control over the Provinces," p. 104. Reprinted from *Politica*, June, 1939, Vol. IV, No. 16.

responsibility by the Court's reply. It was possible that the government would not approve of this decision, and it would be its *duty* not to approve if it did not accept the conclusion of the Court.[14]

While it is to be hoped that federal cabinets will show the fortitude expected of them by Sir John Macdonald, the danger of abuse of the reference power remains.

c Constitutional references – education

Similar problems arise with regard to the appellate jurisdiction of the federal executive in educational matters under s. 93 of the British North America Act, for, in view of the impending storm in Manitoba, it was also Blake's aim in submitting his resolution of 1890 to have the reference power employed in such matters. The arguments he employed were similar to those he used in discussing disallowance. What was the procedure to be followed, he asked, when an educational appeal came before the federal executive? First, it was necessary to determine whether any class of persons had, in virtue of the law or practice at the Union, any right or privilege pertaining to denominational schools, and if so, what was the right. Secondly, it was necessary to determine if a right or privilege had been affected and how by the provincial legislation complained of, and, finally, to determine what legislative action was necessary to repair any harm done. The first two questions, Blake stressed, were legal and not political.[15]

The objection to the executive alone deciding the questions that arose in the case of disallowance was also applicable here. The following passage certainly applied to both:

Ours is a popular government; and when burning questions arise, inflaming the public mind, when agitation is rife as to the political action of the Executive or the Legislature – when action is to be based on legal questions, obviously beyond the grasp of the people at large; when the people are on such questions divided by cries of creed and race; then I maintain

---

[14] Debates, House of Commons, Canada, 1890, Vol. II, 4093-4.

[15] While Blake considered these questions "legal" as opposed to "political" he saw that these legal questions were actually mixed questions of law and fact. It was for this reason that the words "or fact" were inserted into the resolution. Blake discussed the educational aspect in the speech in which he considered the disallowance question. Debates, House of Commons, Canada, 1890, Vol. II, 4084-93.

that a great public good is attainable by the submission of such legal questions to legal tribunals with all the customary securities for a sound judgment; and whose decisions – passionless and dignified, accepted by each of us as binding in our own affairs involving fortune, freedom, honour, life itself – are more likely to be accepted by us all in questions of public concern.

The reference power *was* employed by the Federal Cabinet in the *Manitoba Education Reference*, in 1894,[16] but Blake's hopes that this would significantly reduce controversy were not realized.[17]

d *Other references*

Other special motives for the use of the federal reference power are to be found in the desire of the federal executive for information regarding treaties and other questions touching Canada's relations with foreign powers too important to wait until they come up in a concrete case,[18] and also in the great need for swift judicial clarification of issues at the highest level in the midst of a war emergency.[19]

References have also been used by both the federal and provincial executives simply for assistance in the administration of the federal or provincial laws. This practice is found more often in provincial references,[20] but there is no apparent reason

[16] (1894), 22 S.C.R. 577.

[17] For cases in which the disallowance power was involved see: *Reference re Employment of Aliens*, (1922), 63 S.C.R. 293; *Reference re The Manitoba Act*, [1924] S.C.R. 317; *Reference re Disallowance*, [1938] S.C.R. 71; *Reference re Alberta Securities*, [1938] S.C.R. 100; *Reference re Alberta Railway Act*, (1913), 48 S.C.R. 9.

[18] *Supra*, footnote 9. Also, *Reference re U.S. Forces*, [1943] S.C.R. 483.

[19] *Reference re Validity of the Chemical Regulations*, [1943] S.C.R. 1.

[20] Provincial references: *Reference re Ontario Medical Act*, (1907), 13 O.L.R. 501; *Reference re Bread Sales Act*. (1911), 23 O.L.R. 238; *Reference re Liquor Licence Act*, (1913-14), 29 O.L.R. 475; *Reference re Sessional Allowances*, [1945] 2 D.L.R. 631 (Ont.); *Reference re Power of Municipal Council*, (1957), 7 D.L.R. (2nd) 222 (Ont.); *Re Trades Union Act*, [1945] 2 D.L.R. 163 (N.S.); *Re Labour Act*, [1948] 2 D.L.R. 428 (Alta.); *Reference re Jury Act*, [1946] 3 D.L.R. 457 (Alta.); *Reference re Relief Liability Act*, [1938] 4 D.L.R. 646 (Alta.); *Reference re Charter of City of Vancouver*, [1946] 1 D.L.R. 638; Federal references: *Reference re Validity and Applicability of Industrial Relations and Disputes Investigation Act (Can)*, [1955] S.C.R. 529; *Reference re Adoption Act (Ont.) et al*; [1938] S.C.R. 398; *Reference re Jurisdiction of Tariff Board of Canada*, [1934] S.C.R. 538.

why this should be so. Perhaps it is because provincial boards and agencies are not often empowered to "state a case" for the courts in the manner of the Federal Board of Transport Commissioners. Federal references are also used to aid in settling disputes arising from Dominion-Provincial agreements and arrangements.[21]

THE EFFECT OF REFERENCES

a *Binding?*

Do opinions given on a reference bind the judges rendering them, the executive asking them, or anyone else? The proper legal answer must be that they do not. But what happens in practice is, as we shall see, quite a different matter.

The original federal reference provision, s. 52 of the Supreme Court Act, 1875, did not expressly state that the opinions rendered were to be advisory only, but the Federal Minister of Justice, in introducing the Act to the Commons in 1875 stated that the decision rendered by the Court would not have the character of a judgment but would merely have its moral weight in assisting the government to arrive at a determination.[22] This was entirely in accord with English precedent.

Over a decade later, in 1889, another Minister of Justice, Sir John Thompson, wrote:

Indeed, there seems much reason to doubt . . . that the decision of the Supreme Court on a reference would be binding on any parties or on any interests involved. It would simply advise [the Governor in Council] *as to the opinions entertained by the members of the Court. The precedents in Canada are like those in Great Britain.*[23]

The 1891 amendment to the Supreme Court Act expressly declared that the opinions were to be "advisory only" and this

---

[21] *Reference re Saskatchewan Natural Resources*, [1931] S.C.R. 263; *Reference re Troops in Cape Breton*, [1930] S.C.R. 554.

[22] Debates, House of Commons, Canada, 1875, Vol. I, 286.

[23] (1889), 12 L.N. 284. Of course this was the strict legal view. Sir John was aware of other possibilities.

view was reiterated by Sir John Thompson in the Commons.[24]

The matter was first taken up judicially in the *Manitoba Education Reference*[25] when Taschereau J. declared emphatically that

> . . . *our answers to the questions submitted will bind no one, not even those who put them, nay, not even those who give them, no court of justice, not even this court. We give no judgment, we determine nothing, we end no controversy, and whatever our answers may be, should it be deemed expedient at any time by* [an interested party] *to impugn the constitutionality of any measure that might hereinafter be taken by the federal authorities . . . whether such measure is in accordance with or in opposition to, the answers to this consultation, the recourse in the usual way, to the courts of the country remains open to them.*[25]

Provincial references were regarded in the same manner. The words "although advisory only" were not to be found in the Ontario reference statute, observed Moss C.J.O. in *Re Ontario Medical Act*,[26] but their insertion was scarcely necessary as all the other provisions of the statute went to show that the opinion given was only for the information of the Lieutenant Governor in Council.[27]

These views continued to be emphasized up to 1912. In *Re Criminal Code*,[28] nearly every judge stressed the non-binding, advisory nature of the opinions. As Girouard J. put it:

[24] Debates, House of Commons, Canada, 1891, 3587. The words "advisory only" remained in the reference provisions of the Supreme Court Act until 1956 when the subsection containing them was repealed by 4-5 Eliz. II c. 48, s. 7. The repeal has no effect upon the character of the opinions rendered. The words "advisory only" were inserted in the first place, as a precaution only, to underline that although the opinions were to be regarded as a *final* judgment for *purposes of appeal* to the Privy Council, they were *only advisory for purposes of not binding* the executive or the Supreme Court in future cases. As far as the words "advisory only" were concerned, s. 55 ss. 6 was simply declaratory. The original s. 52 did not contain the words "advisory only" yet the opinions rendered under it were, as we have seen, so regarded.

[25] (1894), 22 S.C.R. 577 at 678.

[26] (1907), 13 O.L.R. 501 at p. 507. The words were subsequently inserted.

[27] A few years earlier, Osler J. A. reserved the right to arrive at a different opinion upon all or any of the questions he had answered. *Reference re Lords Day Act of Ontario*, (1902), 1 O.W.R. 312 at p. 315.

[28] (1910), 43 S.C.R. 434.

. . . our advice has no legal effect, does not affect the rights of parties nor the provincial decisions, and is not even binding upon us.[29]

Shortly afterwards, in *Re References by the Governor in Council*,[30] Fitzpatrick C.J. expressed his adherence to the "advisory only" view and the other justices reiterated their views. Anglin J. was especially emphatic. The words "advisory only" in the Supreme Court Act, he declared, denuded a reference opinion of all the marks of a judgment of the Court leaving the Court itself and every other court throughout Canada – inferior as well as superior – free to disregard it.

This period also saw the approval of the "advisory only" doctrine by the Judicial Committee of the Privy Council in *Attorney General for Ontario* v. *Attorney-General for Canada*[31] and one of the very rare applications of this doctrine in practice in *Kerley* v. *London and Lake Erie Transportation Co.*[32] In the former, Lord Loreburn agreed that the answers given by the Supreme Court were "only advisory" and would have "no more effect than the opinions of law officers."[33] In the latter, an Ontario "concrete case," the judge referred to one of the answers given by the Supreme Court in the 1905 *Sunday Labour Reference* which seemed to be relevant to the point before him. "With all proper deference to the Judges of the Supreme Court," he said, "I cannot regard the opinion expressed on this head as a judgment binding on me, nor can I accept it as the law."[34]

After 1912 virtually nothing more is heard of the "advisory only" approach,[35] and *in practice* the opinions rendered were regarded as binding. Even before 1912 there were phrases uttered judicially and action taken judicially which indicated that judicial practice was going to be quite different than that suggested by the words "advisory only."

[29] *Ibid.*, at p. 436. See also Davies J. at p. 437; Duff J. at pp. 451, 453; Anglin J. at p. 454. Idington J. did not mention the matter but certainly shared their view.

[30] (1910), 43 S.C.R. 536 at p. 592. See also *Reference re Provincial Fisheries*, (1896-97), 26 S.C.R. 444 at p. 539.

[31] [1912] A.C. 571.

[32] (1912), 6 D.L.R. 189, (Ont.).

[33] [1912] A.C. 571 at p. 589.

[34] (1912), 6 D.L.R. 189 at p. 197. The *Sunday Labour Reference* is at (1905), 35 S.C.R. 581. See also *Reference re Bread Sales Act*, (1911), 23 O.L.R. 238 at p. 241.

[35] See, however, *Reference re Bills of Sale Act* et al., [1927] 2 D.L.R. 50 at p. 56.

232 - THE COURTS AND CONSTITUTIONS

In *The King* v. *Brinkley*,[36] Maclaren J.A. was confronted
with the argument that the opinions of the judges of the Supreme
Court in an earlier federal reference[37] touching substantially
the same question as was now before him were not binding upon
him. Maclaren J.A. proceeded to cite the remarks of Taschereau
J. in the *Manitoba Education*[37a] and *Provincial Fisheries*[37b]
references to which we have earlier referred. He noted that the
opinions and answers in the *Fisheries Reference* were subsequently cited as authorities in an opinion, concurred in by a
majority of the judges in a subsequent reference.[38] Moreover,
he continued, in *Attorney-General for Manitoba* v. *Manitoba
License Holders' Association*,[39] Lord MacNaghten, delivering
the judgment of the Board, referred several times to the opinion
of the Board in the *Local Prohibition Reference*[40] as a "decision" and as "the judgment of this Board," and as having settled
and removed objections that were raised to the legislation in the
case in question. In the *Representation in the House of Commons Reference*,[41] the opinions of the Supreme Court were also
referred to as "decisions" in the Privy Council's opinion.

The question of the binding effect of references was never
raised by counsel during their arguments on constitutional
questions during the nineteen-twenties and it was natural for
the courts to sink deeper into the habit, pointed out in *The King*
v. *Brinkley*, of regarding opinions earlier rendered as binding.
An illustration of this habit is found in the *Aeronautics Reference*[42] when it came before the Privy Council. Delivering the
judgment of the Board, Lord Sankey recognized that there had
grown up around the British North America Act "a body of
precedents of high authority and value as guides to its interpretation and application." He pointed to four cases where the
"essential task of taking stock of this body of authority and
reviewing it in relation to its original text" had been performed.
Three of the four cases to which Lord Sankey attached such

---

[36] (1907), 14 O.L.R. 434.
[37] *Reference re Criminal Code Sections Relating to Bigamy*, (1897), 27
S.C.R. 461.
[37a] *Supra*, footnote 16.
[37b] *Supra*, footnote 30.
[38] *Reference re International and Interprovincial Ferries*, (1905), 36
S.C.R. 206 at pp. 217-18.
[39] [1902] A.C. 73.
[40] [1896] A.C. 348.
[41] [1905] A.C. 37, at p. 43.
[42] [1932] A.C. 54.

PART III: THE PROCESS OF INTERPRETATION - 233

importance were references.[43] Finally, his Lordship pointed to
still another reference, *Attorney-General for Canada* v. *Attorney-General for British Columbia*[44] as having "laid down" four
propositions relative to the legislative competence of Canada
and the provinces respectively as "established" by the "decisions" of the Judicial Committee. Two of the four cases cited
by the Board in establishing the propositions are references.[45]

Further illustrations are to be found in the *Natural Products
Marketing Act Reference*,[46] where Duff C.J. cited a group of
cases including a reference as "binding" upon the Supreme
Court, and the *Labour Conventions Reference*,[47] where Rinfret
J. referred to the *Hours of Labour Reference*[47a] of 1925 and
declared that "the opinion then given may be regarded as
binding upon this Court."

How far the habit of regarding opinions rendered on references as true judgments had gone by 1942 is strikingly illustrated
by the *Legal Proceedings Suspension Act Reference*,[48] an
Alberta reference. The circumstances surrounding the reference
are worth going into in some detail. The Alberta Debt Adjustment Act of 1937 enacted, generally speaking, that no action
should be commenced or continued in the Province of Alberta
in respect of any debt or liquidated demand unless a permit to
do so had first been procured from the Debt Adjustment Board.
The Supreme Court of Canada, on a reference by the Governor
in Council, declared the Debt Adjustment Act *ultra vires*,
whereupon the Alberta Legislature enacted the Legal Proceedings Suspension Act of 1942, providing that all actions then or
thereafter commenced which involved the applicability of the
Debt Adjustment Act (excepting those in which no permit was
required under the Debt Adjustment Act, or in which a permit

---

[43] *Attorney-General for Ontario* v. *Attorney-General for Canada*,
[1896] A.C. 348; *Attorney-General for Canada* v. *Attorneys-General
for Ontario, Quebec and Nova Scotia*, [1898] A.C. 700; *Attorney-General for Ontario* v. *Attorney-General for Canada*, [1912] A.C.
571.

[44] [1930] A.C. 111 at p. 118.

[45] *Attorney-General for Ontario* v. *Attorney-General for Canada*,
[1894] A.C. 189; *Attorney-General for Ontario* v. *Attorney-General
for Canada*, [1896] A.C. 348.

[46] The reference was *Attorney-General for Canada* v. *Attorney-General
for Alberta*, [1916] 1 A.C. 588. See [1936] S.C.R. 398 at pp. 404-5.

[47] [1936] S.C.R. 461 at p. 507.

[47a] *Supra*, footnote 9.

[48] [1942] 3 D.L.R. 318.

was granted) should be stayed until sixty days after the determination of an application for leave to appeal to the Privy Council from the opinion of the Supreme Court of Canada, or, if leave was granted, from the determination of the appeal.[49] The Legal Proceedings Suspension Act was then referred by the Lieutenant Governor in Council of Alberta to the Alberta Supreme Court where it was held to be *ultra vires*.

Harvey C.J.A. observed that the stay granted by the Act and the barring of actions for debts, was not for a definite but for an indefinite period which, if there were no attempt to appeal to the Privy Council, would never end. He continued:

For the period of the stay this is a complete setting at nought of the judgment *of the Supreme Court of Canada and it is not without significance that the period of the stay is not limited to the time involved in obtaining the decision of the Judicial Committee, but is for a further period of sixty days. . . .*[50]

The whole affair shows how seriously a reference "opinion" was regarded. The Alberta Legislature seemed to take it for granted that the opinion of the Supreme Court of Canada was much more than "advisory only" and that unless it was overruled by the Privy Council, the Debt Adjustment Act and the debtors' protection under it were at an end. Thus, new legislation was necessary to assist debtors. The Alberta Supreme Court took the "opinion" with equal seriousness. Like the Legislature, it assumed that the pre-Debt Adjustment Act situation between creditors and debtors had been re-established by the Canadian Supreme Court opinion and felt it necessary to strike down the Legal Proceedings Suspension Act to protect the post-opinion position of the creditors.

It was no longer possible to speak of "unconscious habit" after the bold pronouncement of Rinfret J. in 1945 in *Attorney-General of Canada* v. *Higbie et al. and the Attorney-General for British Columbia*.[50a] One of the points at issue was the interpretation to be given to the opinion of Newcombe J. in the earlier *Saskatchewan Natural Resources Reference*.[51]

[49] This statement of the background is taken virtually verbatim from the report on the *Legal Proceedings Suspension Act Reference* [1942] 3 D.L.R. 318. For the report of the Supreme Court decision declaring the Debt Adjustment Act *ultra vires* see [1942] S.C.R. 31.

[50] [1942] 3 D.L.R. 318 at p. 320. Author's emphasis.

[50a] [1945] S.C.R. 385.

[51] [1931] S.C.R. 263.

Rinfret J. had no doubts:

> *It is needless to mention here that, although this was not a judgment in the true sense of the word, but merely what is sometimes referred to as an opinion made in Reference to this Court by the Governor General in Council as provided for by section 55 of the Supreme Court Act and the special jurisdiction therein given to this Court, we should regard an opinion of that kind as binding upon this Court....*[52]

All the more startling, then, after these words, was the course taken by the Supreme Court in 1957 in *C.P.R.* v. *Town of Estevan et al.*[52a] Here the Court was faced, among other problems, with the question of what effect to give to opinions rendered by it and the Judicial Committee upon an earlier reference under the Saskatchewan Constitutional Questions Act[53] which had come before them on appeal.[54] Locke J., speaking for the other judges on this point, held that the Supreme Court and Judicial Committee were not binding as between the parties to this present case, insofar as a particular point was concerned. The matter, he declared,

> *... was not rendered* res judicata *as between the parties to this litigation by the decision of this Court upon the* [earlier] *reference, or by the judgment of the Judicial Committee ... upon ... questions involved in that reference. In so far as the defendant municipalities are concerned, they were not parties to and were not heard upon the reference and, in so far as the present appellant is concerned, even though it was represented* [at all stages] *... I think it is not bound either by the opinions expressed by the Judicial Committee or by this Court. In this respect, matters referred to the Court of Appeal for Saskatchewan under The Constitutional Questions Act of that Province ... do not differ from references to this Court under what is now s. 55 of the Supreme Court Act, R.S.C. 1952, c. 259.*[55]

---

[52] [1945] S.C.R. 385 at p. 403.
[52a] [1957] S.C.R. 365.
[53] R.S.S. 1953, c. 78.
[54] *Reference re Taxation of C.P.R.* [1949] 2 D.L.R. 240; *C.P.R.* v. *Attorney-General for Saskatchewan*, [1951] S.C.R. 190; *Attorney-General for Saskatchewan* v. *C.P.R.*, [1953] A.C. 594.
[55] [1957] S.C.R. 365 at pp. 368-9; Duff J.'s remarks in *Reference re Criminal Code*, (1910), 43 S.C.R. 434 at p. 451 and in *Re References by the Governor General in Council*, (1910), 43 S.C.R. 536 at p. 588 were cited for support.

What is one to make of all this? Theoretically, in law, reference opinions are "advisory only" – no doubt about that. But in practice they are treated with the respect due to judgments. One is reminded of the words of Lord Simon in *Attorney-General for Ontario* v. *Canada Temperance Federation*[56] where, speaking in a somewhat different connection, he said:

Their Lordships do not doubt that in tendering humble advice to His Majesty they are not absolutely bound by previous decisions of the Board. . . . But on constitutional questions it must be seldom indeed that the Board would depart from a previous decision which it may be assumed will have been acted on by governments and subjects.

This seems to sum up the position of the courts on the binding effect of reference. The forceful pronouncements of earlier days that references were only advisory and the holding in *C.P.R.* v. *Town of Estevan et al.* must be taken together with the facts that the pronouncements were all made in cases where there was no need or opportunity to put them into actual effect and that there is not one recorded instance since 1891, with the exception of the *Kerley case*,[56a] where opinions rendered on either federal or provincial references were repudiated in a subsequent reference or concrete case. It is interesting that even in *C.P.R.* v. *Town of Estevan et al.* Locke J., having uttered the words quoted above, went on, nevertheless, to declare his agreement with the opinions rendered on the earlier reference, and so the necessity for actual repudiation did not arise.

b *Useful?*

The usefulness of reference cases has long been in issue in the courts. We have seen in the remarks of Maule J. in *M'Naghten's case*[56b] the difficulties experienced by English judges in preparing a satisfactory reply. The remarks of Lord Chief Justice Tindal in the same case, put the point with even greater effect. The judges, he declared, had

. . . foreborne entering into any particular discussion upon these questions from the extreme and almost insuperable difficulty of applying those answers to cases in which the facts are not

---

[56] [1946] A.C. 193 at p. 206.
[56a] *Supra*, footnote 32.
[56b] 10 Cl. & F. 200.

brought judicially before them. The facts of each particular case must of necessity present themselves with endless variety, and with every shade of difference in each case; and as it is their duty to declare the law upon each particular case, on facts proved before them, and after hearing argument of counsel thereon; they deem it at once impractical and at the same time dangerous to the administration of justice, if it were practicable, to attempt to make minute applications of the principles involved in the answers given by them to your Lordships' questions.[57]

Similar sentiments have frequently been voiced in Canadian courts and in the Privy Council with regard to Canadian references.[57a] In the *Local Prohibition Reference*, Lord Watson criticized the six general questions as "academic" rather than "judicial" and as "better fitted for the consideration of the officers of the Crown than of a court of law." The replies to them must necessarily, he said, depend upon the circumstances in which they might arise for decision and the circumstances were, in this case, left to speculation.[58] A much harsher criticism of questions submitted was voiced by the Board in *Attorney-General for Ontario* v. *Hamilton Street Railway*,[59] again directed against the general questions in a mixed submission. They were questions, the Board declared, proper to be considered in concrete cases only and opinions expressed upon them would be worthless "as being speculative opinions on hypothetical questions." Similar remarks had earlier been made in the Ontario Court of Appeal when the same questions were being considered there,[60] while in 1905 the Supreme Court of Canada declined to answer a question dealing with *specific* pieces of legislation on the grounds that useful or satisfactory answers

[57] *Ibid.*, at p. 208.

[57]a *Attorney-General for British Columbia* v. *Attorney-General for Canada*, [1914] A.C. 153 at p. 162; *Reference re Alberta Railway Act*, (1914), 48 S.C.R. 9 at p. 25; *Attorney-General for Ontario* v. *Attorney-General for Canada*, [1916] 1 A.C. 598; *Hirsch* v. *Protestant Board of School Commissioners*, [1928] A.C. 200 at p. 215; *Re Waters and Water Powers*, [1929] S.C.R. 200 at pp. 226, 227; *Re Bills of Sale Act et al*, [1927] 2 D.L.R. 50 at p. 52; *Reference re Alberta Debt Adjustment Act*, [1942] S.C.R. 31 at p. 52; *Aeronautics Reference*, [1932] A.C. 54 at p. 66; *Companies Reference*, (1914), 48 S.C.R. 331 at p. 359.

[58] [1896] A.C. 348 at p. 370.

[59] [1903] A.C. 524 at p. 529.

[60] [1902] O.W.R. 312 at pp. 314, 315, 316.

could only be given to them when they arose in concrete cases.[61]

In *John Deere Plow Co. Ltd.* v. *Wharton*[61a] Lord Haldane referred to the attempts made by the Supreme Court in the *Companies Reference*, to carry out the task imposed upon them by the submission. In Lord Haldane's view, the task had been an impossible one, owing, he said, to the abstract character of the questions put. Earlier in the judgment he delivered a caution on the use of reference cases in constitutional matters:

The structure of ss. 91 and 92, and the degree to which the connotation of the expressions used overlaps, render it, in their Lordships' opinion, unwise . . . to attempt exhaustive definitions of the meaning and scope of these expressions. . . . It is in many cases only by confining decisions to concrete questions which have actually arisen in circumstances the whole of which are before the tribunal that injustice to future suitors can be avoided. . . . It is the wise course to decide each case which arises without entering more largely upon an interpretation of the statute than is necessary for the decision of the particular question in hand. . . . It must be borne in mind in construing the two sections that matters which in a special aspect and for a particular purpose may fall within one of them, may in a different aspect and for a different purpose fall within the other. In such cases, the nature and scope of the legislative attempt of the Dominion or the Province, as the case may be, have to be examined with reference to the actual facts if it is to be possible to determine under which set of powers it falls in substance and in reality.[62]

These words, taken together with the fact that the reference power has been very frequently employed by federal and provincial executives to determine the division of legislative jurisdiction, raise the further question as to what effect this use of references has had on the interpretation of those sections. In particular, have references contributed noticeably to the marked judicial diminution of the scope of federal legislative jurisdiction from that envisaged by the Fathers of Confederation and the text of the British North America Act?

[61] *Reference re Legislation Respecting Abstention from Labour on Sunday*, (1905), 35 S.C.R. 581 at p. 591. See also *Reference re Ontario Medical Act*, (1907), 13 O.L.R. 501 at pp. 507-9 and *Reference re Bread Sales Act*, (1911), 23 O.L.R. 238 at p. 240.

[61a] [1915] A.C. 330.

[62] *Ibid.*, at pp. 338-9.

Some writers maintain that they have. Jennings[63] hints at such a connection. Others are more explicit. Clokie[64] states, "Judicial nullification of Dominion legislation began in the field of advisory opinions" and sees significance in the fact that they were favoured by Blake, "a 'provincial rights' man." Macdonald[65] considers it "not without point" to observe that the Privy Council's contribution to the elucidation of the Canadian Constitution has been made in reference cases where the realities of Canadian life and problems were not presented in the way that they might have been in concrete cases. Other writers[66] have, in effect, come to the same conclusion. Echoing many of the judicial objections to references, they stress the absence of a factual, "real-life" background in the questions submitted and the consequent unreality of many of the opinions rendered.

Davison,[67] examining the Bennett New Deal references, finds the factual background "necessarily meagre." In economic terms he notes the *Employment and Social Insurance Act Reference* where counsel for Canada presented statistics relating to unemployment and unemployment expenditures for the period 1930-35 which were analysed in the arguments of provincial counsel before the Judicial Committee, but not, be it noted, in the opinion itself.[68] He is especially critical of the key *Natural Products Marketing Act Reference* where neither the arguments nor opinion scrutinize factual material.[69] The upholding of virtually the entire *Dominion Trade and Industry Commission Act*[70] he regards as miraculous.

[63] Jennings, W. Ivor, Constitutional Interpretation: The Experience of Canada, (1937), 51 Harvard L. R. 1, at p. 12.

[64] Clokie, H. McD., Judicial Review, Federalism and the Canadian Constitution, (1942), 8 Canadian Journal of Economics and Political Science 537, at p. 543. Parenthetically, it seems grossly unfair to speak of "judicial pretensions" in the matter of advisory opinions, as Clokie does, considering the long history of judicial resistance to the use of the reference power on grounds that references were of limited value, unethical and unconstitutional.

[65] Macdonald, Vincent C., The Privy Council and the Canadian Constitution, (1951), 29 Can. Bar Rev. 1021, at p. 1028.

[66] Freund, Paul A., A Supreme Court in a Federation: Some Lessons from Legal History, (1953), 53 Columbia L. R. 597, at p. 613.

[67] Davison, J. F., The Constitutionality and Utility of Advisory Opinions, (1937-38), 2 University of Toronto L. J. 254, at pp. 275-6.

[68] [1937] A.C. 355 at p. 359 for the statistics. See [1936] S.C.R. 427 at p. 451 where the "emergency" question is touched on. The arguments of counsel before the Supreme Court were not reported.

[69] [1936] S.C.R. 398; [1937] A.C. 377.

[70] [1936] S.C.R. 379; [1937] A.C. 405.

LaBrie[71] stresses that many important considerations relevant to a determination of pith and substance can only be determined from the form of the legislation considered along with the circumstances which surround its enactment and operation and that even where fully drafted legislation is referred to a court, it would be difficult to prove the implications that might arise from its enactment. LaBrie is also critical of confining the courts to facts set out in the order of reference. But the examples he cites, while interesting, are inconclusive in terms of our present discussion, namely, the federal-provincial conflict over legislative jurisdiction.[72]

The critics are surely right in suggesting that there is some relationship between the use of references and the trend of judicial interpretation, but the extent of that relationship is not easy to determine. The very lack of concrete cases with which the references might be compared makes the task of measuring their influence itself rather abstract and hypothetical. Those concrete cases that did arise seem inconclusive. There is a *Russell's* case[73] but there is a *Snider's* case.[74] The companies cases[75] may be significant, but afford no firm basis for conclusions. A statement which purported to reduce "The Regulation of Trade and Commerce" to the same degree of weakness as the federal residuary power[76] was made in a concrete case.[77] The "emergency" doctrine was expounded in still another concrete

---

[71] LaBrie, F. E., Constitutional Interpretation and Legislative Review, (1950), 8 University of Toronto L. J. 298, at p. 347.

[72] *The Alberta Statutes Reference* [1939] A.C. 117; went against the province. *The Margarine Reference* [1951] A.C. 179; went against the Dominion. *The Canada Temperance Act Reference*, [1939] O.R. 570, and the *Leasehold Regulations Reference*, [1950] S.C.R. 124 saw the confinement to the terms of reference work in favour of the Dominion with regard to the continuance of an emergency. But it is easy to conceive of situations where the reverse could be true.

[73] (1882), 7 A.C. 829.

[74] [1925] A.C. 396.

[75] *John Deere Plow Co.* v. *Wharton*, [1915] A.C. 330; *Great West Saddlery Co.* v. *The King*, [1921] 2 A.C. 91. Lord Haldane was driven in these cases to "peace, order and good government" for the incorporation of companies with Dominion objects.

[76] *Attorney-General for Ontario* v. *Attorney-General for Canada*, [1896] A.C. 348.

[77] *City of Montreal* v. *Montreal Street Railway*, [1912] A.C. 333 at p. 344

case.[78] Conversely, a number of important references have gone in favour of the Dominion.[79]

The *Aeronautics Reference* and the *Canada Temperance Act Reference* suggest that what may be equally important is the approach of the judges. If they are prepared, as Lord Sankey urged, to treat the British North America Act as a "living tree, capable of growth,"[80] to eschew narrow canons of interpretation[81] and slavish adherence to *stare decisis*,[82] the form in which the case comes before them will not be an insuperable obstacle to a decision based upon the text of the Act and the realities of Canadian life.

There are, of course, other factors to be weighed in considering the usefulness of reference cases besides those we have touched upon. In particular, references have been forwarded as a technique for determining important legal questions speedily and without expense to private litigants. Blake, during the dis-

[78] *Fort Frances Pulp and Paper Co.* v. *Manitoba Free Press Co.*, [1923] A.C. 695.

[79] The *Aeronautics Reference*, [1932] A.C. 54; the *Radio Reference*, [1932] A.C. 304; the *Alberta Statutes Reference*, [1939] A.C. 117, the *Canada Temperance Act Reference*, [1946] A.C. 193. See also *Reference re Prohibitory Liquor Laws* (1895), 24 S.C.R. 170, where the Supreme Court held in favour of the Dominion, the same result, be it noted, that it reached with a somewhat differently composed court in the concrete case of *Huson* v. *Township of South Norwich* (1895), 24 S.C.R. 145. The Supreme Court was overruled in *Attorney-General for Ontario* v. *Attorney-General for Canada*, [1896] A.C. 348.

[80] The "living tree" metaphor was employed in *Edwards* v. *Attorney-General for Canada*, [1930] A.C. 124, a reference, but one not involving the question of legislative jurisdiction. It is possible to discern much of the same approach in Lord Sankey's opinion in the *Aeronautics Reference*, particularly in his "sixty colours" analogy and his statement that aeronautics had attained such dimensions as to affect the body politic of the Dominion. This is not, of course, to ignore the note played by s. 132 in the case.

[81] Three canons that proved particularly disastrous to the scope of federal jurisdiction were, first, that the Act was to be interpreted like an ordinary statute, *Bank of Toronto* v. *Lambe*, (1887), 12 A.C. 575 (a concrete case), that the specific inclusion of Banking in s. 91 excluded other particular trades, *Citizen's Insurance Co.* v. *Parsons*, (1881), 7 A.C. 96 (a concrete case) and that regulation did not include prohibition, *Attorney-General for Ontario* v. *Attorney-General for Canada*, [1896] A.C. 348 (a reference). Also with regard to the attitude of the judges, see E. R. Richard, Peace, Order and Good Government, (1940), 18 Can. Bar Rev. 243 at pp. 256-8 where evidence is offered that the Act was deliberately twisted in favour of the provinces by Lord Watson for reasons of policy.

[82] See Jennings, *op. cit.*, pp. 37-8.

cussion of his resolution of 1890,[83] cited Bryce's exposition of the disadvantages which resulted from the absence of reference provisions in the United States. An immediate and final decision, wrote Bryce, of a contested point of constitutional law would often be of benefit both to the citizen individually and to the various organs of government. As things actually stood, no one knew with certainty when, if ever, a point of this type would be decided. No one liked incurring the cost and effort necessary to bring it before the courts and the case might be ended by a settlement or dropped entirely. If it did happen that, after many years, it came before the Supreme Court and was decided, it might be that the decision would differ from that which lawyers in general had foreseen, that it would modify what was thought to have been the law and that it would ruin private interests based on opinions that this decision now declared to be unfounded.[84]

To these arguments might be added the special necessity for speedy determination of questions relating to war emergencies and Canada's relations with foreign powers.[85] On the other hand, as we have seen with regard to disallowance, there is the possibility that reference will be abused by the executive. This leads us to our next major area, the ethics of references.

c *Ethical?*

The judges have objected to the submission of references from an ethical viewpoint because, they argued, references affect private rights without affording parties affected an opportunity to be heard and because, though theoretically merely advisory, opinions rendered are bound to embarrass the administration of justice when the subject of an earlier reference is brought before the courts on a later occasion by genuine litigants.

In 1898, the Privy Council, in an important constitutional reference, made its position known on this question in a pronouncement that has often been judicially cited. Delivering the opinion of the Board, Lord Herschell declared:

[83] Debates, House of Commons, Canada, 1890, Vol. 2, 4084-93.
[84] These views have been echoed but rarely in the courts, where there has been much hostility to the use of references. But see *Re References*, (1910), 43 S.C.R. 536 at p. 587 and *Reference Re Local Option Act*, (1890-91), 18 O.A.R. 572 at pp. 584-85.
[85] *Reference re Chemical Regulations*, [1943] S.C.R. 1.

*Their Lordships must decline to answer the last question sub-
mitted as to the rights of riparian proprietors. These proprietors
are not parties to this litigation or represented before their
Lordships, and accordingly their Lordships do not think it
proper when determining the respective rights and jurisdictions
of the Dominion and Provincial Legislatures to express an
opinion upon the extent of the rights possessed by riparian
proprietors.*[86]

In *Re References*[87] Idington J. considered the question from
its second aspect: embarrassment of the administration of justice. What would be the thought of a judge, he asked, who had
expressed to a private litigant an opinion more or less deliberate
upon questions the answers to which determined that litigant's
rights and who had afterwards sat in that litigant's case and
judged it? Was there not involved in the very essence of what
was attempted the taking away of men's rights and liberties
without due process of law?

But it was in the *Marriage Laws Reference*[88] that the private
rights question received the fullest discussion. There, counsel
for Quebec, citing the views of Lord Herschell as quoted above,
objected to the Supreme Court answering one of the questions
on grounds that it was a question which affected private rights
and private interests which were not represented before the
Court. The question was whether the law of Quebec rendered
null and void, unless contracted before a Roman Catholic priest,
marriages between persons of certain religious faiths. In the
view of counsel for Quebec a question could hardly be submitted which involved more private rights than this one. It
involved a declaration which would not only cause disturbance,
but would put the ban of absolute nullity upon scores of marriages of persons who were not represented before the Court.
It was well and good to say that the opinion rendered would be
only advisory, yet if the opinion favoured nullity, it would affect
the name and fame and standing of every person married under
the conditions set forth in the question as well as that of the
children.

[86] *Attorney-General for Canada* v. *Attorneys-General for Ontario, Quebec and Nova Scotia*, [1898] A.C. 700 at p. 717.

[87] (1910), 43 S.C.R. 536 at pp. 573, 583. It seems clear here that what
Idington J. means by due process is simply an ordinary trial not the
technical meaning of the American term.

[88] [1912] 46 S.C.R. 132 at p. 289.

Counsel for Canada took up this argument in reply and pointed out that the same was true of *every* case that was heard in the Court. Interests which were not represented and could not be represented were affected and determined as much in ordinary cases as in any reference. Moreover, there was a public interest in having the answers which outweighed the private interest.[89]

Fitzpatrick C.J., Idington and Anglin JJ. agreed with counsel for Quebec that the question was improper.[90] Idington J. was very bitter:

As to the objections strongly pressed by counsel for Quebec that we should not answer the second question . . . in a recent reference I assumed that private rights might be touched and urged all I could in the same direction. . . . The Judicial Committee's judgment indicates such objections were hardly worthy of notice. . . . I admit this case involves . . . what I had conceived to be the vicious principle of interrogating judge.

It . . . imperils private rights in a way that seems to deprive those concerned of trial by the process of law.[91]

A very recent echo of the private rights controversy was heard in *Attorney-General of Canada* v. *C.P.R. and C.N.R.*[92] where Rand J., delivering the judgment of Kerwin C.J. and Taschereau, Cartwright and Fauteux JJ., objected to answering three of the questions on grounds that

. . . we would be expressing an opinion that might seriously affect private rights in the absence of those claiming them, a step which would be contrary to the fundamental conception of due process, the application of which to opinions of this nature has long been recognized.[93]

These remarks show that the private rights question is by no means closed. They also, when taken together with the other cases considered, suggest a criterion used in evaluating a "private rights" complaint, namely, that where the questions, although part of a larger constitutional reference, directly touch private interests, as in *Attorney-General for Canada* v. *Attorneys-General for Ontario, Quebec and Nova Scotia*[94] and *Attorney-General for Canada* v. *C.P.R. and C.N.R.*, the courts

[89] *Ibid.*, at pp. 308-9.
[90] *Ibid.*, at pp. 336, 421-22.
[91] *Ibid.*, at p. 395.
[92] [1958] S.C.R. 285.
[93] *Ibid.*, at p. 294.
[94] *Supra*, footnote 87.

will decline to answer,[95] but where, as Anglin J. put it in the *Aeronautics Reference*, the interests are affected only obliquely because the questions are directed to the problem of legislative jurisdiction the courts will proceed.

d Constitutional?

Are references constitutional? It has been decided on the highest authority that they are. The arguments advanced in favour of the contrary view are such as may involve us in some slight repetition of points covered earlier in this paper, for, as Lord Loreburn observed in 1912:[96]

What in substance their Lordships are asked to do is to say that the Canadian Parliament ought not to pass laws like this because it may be embarrassing and onerous to a Court, and to declare this law invalid because it ought not to have been passed.

Protests from the bench that the federal reference legislation was unconstitutional were heard as far back as 1892 and 1894, shortly after the passage of the amendment to the Supreme Court Act in 1891. In 1894, in the *Manitoba Education Reference*,[97] Taschereau J. expressed his doubts as to whether the amendment was *intra vires* the Dominion. What section of the British North America Act, he asked, empowered Parliament to confer on the Supreme Court, a statutory court, any other jurisdiction than that of a court of appeal under s. 101 of that Act? In his view, the reference legislation had made the court a court of first instance, or rather an advisory board to the executive, performing neither the usual functions of a court of appeal nor of any court of justice whatever.

It was only in 1910, however, that the constitutional issue was put squarely before the Court.[98] In that year the Governor-in-Council submitted a number of questions for the consideration of the Court dealing with a mixture of topics, including the

[95] The *Marriage Laws Reference* is somewhat unique. Since Question 2 directly affected private rights, Fitzpatrick C. J., Idington and Anglin JJ. protested it, yet it was answered by all the judges except Fitzpatrick C. J.

[96] *Attorney-General for Ontario* v. *Attorney-General for Canada*, [1912] A.C. 571 at p. 589.

[97] (1894), 22 S.C.R. 577 at p. 677. Taschereau J. had also expressed his doubts on this score in *Reference re County Courts of British Columbia*, (1892), 21 S.C.R. 446 at pp. 454-55.

[98] *References by the Governor-General in Council*, (1910), 43 S.C.R. 536 at p. 537.

limitations placed by the British North America Act, 1867, upon the provincial power to incorporate companies, the competency of British Columbia to grant certain fishing rights in certain waters, and the validity of some sections of the Insurance Act (Can.) of 1910. British Columbia consented to the reference on the fishing question and Quebec to the reference on both the fishing and insurance questions. However, all the other provinces, with the exception of Saskatchewan, moved that the Court should not consider the questions "as not being matters which can properly be considered by the court as a court or by the individual members thereof in the proper execution of their judicial duties." The motion of the provinces was dismissed by the Supreme Court, four to two.

On appeal,[99] counsel for the appellant provinces noted that the point involved in references might afterwards arise in the course of legal proceedings between private suitors or between the province and the Dominion. The contribution of counsel for Canada, on the other hand, is noteworthy too for pointing out that reference legislation had been enacted by most of the provinces. His remarks, together with those of provincial counsel, raised for the first time the constitutionality of provincial reference legislation. The Supreme Court had confined its attention entirely to references by the Governor-in-Council.

Earl Loreburn, delivering the judgment of the Board, proceeded to define the basic issues generally thus:

It is argued . . . that the Dominion Act authorizing questions to be asked of the Supreme Court is an invasion of provincial rights, but not because the power of asking such questions belongs exclusively to the provinces. The real ground is far wider. It is no less than this – that no Legislature in Canada has the right to pass an Act for asking such questions at all;[100]

and with regard to the Supreme Court in particular, as follows:

The provinces . . . say that when a Court of Appeal from all the provincial Courts is authorized to be set up, that carries with it an implied condition that the Court of Appeal shall be in truth a judicial body according to the conception of judicial character obtaining in civilized countries and especially obtaining in Great Britain, to whose Constitution the Constitution of Canada is intended to be similar. . . . And they say that to place the duty of

[99] Supra, footnote 96.
[100] Ibid., at p. 581.

answering questions, such as the Canadian Act under considera-
tion does require the Court to answer, is incompatible with the
maintenance of such judicial character or of public confidence
in it, or with the free access to an unbiased tribunal of appeal to
which litigants in the provincial Courts are of right entitled.
This argument in truth arraigns the lawfulness of so treating a
Court upon the ground that a Court liable to be so treated ceases
to be such a judiciary as the Constitution provides for. . . . If,
notwithstanding the liability to answer questions the Supreme
Court is still a judiciary within the meaning of the British North
America Act, then there is no ground for saying that the
impugned Canadian Act is ultra vires.[101]

His Lordship went on to reject the provincial contentions in
general because to assume that any point of internal self-
government had been withheld from Canada would be "sub-
versive of the entire scheme and policy" of the British North
America Act,[102] and in particular, on three grounds: United
Kingdom practice, the fact that reference had been answered
before 1910 by the Supreme Court and Privy Council, and the
fact that nearly all the provinces had enacted legislation similar
to the federal legislation now being considered. Of these three,
Earl Loreburn attached the greater weight to the last two, since,
as he put it, "Canada must judge of Canadian requirements."[103]

His Lordship noted that reference legislation had been on the
federal statute books in one form or another since 1875 and that
the Supreme Court had frequently answered questions submitted under it. More important, the Judicial Committee had
heard several appeals from such answers without ever having
questioned the validity of such proceedings. It was quite true,
he admitted, that no interested party had ever raised the issue
before 1910 and these bodies would be reluctant to raise it on
their own, but surely this would not be the case where the practice involved the very foundations of justice. The only inference
which could be drawn from the past silence of the Board in
Canadian references was that it did not consider such submis-
sions prejudicial to the independence and character of courts of
justice.[104] Moreover, there was the provincial reference legislation to consider. The proposition that this legislation could be

[101] *Ibid.*, at pp. 584-85.
[102] *Ibid.*, at p. 581.
[103] *Ibid.*, at p. 587.
[104] *Ibid.*, at pp. 587-88.

valid while similar federal legislation was invalid was dismissed by his Lordship as "very strange." There only remained, then, the conclusion that the provincial legislation was also invalid "upon the general ground . . . that a court of justice ceased in effect to be a court of justice when such a duty is laid upon it." But this was unacceptable.

Certainly it is remarkable that for thirty-five years this point of view has apparently escaped notice in Canada, and a contrary view, now said to menace the very essence of justice has been tranquilly acted upon without question by the Legislatures of the Dominion and provinces, by the Courts in Canada, and by the Judicial Committee ever since the British North America Act established the present Constitution of Canada.[105]

His Lordship then expressed his agreement with the proposition that federal references could not affect the administration of justice because they were only advisory, issued a reminder that the Board was not concerned with whether references were good policy, and dismissed the appeal.

The judgment, by implication, upheld the provincial reference legislation as well as that of the Dominion. The holding declares that "it was *intra vires* of the *respective Legislatures*" to impose this duty upon the courts. Left more obscure is the question of basis in the sections of the British North America Act. Presumably, it is s. 92 (14) for the provinces, but the source of federal jurisdiction is more uncertain. In *Re References* Davies and Fitzpatrick JJ. felt that s. 101 would be adequate for this purpose, but that the necessary clause of s. 91 would do equally well. Duff J. considered s. 101 only, while Anglin J. did likewise with s. 91. Perhaps since Anglin J. forcefully rejected s. 101 while Duff J. did not consider s. 91, the edge should go to the latter section. Macdonald[106] lists references among the few matters with which the Dominion may deal in normal times in virtue of the opening words of s. 91. Since we have it on the authority of both the Supreme Court and the Privy Council that federal references involve no interference with any of the classes of subject assigned to the province in s. 92, such a solution would be entirely proper.

[105]*Ibid.*, at p. 588.
[106] Macdonald, *op. cit.*

THE CONTRIBUTORS

ALEXANDER BRADY, Ph.D., F.R.S.C.,
> Professor of Political Economy,
> University of Toronto,
> Toronto, Ontario.

BORA LASKIN, Q.C., M.A., LL.B., LL.M., F.R.S.C.,
> Professor of Law,
> University of Toronto,
> Toronto, Ontario.

THE HONOURABLE VINCENT C. MACDONALD, B.A., LL.B., LL.D., F.R.S.C.,
> Justice of The Supreme Court of Nova Scotia,
> formerly Dean of The Faculty of Law,
> Dalhousie University,
> Halifax, Nova Scotia.
> *The editor deeply regrets to report that the death of* Mr. Justice MacDonald *occurred in the early summer of 1964 while this book was in the press.*

FRANK MACKINNON, M.A., Ph.D., LL.D.,
> Principal,
> Prince of Wales College,
> Charlottetown, Prince Edward Island.

LOUIS-PHILLIPPE PIGEON, Q.C., B.A., LL.L.,
> Professor of Law,
> Laval University,
> Quebec City,
> Special legal adviser to the Premier of Quebec.

GERALD RUBIN, M.A., B.C.L.
> (McGill University),
> Segal and Rubin, Notaries,
> Montreal, Quebec.

FRANK R. SCOTT., Q.C., B.A., B.Litt., B.C.L., LL.D., F.R.S.C.,
> Macdonald Professor of Law,
> McGill University,
> Montreal, Quebec;
> formerly Dean of the Faculty of Law, McGill University.

THE CARLETON LIBRARY